The Future of Modernism

The Future of Modernism

Edited by
Hugh Witemeyer

Ann Arbor
THE UNIVERSITY OF MICHIGAN PRESS

2000   1999   1998   1997   4   3   2   1

A CIP catalog record for this book is available from the British Library.

Library of Congress Cataloging-in-Publication Data

The future of modernism / edited by Hugh Witemeyer.
    p.   cm.
    Includes bibliographical references and index.
    ISBN 0-472-10835-2
    1. American literature—20th century—History and criticism.
2. Modernism (Literature)—United States.   3. English
literature—20th century—History and criticism.   4. Modernism
(Literature)—Great Britain.   I. Witemeyer, Hugh.
    PS228.M63F87   1997
    810.9'112—dc21   97-17841
                                             CIP

Grateful acknowledgment is made to the following publishers for permission to reprint previously published materials. Faber and Faber, Inc. for excerpts from *On Poetry and Poets* by T. S. Eliot. Reprinted by permission of Faber and Faber, Inc. Faber and Faber, Ltd. for excerpts from *On Poetry and Poets* by T. S. Eliot; for excerpts from *Collected Poems and Plays* by T. S. Eliot; and for excerpts from *Selected Essays* by T. S. Eliot. Reprinted by permission of Faber and Faber, Ltd., Publishers. Farrar, Straus & Giroux, Inc. for excerpts from "The Frontiers of Criticism" from *On Poetry and Poets* by T. S. Eliot. Copyright © 1957 by T. S. Eliot, and copyright renewed © 1985 by Valerie Eliot. Reprinted by permission of Farrar, Straus & Giroux, Inc. Harcourt Brace & Company for excerpts from *Collected Poems 1909–1962* by T. S. Eliot, copyright 1936 by Harcourt Brace & Company, copyright © 1964, 1963 by T. S. Eliot; for excerpts from "In the Field" in *Walking to Sleep: New Poems and Translations,* copyright © 1968 by Richard Wilbur; for excerpt from "A Miltonic Sonnet for Mr. Johnson" in *Walking to Sleep: New Poems and Translations,* copyright © 1967 by Richard Wilbur; and for excerpts from "Love Calls Us to the Things of This World" and "For the New Railway Station in Rome" in *Things of This World,* copyright © 1956 and renewed 1984 by Richard Wilbur, reprinted by permission of Harcourt Brace & Company. Stephen James Joyce for excerpts from *Ulysses* by James Joyce. Penguin Books USA Inc. for excerpts from *A Portrait of the Artist as a Young Man* by James Joyce, copyright 1916 by B.W. Huebsch, copyright 1944 by Nora Joyce, copyright © 1964 by the Estate of James Joyce; and for excerpts from *The Critical Writings of James Joyce* by James Joyce, E. Mason, and R. Ellmann, editors, copyright © 1959 by Harriet Weaver and F. Lionel Monro, as Administrators for the Estate of James Joyce, renewed © 1987 by F. Lionel Monro. Used by permission of Viking Penguin, a division of Penguin Books USA Inc. Simon & Schuster for excerpt from "The Circus Animals' Desertion." Reprinted with the permission of Simon & Schuster from *The Poems of W. B. Yeats: A New Edition,* edited by Richard J. Finneran. Copyright © 1940 by Georgie Yeats, renewed 1968 by Bertha Georgie Yeats, Michael Butler Yeats, and Anne Yeats. New Directions Publishing Corporation for "The Old Steps of the Passaic General Hospital" and "My Nurses" copyright © 1997 by Paul H. Williams and the Estate of William Eric Williams; used by permission of New Directions Publishing Corporation, agents.

For A. Walton Litz

Contents

Introduction:
Modernism Resartus

Hugh Witemeyer

"Modernism," Julian Symons observes, "is a word often used but rarely defined" (9). The term is "subject to extreme semantic confusion," and "no international agreement has ever been reached on [its] use and significance" (Bradbury and McFarlane 22; Chefidor 1). It is construed differently by scholars trained in different countries and disciplines. Its "mercurial character" has prompted some critics to abandon the singular form of the word and to speak instead of a "plurality of modernisms" (Chefidor 1; Brooker 5; see also Nicholls vii; Perloff 170).

Among scholars of British, Irish, and American literature, however, the term *modernism* has acquired a somewhat firmer denotation. In their discourse it often designates an experimental trend in English-language literature that flourished from about 1890 to 1945. Taxonomies of the trend frequently include: (1) a revulsion against urban, industrial, bourgeois society, with its technologies of mass warfare; (2) a disposition to interpret modern experience in terms of patterns derived from archaic cultures and ancient mythologies; (3) a fascination with the unconscious and irrational activities of the human psyche; and (4) a rejection of post-Renaissance techniques of naturalistic representation in favor of spare, elemental, disjunctive, and ironic modes. The canon of this Anglo-American literary modernism is undergoing redefinition, but its central figures are perhaps W. B. Yeats, James Joyce, T. S. Eliot, Ezra Pound, William Carlos Williams, Wallace Stevens, e. e. cummings, Hilda Doolittle ("H.D."), Marianne Moore, Gertrude Stein, Virginia Woolf, E. M. Forster, D. H. Lawrence, Joseph Conrad, Ford Madox Ford, Wyndham Lewis, William Faulkner, and Ernest Hemingway. Most of the contributors to *The Future of Modernism* employ the term in this general sense.

In the past fifteen or twenty years Anglo-American modernism has come under scrutiny from the perspective of emergent theories that challenge the foundational assumptions of all cultural categories. These theories include poststructuralism, deconstruction, feminism, and postcolonial historicism. The new perspectives sometimes join forces under the umbrella term *postmodernism*. As Sanford Schwartz notes in the opening essay of this collection, "the arrival of postmodernism has significantly reshaped the terrain upon which the study of modernism takes place."

To oversimplify a complex debate, postmodernism has generally taken an oppositional or antagonistic view of modernism. Defining itself in contrast to its predecessor, postmodernism tends to paint modernism as a dominant, hegemonic, sometimes repressive force (see, e.g., Nelson 54–55; Clark 3–6). In some of the cruder formulations no evidence or argument is offered in support of these judgments; modernism is simply assumed to be synonymous with authority, hierarchy, patriarchy, phallogocentrism, elitism, fascism, racism, formalism, and universalism (the denial of historical contingency). Such casual maligning leads George Bornstein, in his contribution to the present volume, to describe modernism as "the roadkill of contemporary theory."

Insofar as this book has a polemical intent, it is to contest facile dismissals of modernism. Rejecting caricature or strawman versions of the movement, the contributors emphasize the complex and vital legacy of the major modernist authors. In contrast to scholarly obituaries that memorialize modernism as "thankfully past," these essays "affirm that modernism is very much alive" and that it will continue to invigorate our imaginative activities well into the twenty-first century (Jospovici xiv; Robbins 231).

To affirm the future of modernism, however, is not to replicate its past. Postmodernist critiques have permanently altered conceptions of the program and canon of modernism. As Bornstein notes, "future views of modernism will construct their subject far differently than the New Critics did." The contributors to the present volume take this sea change into account, acknowledging and learning from the criticism of recent years.

Thus, in the opening essay Sanford Schwartz argues against simplistic binary oppositions and for a suppler approach that recognizes "The Postmodernity of Modernism." "The rereading of modernism from a postmodern perspective," Schwartz maintains,

. . . has introduced a more variegated understanding of the modernist enterprise, contributed to the retrospective expansion of its canon, and prompted the claim that modernism (or certain elements of modernism) may be more postmodern than we ordinarily assume.

Schwartz interrogates "the modern/postmodern divide" without denying its hermeneutic usefulness.

The next contributor, Jeffrey M. Perl, sounds a note heard in many of the other essays as well. In "Passing the Time: Modernism versus New Criticism" Perl contends that reductive postmodernist accounts of modernism often derive from a confusion between it and New Critical formalism. It is essential, Perl argues, to divorce modernism from the New Criticism, because "the New Critical reading of modernism was impossibly wrong." Later in the collection Vicki Mahaffey makes a similar point when she writes, "more and more frequently, what is being attacked in the name of modernism is . . . the dominant critical theory of the time—the New Criticism—so often confused with it."

In decoupling modernism from formalism, Perl maintains that James Joyce's treatment of the aesthetic of Stephen Dedalus in *A Portrait of the Artist as a Young Man* is ironic. A somewhat different view of Joycean irony lies at the heart of Ronald Bush's essay "James Joyce, Eleanor Marx, and the Future of Modernism." For Bush a saving grace of Joyce's work is its "modernist philosophical aestheticism, an ironic reduction of all truth to the status of as-if and an unequivocal rejection of assumptions . . . of univeral progress." Bush traces this skeptical irony in the work of Joyce's nineteenth-century mentors, Gustave Flaubert and Henrik Ibsen. He contrasts it to the confident, reformist rationalism of Karl Marx's daughter, Eleanor, who was instrumental in introducing the work of Flaubert and Ibsen into England. Extending his analysis to the present, Bush contrasts "philosophical aestheticism" to the reformist outlook of recent postcolonialist critics of modernism, whose political assumptions descend in part from those of Marx.

From irony the focus moves to satire and absurdity in Holly Laird's essay "Laughter and Nonsense in the Making and (Postmodern) Remaking of Modernism." Laird suggests that a postmodernist attention to the "contentious, alternately debunking and canonizing laughter" in women's writing will enrich our views of modernist attitudes and the modernist canon. Thus, the mocking humor of Edith Sitwell and the "laughing indeterminacy" of Zora Neale Hurston suggest new perspectives upon the work of T. S. Eliot and the writers of the Harlem Renaissance. Like other contributors to the collection, Laird welcomes the opening of the canon and the challenge to received notions of gender, race, and class that postmodernism has brought to bear. But she sees these developments as illuminating, not negating, the achievement of modernism.

The next three essays reverse the perspective of Schwartz and Laird. Instead of viewing modernism from postmodernist perspectives, they view later-twentieth-century poetry from modernist perspectives. Vicki Mahaffey, Christopher MacGowan, and James Longenbach show how the legacies of W. B. Yeats, William Carlos Williams, Marianne Moore, and Wallace Stevens enrich the work of their successors. The implicit argument of these essays is that modernism enacts its future by shaping the creative and critical sensibilities of its inheritors.

Thus, Mahaffey's essay "Heirs of Yeats: Eire as Female Poets Revise Her" shows how contemporary Irish women poets such as Eavan Boland, Paula Meehan, and Sara Berkeley have revised the traditional allegorical personification of Ireland as female that they inherited from Yeats and other male predecessors. Rather than an abstract spiritual ideal, Mahaffey argues, the women poets of today embody Ireland in the full "diversity of femaleness."

Mahaffey's concern with poetic representations of community is shared by Christopher MacGowan in "'Caresses—Withheld': William Carlos Williams's Dialogue with the Future." MacGowan examines poems by Williams that deal "with the local community, or a contemporary public event." The examples range from *Paterson* to newly rediscovered verses printed in local newspapers. MacGowan discusses issues of distance and engagement in this public and occasional poetry, and he compares Williams's strategies to those of three younger poets who were influenced by him: Allen Ginsberg, Denise Levertov, and Thom Gunn.

James Longenbach likewise stresses public issues in his discussion of "Modern Poetry after Modernism: The Example of Richard Wilbur." Longenbach mounts a revisionist reading of Wilbur by viewing his work through a series of modernist filters. Wilbur, Longenbach maintains, "has gleefully gone back to modernism to learn from Moore, Stevens, Eliot, Frost, and Williams; at the same time, he has moved past it precisely because of his openness to modernism's variety of poetic practices." Among the things Wilbur learned, according to Longenbach, is how to deal with "the public events of his time," from Mc-Carthyism to the Vietnam War. By stressing the modernist legacy of engagement with contemporary political and social events, Mahaffey, MacGowan, and Longenbach implicitly challenge postmodernist characterizations of modernism as an ideology that denies history (see, e.g., Smith 19).

If the inclusion of women and ethnic minority writers has expanded the canon of Anglo-American modernism, so also have changes in editing and copyright. As modernist works enter the public domain, multiple and competing editions of them will be produced. Previously unpublished texts will be newly edited. Moreover, these new editions will reflect the radical transformations now taking place in editorial theory and publishing technology. The last four essays in the collection argue in various ways that modernist texts of the future will differ significantly from those of the past.

In "The Once and Future Texts of Modernist Poetry" George Bornstein offers an informed and witty overview of new developments in textual editing. Definitive texts, final authorial intentions, and immutable canons are no longer tenable ideals, Bornstein contends. Instead, future texts of modernist poetry will be "protean, existing in multiple and equally authorized forms." Editing will be further complicated by the impact of copyright law and electronic hypertext technology. Bornstein illustrates his argument with key examples from the work of Marianne Moore, Ezra Pound, and W. B. Yeats.

Each of the next three essays focuses upon one of the developments identified in Bornstein's survey. Thus, in Michael Groden's essay "Wandering in the *Avant-texte:* Joyce's 'Cyclops' Copybook Revisited" the new editorial theory is applied to a classic work of modernist prose. As European concepts of textuality have arisen to challenge Anglo-American notions in recent years, Joyce's *Ulysses* has provided the battlefield on which some of the fiercest engagements have been fought. Continental theory treats the "avant-texte" (manuscripts, proofs, periodical versions) of a work as no less important than the "final," or "authorized," version. In his discussion of the "Cyclops" episode of *Ulysses* Groden shows how a consideration of "prepublication documents" can alter critical interpretations of structure, characterization, and "the role of the author in the text." Instead of a unitary opus created by a genius, *Ulysses* becomes "various systems of discourse in dialogue with one another."

The modernist canon is also being expanded by the editing and publication of previously unpublished manuscripts and works long out of print. In "H.D. Prosed: The Future of an Imagist Poet" Robert Spoo describes and assesses the recent wave of new editions of unknown or little-known prose writings by Hilda Doolittle. "Of all the modernists-in-progress none has been more dramatically altered by archival revelations than H.D.," Spoo argues. "The recent spate of memoirs and autobiographical novels has given us a wholly different H.D." Spoo discusses the history of H.D.'s manuscripts and summarizes feminist critical interpretations of them. He stresses the importance of careful editing to an accurate representation of H.D.'s "subtle *écriture feminine*."

Finally, the future texts of modernism may differ in their physical format from the texts we now have. In "The Electronic Future of Modernist Studies" Mary FitzGerald speculates upon the impact that electronic publishing will have upon teaching and scholarship in the humanities. Of all the essays in the collection FitzGerald's is the most "futuristic" in the popular, Alvin Toffler sense of the term.

As books give way to CD-ROMs and on-line editions employing hypermedia formats, students of the twenty-first century may well encounter modernist works through "interactive multimedia software" instead of a "fixed codex format." FitzGerald is optimistic about this prospect, arguing that electronic technology is superior to print technology in most respects. She contends that the study of early-twentieth-century literature is especially good preparation for "future shock" because "the advances offered by electronic technology owe a debt to modernism."

> The high modernists and their heirs in the literary, visual, and musical arts produced a set of metaphors that not only parallel the scientific insights of the twentieth century but created the mind-set that gave rise to them. The verbal and dissonant structures that they employed and the blessed rage for order that drove them to create prefigure the ramifying networks and binary universes of our present mode of information processing.

Thus, FitzGerald closes the collection with a challenging preview of new modes of teaching and learning.

These essays embody no unified vision of the future of modernism. Rather, they suggest a variety of trajectories into the next century. They share starting points rather than finishing lines. Their principal common denominators are a grounding in historical, as opposed to exclusively theoretical, modes of approach, and an unshakable conviction of the enduring value of modernist writing.

Both the family resemblance and the diversity of the essays owe much to the teaching and scholarship of Professor A. Walton Litz of Princeton University. His sustained commitment to modernist literature has inspired several generations of students; indeed, all of the contributors to the present volume wrote their doctoral dissertations under his direction or advisement. That the subsequent, independent work of Litz's students has taken a variety of directions is also a tribute to his influence: to the range of his scholarship, the openness of his teaching, and the generosity of his mentoring. We therefore dedicate *The Future of Modernism*, with affection and gratitude, to A. Walton Litz.

WORKS CITED

Bradbury, Malcolm, and James McFarlane. "The Name and Nature of Modernism." In *Modernism 1890–1930,* ed. Malcolm Bradbury and James McFarlane. Sussex: Harvester Press, 1978.

Brooker, Peter. "Introduction: Reconstructions." In *Modernism/Postmodernism,* ed. Peter Brooker. London: Longman, 1992.

Chefidor, Monique. "Modernism: Babel Revisited." In *Modernism: Challenges and Perspectives,* ed. Monique Chefidor, Ricardo Quinones, and Albert Wachtel. Urbana: U of Illinois P, 1986.

Clark, Suzanne. *Sentimental Modernism: Women Writers and the Revolution of the Word.* Bloomington: Indiana UP, 1991.

Jospovici, Gabriel. *The Lessons of Modernism and Other Essays.* 2nd ed. Houndmills: Macmillan, 1987.

Nelson, Cary. *Repression and Recovery: Modern American Poetry and the Politics of Cultural Memory, 1910–1945.* Madison: U of Wisconsin P, 1987.

Nicholls, Peter. *Modernisms: A Literary Guide.* Berkeley and Los Angeles: U of California P, 1995.

Perloff, Marjorie. "Modernist Studies." In *Redrawing the Boundaries: The Transformation of English and American Literary Studies,* ed. Stephen Greenblatt and Giles Gunn. New York: Modern Language Association, 1992.

Robbins, Bruce. "Modernism in History, Modernism in Power." In *Modernism Reconsidered,* ed. Robert Kiely. Cambridge, MA: Harvard UP, 1983.

Smith, Stan. *The Origins of Modernism: Eliot, Pound, Yeats, and the Rhetorics of Renewal.* Hemel Hempstead: Harvester, 1994.

Symons, Julian. *Makers of the New: The Revolution in Literature, 1912–1939.* London: Andre Deutsch, 1987.

The Postmodernity of Modernism

Sanford Schwartz

In the last few decades the concept of modernism has been altered significantly by the emergence of postmodernism as an axial notion in our cultural vocabulary. It has long been recognized that it is impossible to characterize postmodernism without presupposing some conception of the anterior dispensation embedded in its name. But in recent years it has also become increasingly difficult to consider modernism without reference to the prefix that presumes to mark its temporal and conceptual limits. Most discussions of the relationship between modernism and postmodernism assume a particular definition of the former—as if the historical closure of modernism has settled the question of its identity—and proceed to consider the emergent character of the latter. But the arrival of postmodernism, which has imposed temporal closure upon modernism, also invites us to take another look at modernism in light of the putative passage beyond it. If nothing else, the sheer variety of modernisms that have surfaced in the ever-widening debate over the postmodern indicates that the issue of modernism·—its characteristic features, its ties to the related notion of modernity, and its ghostly presence in the very name of its successor—is far less settled than many intellectuals would like to believe. Modernism may be receding into the cultural past, but it seems to have found new life in the posthumous encounter with its heir.

The focus of this essay is the peculiar afterlife of Anglo-American literary modernism in its entanglement with the postmodern. I will begin by examining some problematic features of the modern/postmodern divide in literary criticism: the polemical use of unmediated oppositions, notwithstanding disclaimers to the contrary; the appropriation of the modern/postmodern distinction from other disciplines, such as philosophy, and from the other arts; and the fixation on the particular conception of modernism—and the selective "modernist" canon—that rose to hegemony during the decade after World War II. The point of such an interrogation is not to deny the distinction between the modern and the postmodern but, rather, to call into question the way this distinction is usually conceived. I will then proceed to consider one of the recent unsung consequences of the modern/postmodern debate—the rereading of modernism from a postmodern perspective, which has introduced a more variegated understanding of the modernist enterprise, contributed to the retrospective expansion of its canon, and prompted the claim that modernism (or certain elements of modernism) may be more postmodern than we ordinarily assume. Ironically, this revisionist modernism subverts the use of *modernism* as a stable term of reference in discussions of its successor and thereby undercuts the antitheses upon which the division between modernism and postmodernism has been constructed. On the other hand, the suspicious ease with which modernism has been postmodernized in recent years also raises a new set of critical questions and introduces some interpretive difficulties that mirror the flaws in the original partition between the two terms.

The ultimate aim of this inquiry is neither to dissolve nor to defend the distinction between modernism and postmodernism but, rather, to understand the difference that the latter has made to the former. On one side, the various formulations of the modern/postmodern divide may crumble upon critical scrutiny, but for better or worse they have solidified the particular image of modernism regnant in the postwar era. On the other side, the project of postmodernizing modernism may overshoot its target, but it has uncovered some forgotten or previously unnoticed aspects of modernist poetics. In this respect the arrival of postmodernism has significantly reshaped the terrain upon which the study of modernism takes place. It has produced some reductive caricatures of modernism, but it has also engendered a new view of modernism that may eventually come full circle to engage the postmodern perspective from which it has issued.

I

One of the main attractions of the postmodern debate, now well into its third decade, is the ongoing attempt to name the difference signified by the *post* before the *modern*. None of the major players has been willing to settle for the purely chronological solution of dividing the twentieth century in half around the year 1945. As mere period labels *modernism* and *postmodernism* are drained of their provocative cultural significance and lose the distinctive bond that simultaneously unites and distinguishes them. Virtually all theorists of postmodern literature opt for some sort of typological distinction that elicits discernible differences in modes of thought, social values, and artistic styles. A few critics, such as Umberto Eco, are prepared to elevate the modern and postmodern into transhistorical categories that manifest enduring alternatives or tensions within Western culture. But the great majority, aiming for a higher degree of historical particularity, want their formulations to say something about the trajectory of our own times. Unfortunately, this attempt to project a binary distinction onto the historical process raises any number of difficulties that overwhelm some ingenious attempts to resolve them.

Theorists of postmodern literature often begin by acknowledging the complexity of the modern/postmodern relationship but then proceed to the unpostmodern practice of employing traditional antinomies to define the difference between them. The preliminary debates of the 1960s revolved around the distinction between elite and popular, "high" and "low," culture, as a new generation of artists and intellectuals, spurred on by critics such as Leslie Fiedler, Ihab Hassan, and Susan Sontag, launched the rebellion against the ostensibly conservative and purist standards of midcentury modernism.[1] But, as critics of the late 1960s and 1970s began to appropriate the alluring terminology of poststructuralist theory, the distinction between modernism and postmodernism came to turn on some fashionable philosophical antitheses—identity/difference, presence/absence, determinacy/indeterminacy, structure/play (mistranslated as "free play"), transcendence/immanence, among others.

In Derridean deconstruction such binary oppositions were employed strategically to destabilize the metaphysical tradition they sustained. In American literary circles, however, these antitheses were employed without their deconstructive edge to name the difference between modernism and postmodernism. Modernism was associated with identity, unity, and homogeneity, postmodernism with difference, multiplicity, and heterogeneity, and caveats to the effect that such antitheses were "unstable" and "equivocal" served more to reinforce than subvert the oppositions they qualified.[2] These dichotomies were buttressed by related pairs imported from fields such as rhetoric (metaphor/metonymy, paradox/aporia), linguistics (hypotaxis/parataxis, signified/signifier), and literary criticism (symbol/allegory) and put to work to distinguish the modernist fidelity to totality, hierarchy, and closure from the postmodernist emphasis upon fragmentation, subversion, and open-endedness. As a result of this process, the modern/postmodern distinction was secured by an imposing array of homologous oppositions. As we shall see, however, this set of oppositions (though differently named) once played a major role within modernism itself, a role obscured by the institutionalization of modernism in the postwar era and perpetuated in the successive reactions against it.

The theory of postmodern literature has also been conditioned by the critique of modernity among influential theorists such as Theodor Adorno, Jean Baudrillard, Gilles Deleuze, Michel Foucault, and Jean-François Lyotard. All of these figures identify modernity with systemic and coercive rationality, and, though they differ significantly in their response to the modern condition, they seem to support the equation of the postmodern with resistance to (or at least the recognition of) the pervasive rationalization of modern life. In his well-known account Lyotard associates modernity with the project of Enlightenment rationality, which in his view achieved its ultimate and grotesque realization in the death camps at Auschwitz. The postmodern condition involves a renunciation of all totalizing projects along with the historical myths that legitimate them—an "incredulity toward metanarratives"—and the recognition of the incommensurable plurality of human interests, needs, and desires.[3] Somewhat incongruously, theorists of postmodern literature are prone to conflate the modernity/postmodernity problematic of contemporary theory with that of modernism/postmodernism in the arts. Never mind that modernism was once regarded as a reaction against modernity, and the exemplary artists in contemporary theory (e.g., Mallarmé, Joyce, Brecht) are generally associated with literary modernism. The temptation to equate postmodernism and postmodernity ends up reducing modernism to another manifestation of modernity and relegating to the postmodern some of the functions once attributed to its predecessor.[4]

Another element of contemporary theory also enters into literary formulations of the postmodern. It is now common to associate modernity with the philosophical epoch inaugurated by Descartes and to define postmodernity in terms of the decentering of the Cartesian cogito, the loss of a secure division between subjective and objective realms, and the breakdown of representational theories of knowledge. Literary critics have adopted this conception to distinguish "modern" subjectivism, foundationalism, and realism from the "postmodern" disruption of consistent subject positions, its nonfoundationalist *mise en abyme,* and the search for an aesthetic beyond the traditional canons of representation. But this transposition from philosophy to literature ignores the fact that the postmodern unraveling of Cartesian modernity by Nietzsche, James, and others around the turn of the century plays a major role in the poetics of modernism. It may be argued that Anglo-American modernists resisted the more radical Nietzschean implications of this critique, but, unless we qualify the wholesale equation between the postmodern and the dissolution of Cartesian dualism, we must acknowledge the postmodern character of modernist poetics. As we shall see, the literary appropriation of the philosophical distinction between modernity and postmodernity has become one of the more enticing strategies for converting modernists into vintage postmodernists.

Theorists of postmodern literature also draw on stylistic developments in the other arts to uphold the modern/postmodern divide. Painting, sculpture, music, and the mass media have provided some interesting parallels, but the most popular source has been architecture, in which the contrast between modern and postmodern styles appears especially sharp.[5] The turn from the allegedly severe formalism of Mies van der Rohe to the playful stylistic melange of Michael Graves, John Portman, and other contemporary architects is considered paradigmatic of the sweeping cultural shift from the modern to the postmodern. The architectural paradigm seems to coalesce with, and is often used to exemplify, the "high"/"low" distinction of the 1960s, the identity/difference constellation from poststructuralist theory, and the modernity/postmodernity problematic of theorists such as Lyotard. But major problems arise when this compelling if sometimes exaggerated illustration of cultural change is projected onto the less clear-cut development of twentieth-century literature, thereby reducing literary modernism to an ahistorical, elitist formalism and ignoring its complex reinscriptions of the past, its appropriations of popular culture, and the referential aims of its putatively nonreferential aesthetic.[6]

The difficulties of upholding the literary distinction between modernism and postmodernism vary with the particular type of definition and the degree to which postmodernism is considered a radical break with its predecessor. The most conspicuous embarrassment comes from the projection of categorical distinctions onto the messy scene of history. It is difficult to avoid the charge that modernist texts exhibit many of the defining features of postmodernism, while postmodernist texts exploit the techniques once associated with modernist literature and contemporaneous developments in the visual arts. For instance, many commentators have noted that the distinction between elite and popular, high and low, culture depends upon a particular midcentury view of modernism—a formalist aesthetic exemplified by the international style in architecture; "abstract" painting, sculpture, and design; and the poetics of New Criticism—which obscures the fascination with popular culture in Joyce, Eliot, and other "high" modernists. The detractors of postmodernism may lament the decline of artistic standards, while supporters revel in their demise, but both factions rely on the same questionable premise that neglects a significant aspect of the modernist enterprise.

A similar problem occurs when modernism is turned to an ahistorical formalism and set against the double-coded historicism of the postmodern. In her influential study *A Poetics of Postmodernism* (1988) Linda Hutcheon overplays her hand by amplifying a commendable treatise on historiographic metafiction (e.g., *Ragtime, The French Lieutenant's Woman, The White Hotel*) into a full-fledged theory of postmodernism. Adopting the model of twentieth-century architecture, she contrasts the spare geometrical forms of modernist design to the historical playfulness and contextual sensitivity of the postmodern. This distinction may or may not do justice to the complexities of modernist architecture (see n. 6), but it disintegrates entirely when transposed to the history of twentieth-century fiction. The historical referentiality of postmodern architecture lines up reasonably well with historiographic metafiction, but it takes a rather severe lapse of cultural memory to pin an "ahistorical" label on a literary movement represented by Faulkner and Joyce, not to mention Pound and Eliot, without doing major violence to the term. The issue of "formalism" (an often used if contested designation throughout the history of modernism) is more complicated, but it would require a nuanced and highly qualified definition of the term to restrict its application to modernist (as distinct from postmodernist) fiction.[7]

Many critics acknowledge the seepage across the modern/post-modern divide and offer some interesting solutions to the problem. In *Postmodernist Fiction* (1987) Brian McHale distinguishes between the "epistemological" concerns of modernist works and the "ontological" character of the postmodern. (The terms echo Heidegger's attempt to reorient philosophy from the epistemological project of the Cartesian epoch and therefore subtly link modernist fiction to a pre-Heideggerian project.) McHale softens his distinction with the claim that the passage from modern to postmodern is not a simple replacement of one mode by another but, rather, a shift in the literary "dominant," and he points to the occasional surfacing of the postmodern in works such as Faulkner's *Absalom, Absalom!* or the second half of Joyce's *Ulysses*. But, by activating the familiar organic image of a new mode trying to emerge out of the old, McHale's apparent concession to historical complexity lends further weight to the dichotomy he is presumably attempting to qualify.[8]

In his more recent book, *Constructing Postmodernism* (1992), McHale becomes more circumspect about the fence-posting of his previous work, admitting that his narrative of a comprehensive literary transformation belies the nontotalizing spirit of the postmodern. But, rather than follow this insight to its ultimate conclusion, McHale attempts to enlist it in support of his original theory. The postmodern has produced an "anxiety of metanarratives," but, since we are compelled to tell stories to make sense of our experience, we must "tolerate the anxiety" and learn to live with convenient fictions.[9] In the boldest move of the book he reckons with the postmodern aspects of modernism by shifting the ground of the distinction from the intrinsic character of the texts themselves to the strategies of interpreting them. Hence, we may now have a postmodernist *Ulysses* as well as a modernist *Gravity's Rainbow*, since the issue of whether a text is modern or postmodern depends upon the way we read it.

Once again McHale retreats from the implications of one nonfoundationalist position by invoking another. In the absence of an absolute criterion for deciding between one reading and the other, the choice between modernist and postmodernist orientations is a matter for practical, or "strategic," interests to decide. Given this objective undecidability, McHale opts for the "modernist" reading of canonically modernist texts (allowing for a few exceptions) on the grounds that it is "the construct likeliest to shed light on the regularities of modernism and the specific 'otherness' of postmodernism."[10] Such attempts to re-erect the wall between modern and postmodern only aggravate the difficulties they attempt to resolve. Moreover, the allegedly postmodern procedure of choosing "a strategically useful and satisfying fiction, in the key of 'as if'"—an interesting amalgam of William James's "Will to Believe" (1896) and Hans Vaihinger's philosophy of "As If" (1910)—is one of the most characteristic stances of modernism itself.[11]

Some of McHale's troubles issue from his willingness to consider objections to a sharp cut between modernism and postmodernism. Specifically, he is concerned with Hans Lethen's claim that theorists of postmodern literature adopt a view of modernism that excludes the more radical moments within it. In order to keep modernism distinct from postmodernism, Lethen maintains, Dada and other avant-garde movements have been subtracted from the former and their subversive aesthetic ascribed to the latter. The list of polarities commonly used to distinguish modernism and postmodernism—ontological certainty/ ontological uncertainty, presence/absence, determinacy/inde- terminacy, hierarchy/anarchy, and so on—"shows the battlefield on which Modernism itself operates."[12] The prevailing division between modern and postmodern is simply "modernism cut in half," and what we call the postmodern is nothing other than the forgotten side of modernism. Susan Suleiman offers a slight twist to the same point, claiming that the modern/postmodern debate is a distinctively Anglo- centric development owing to the fact that "many of the movements that existed on the Continent—such as Dadaism, Surrealism, or Rus- sian and Italian Futurism—were never integrated into the Anglo- American notion of literary Modernism."[13] The binary oppositions that came to isolate the modern from the postmodern are based on the restricted and conservative view of modernism that developed in the English-speaking world.

Both Lethen and Suleiman remind us of the diversity of literary movements that once coexisted under the banner of modernism. They also show that the postmodern debate as it developed in the 1960s and 1970s was prompted by the New Critical codification of modernism that dominated the academy after World War II. But their corrective also introduces some distortions of its own. Lethen and Suleiman relo- cate the antitheses of the modern/postmodern divide within modern- ism itself but then assign the opposing terms to different groups within the larger movement. What is misleading about their argument is that the same polarities they use to define differences *between* main-line and radical modernists also operate as significant tensions *within* the works of the former. The tensions and oscillations between identity and difference, determinacy and indeterminacy, conceptual form and aleatory flux, are constitutive of modernist poetics in the English-speaking world. Hence, it is no accident that contemporary scholars continue to uncover a "postmodern" strain in Pound, Eliot, Stevens, and Williams or in Conrad, Faulkner, Joyce, and Woolf. The same categories employed to sequester these writers from their postmodern successors occupy a crucial position in their works.[14]

For the most part the theorizing of the postmodern has cast a dark spell over its predecessor. The propensity to conceptualize the modern/postmodern relationship in terms of stark antitheses has consigned the former to a conservative ghetto and relegated its more heterodox elements to the latter. Both supporters and detractors of postmodern literature have exhibited a tendency to caricature modernism, the first to clear an oppositional space for its successor, the second to uphold a view of modernism that obscures some of its most interesting features. Of course, such antitheses have never gone unchallenged, even by those who have posited them, if only because the vaunted double coding of the postmodern calls into question the binary pairs employed to distinguish it from modernism, thereby confirming its identity with modernism in the very process of marking the difference between them. But, if theorists of the postmodern have hesitated to delve too deeply into the problem, it would be a mistake to leap too quickly to the opposite conclusion that we should simply dissolve the distinction between modernism and postmodernism, something that is unlikely to occur in any case. If the theorizing of postmodernism has produced some untenable oppositions to modernism, the recent efforts to reveal the postmodern within modernism, as I hope to show, may be obscuring some significant differences.

II

For several decades the same literary developments that have consigned modernism to cultural oblivion have also brought forth new ways of reading it. The revolt against modernist poetry and New Critical poetics in the late 1950s and 1960s also created a new awareness of the once concealed continuities between romanticism and modernism.

The deconstructive turn in the 1970s and 1980s, while challenging modernist/New Critical poetics, also instigated some significant re-readings of modernist texts. More recently, the widespread preoccupation with issues of gender, class, race, region, and ethnicity has produced a retrospective expansion of the modernist canon, a reassessment of its sociopolitical contexts, and the establishment of a more internally variegated conception of the modernist enterprise.[15] In other words, since its codification during the heyday of New Criticism, Anglo-American modernism has been at once static and mobile—primarily an inert and reified target for new movements seeking self-definition but also a protean phenomenon continually altering its configuration as it is viewed from new perspectives. The rise of postmodern literary theory (which is closely related though not identical to these other movements) has produced the same double effect on modernism, but with the ironic result that the postmodern is now undermining the very conception of modernism upon which it continues to depend.

In recent years we have witnessed the postmodernizing of virtually every author associated with high modernism in the Anglo-American scene. The list ranges from canonical eminences, such as Yeats and Eliot, to those like Gertrude Stein who never fit comfortably within the orthodox mold. In the 1970s, J. Hillis Miller and Joseph Riddel launched the new wave with provocative if controversial readings of Stevens, Pound, and Williams.[16] But several factors obscured the implications of these essays for the future of modernism. As a mode of textual analysis, American deconstruction (like New Criticism) was at once too narrow and too broad. The unobjectionable focus on individual writers left intact the more general notion of modernism, while the profligate use of deconstruction to scrutinize texts from Homer to the present obfuscated its particular relevance to the first generation of poets writing in the wake of the intellectual revolution associated with Nietzsche, James, and others at the turn of the century. Furthermore, this type of analysis ignored the structural tensions that characterize many modernist texts: while uncovering the element of flux, indeterminacy, and open-endedness in modernist poetics, it neglected or re-described the countervailing impulse to project organizing forms, if only in the tentative mode of "as if," upon the uncontainable play of textual difference. If New Criticism neutralized textual flux by means of tropes that establish unity-in-difference—paradox, metaphor, and the tamer forms of irony and ambiguity—deconstruction lifted the constraints of form and thereby converted modernists (and many others too) into exemplary postmodernists.

American deconstruction contributed to the more general shift in critical orientation that took place during the 1970s. With the decline of the New Critical hegemony came a new model of inquiry that altered prevailing notions of authorial intention, textual structure, and reader appropriation, all of which pointed to the irreducibly plural character of literary interpretation. The author was transformed from a unifying consciousness to the conduit for disparate or conflicting desires, discursive structures, and ideological formations of which he or she may be unaware. The literary text, previously considered a coherent organic entity, became the site of dissonant voices, unassimilated fragments, and irreconcilable discrepancies among its constituent elements. At the same time, critics began to emphasize the constitutive role of transient personal interests, social conditions, and interpretive conventions in the process of textual comprehension. The application of this new paradigm transcended the specificities of literary history, but, given the distinctive features of modernist texts such as *The Waste Land, The Cantos,* and *Ulysses,* the effects on modernism were especially profound. If Eliot and the New Critics offered readers a procedure for reducing these bewildering texts to formal unity, the critics of the 1970s began to emphasize the intricacies of the compositional process and the proliferation of disparate voices and modes that undercut traditional conceptions of literary form.[17] Eventually, the same strategy was extended from the level of individual texts to the history of the modernist movement as a whole. In *A Genealogy of Modernism* (1984) Michael Levenson focuses on the established modernist canon but resolves modernist poetics into a complex series of historical shifts and reversals later effaced by the construction of modernist orthodoxy.[18] More recently, Marjorie Perloff has taken the final step in this process by suggesting that we simply abandon the unitary notion of modernism in favor of an irreducible variety of "modernisms."[19] This is the logic of disintegration with a vengeance, but it is symptomatic not only of the new critical dispensation but also of the difference it has made to the study of modernism.

Another means of fissuring the unitary character of modernism came from the very antitheses originally employed to separate it from the postmodern. As critics struggled to define the new literature taking shape in the 1960s and 1970s, they also began to identify postmodernist strains in the previous era. The same binary oppositions that distinguished modernism and postmodernism were redeployed to define competing forms within modernist or even romantic tradition. In a seminal essay Charles Altieri celebrates the "immanence" of contemporary poetry but argues that the conflict between "immanent" and "transcendent" modes may be traced back to the alternatives previously laid out by Wordsworth and Coleridge. Hence, the postmodern revolt against Eliot and canonical modernism is only the latest round in an ongoing struggle within the (broadly defined) modern tradition.[20] In studies prior to her declaration of unlimited modernisms Marjorie Perloff distinguishes between Symbolist poetics (Baudelaire, Eliot, Stevens, Auden) and an alternative tradition of "indeterminacy" originating with Rimbaud and associated both with "modernists" such as Stein, Williams, and Pound and with "the poetry now emerging."[21]

These attempts to rethink literary tradition have the beneficial effect of dissolving simple chronological divisions without abandoning history altogether. In postulating a postmodern tradition within modernism, they identify specific literary practices obscured by previous accounts of modernist technique. But this manner of "cutting modernism in half" suffers from the same liabilities as the antitheses between modern and postmodern from which it derives. Perloff provides a fruitful typological distinction, though the attributes of one type appear in poets she assigns to the other, and passages designed to illustrate an author's allegiance to one poetic mode occasionally seem just as well suited to the alternative mode. The legitimacy of the distinction is compromised by the very efforts to patrol the border that holds it in place. In this respect a binary opposition can be as problematic as the monolithic framework it is meant to replace.

Perhaps the most compelling strategy for postmodernizing modernism comes from contemporary philosophy, which tends to identify the postmodern divide with Nietzsche, James, and other turn-of-the-century philosophers. The approach from philosophy is especially attractive because it appears to anchor the rereading of modernism in a roughly contemporaneous movement. The philosophical watershed comfortably precedes and overlaps the early modernist movement, and the influence of philosophers associated with this revolution is a well-documented phenomenon in literary modernism. Furthermore, the various touchstones of the new philosophical dispensation are central concerns of modernist poetics: the recognition that consciousness is not fully transparent to itself but conditioned by forces of which it is un-aware; the loss of a clear division between subject and object, mind and world, knowledge and reality; the claim that our conceptual systems are not the reflection of a transcendent order beneath the sensory flux but convenient and transient devices for projecting order upon it. Thus, by transferring the philosophical definition of postmodernism to the literary realm, we can readily demonstrate the postmodernity of the modernist enterprise.[22]

The approach from philosophy is also fraught with dangers. From a contemporary perspective it is tempting to focus upon Nietzsche (sharpened by contemporary French theory), or upon a Nietzschean version of James, and ignore the distinctive stances of other philoso-phers, including Bergson and Bradley, who participated in the same philosophical revolution.[23] All of these philosophers agree that concep-tual systems should be construed as instrumental grids for ordering a stream of sensations irreducible to any rational schema. Yet they differ considerably in their descriptions of immediate experience and on the status of the concepts we use to order it.

At least two lines of comparison are significant for the postmodern rereading of modernism. Bergson and the early James emphasize the personal and subjective nature of the sensory flux: the former's *durée réelle* (real duration) and the latter's "stream of thought" inform the more traditional interpretations that associate modernism with the ren-dering of individual consciousness. By contrast, Nietzsche, Bradley, and the later James assume the more radical position that immediate experience precedes the very distinction between subject and object and that the point at which we mark the boundary between them is a matter for transient and practical interests to decide. This stance points to the more equivocal structure evident in poems such as "The Love Song of J. Alfred Prufrock," in which the poetic "voice" oscillates be-tween subjective and objective viewpoints and in which it is difficult, if not impossible, to determine whether we are apprehending an internal stream of consciousness, as most readers still assume, or listening to a speaker's presentation of himself to another person ("Let us go then, you and I"), as Eliot once maintained.

It is easy to confuse the Bergsonian flux with its Nietzschean coun-terpart, but in the current critical climate the consequences of mistak-ing one for the other are significant: modernism remains modernist when the contemporary critic identifies the text with a Bergsonian or

Jamesian stream of consciousness; it becomes postmodernist when the critic assumes a problematic blurring of the subject/object divide. In principle, modernist and postmodernist readings imply distinct textual structures, but in practice it is common for different critics to regard the same text in one way or the other and for the same critic to detect (or imagine) an author's development from a modernist to a postmodernist orientation.[24]

A similar distinction must be made between Nietzschean and Jamesian positions regarding the instrumental nature of concepts. The more familiar Nietzschean stance is that concepts are merely convenient fictions, though Nietzsche deconstructs the very distinction between "truth" and "fiction" in order to free the latter from its traditional role as the dialectical counterpart of the former. The Jamesian position is that concepts are true to the degree that they guide us efficaciously through the sensory flux. Conceptual networks are human inventions, but they may disclose real relations—that is, aspects of reality itself. Unlike Nietzsche, who subverts the traditional hierarchy that privileges conceptual abstraction over concrete sensation, form over flux, identity over difference, James retains the opposing terms and attempts to establish a new and more productive relationship between them.

It is easy to conflate Nietzsche and James, since they share the same recognition of the constructed character of human knowledge, and contemporary philosophers such as Richard Rorty see that for certain purposes the differences between them can be ignored.[25] Rorty strategically nudges James in the direction of Nietzsche, but in the reading of modernist literature it would be a mistake to disregard the distinctions between them. Modernist texts often display a more Jamesian attempt to establish interactive or tensional relationships between conceptual unity and sensory multiplicity, organizing form and unstable flux. If some critics regard these tensional constructs as the endgame of traditional aesthetics, the postmodernizers of modernism are prone to the opposite extreme of effacing a significant difference.[26]

Another hazard of the philosophical approach issues from the propensity to construct a narrative of authorial development from modernist to postmodernist modes. This problem is especially evident in Richard Shusterman's formidable reinterpretation of T. S. Eliot's literary criticism.[27] Well aware of Eliot's extensive philosophical training, Shusterman claims that the poet's intellectual development mirrors the course of Anglo-American philosophy in the last hundred years: an

initial commitment to Bradley's idealism; then a relatively abrupt trans-
formation, influenced by Russell's rejection of Bradley, to the analytical
realism that presumably informs Eliot's early criticism; and, finally, in a
move that foreshadows the new postmodern configuration, a shift from
realism and objectivism toward a nonfoundationalist position strik-
ingly similar to that of future luminaries such as the later Wittgenstein,
Gadamer, Derrida, and Rorty. In this way Shusterman rescues Eliot
from the image he imposed upon himself and the one imposed upon
him by his putative association with the poetics of Brooks, Warren,
Ransom, and Tate. Eliot the New Critic becomes Eliot the postmodern
theorist, endowed with a finely attuned sense of the radically historicist
and nonfoundational philosophy that would move to the center of the
philosophical stage in the decades after his death.

Unfortunately, for all its conceptual elegance this sequence slides
over Eliot's early philosophical prose, which indicates that by Shuster-
man's own definition Eliot was postmodern from the outset of his
career. The Bradley who appears in Eliot's doctoral dissertation (1916)
is not a typical philosophical idealist: Bradley begins with a post-
Cartesian notion of "immediate experience" that precedes the division
between subject and object, and he proposes a theory of knowledge as
thoroughly instrumental as that of James and the pragmatists.[28] More-
over, a look at Eliot's early philosophical papers shows that he had
already assimilated the realist attack on Bradley and commits himself
neither to idealism nor to realism but, rather, to a dialectical strategy
designed to undercut the one-sided claims of both. In response to philo-
sophical idealism Eliot shows that the mind can be understood entirely
in terms of the objects to which it is directed, while in response to
realism he demonstrates that all objects depend ultimately upon the
minds that constitute them.

Therefore, it is a mistake to maintain that Eliot converted from
Bradley's idealism to Russell's realism, since the realist critique of ideal-
ism, like the idealist critique of realism, is a conspicuous feature of
Eliot's work from the very start. In Eliot's early writings the very dis-
tinction between subject and object is ultimately a relative one, and
idealism and realism cannot be regarded as independent options, since
each exists only as the differential counterpart of the other.[29] In other
words, the story of Eliot's development from one stage to the next
depends upon the artificial separation between two positions that are
not successive but simultaneous aspects of his work. Shusterman seems

on firmer ground when he considers the later Eliot, but, in bypassing the postmodern features of the early writings, he drifts into a questionable narrative of progression from modern to postmodern modes.[30]

Shusterman's study raises a final issue that complicates the postmodern appropriation of modernism. It is at once stimulating and unsettling to find that Eliot's orientation to language, interpretation, and tradition anticipates some of the leading tenets of contemporary theory, including the focus on the historicity of understanding, the skeptical attitude toward the rational-scientific model of knowledge, and the turn to Aristotelian *phronesis* (or practical wisdom) as an alternative to the Enlightenment model of rationality. Many of these ideas, however, have been part of the conservative intellectual tradition since the later eighteenth century, and what Shusterman may actually have hit upon in his discovery of a postmodern Eliot is the striking similarity between conservative and radical attacks upon the rationalist heritage of the Enlightenment.[31] This convergence of antithetical ideologies raises the question, articulated most forcefully in the debate between Habermas and Lyotard, of the ideological affiliations of postmodernism.[32] Should the postmodern be regarded as a major departure from modernity or as another manifestation of a long-standing ideological debate constitutive of modernity? Or, to put it somewhat differently, does the postmodern introduce a new orientation that reconfigures the ideological divisions of the preceding centuries, or is it another phase of the ongoing critique of Enlightenment rationality that looms large in romanticism and modernism alike? Such questions may resist instant resolution, but, given that the same perspectives, arguments, and tropes may proceed from opposite ends of the ideological spectrum, the critic who aspires to reread the modern through the lens of the postmodern cannot afford to ignore them.

III

In large measure the problems of the postmodernizing of modernism reflect those of the original modern/postmodern divide. If the theorists of postmodern literature amplified some discernible differences into pronounced antitheses, revisionary modernists tend to elide subtle differences and subsume the modern (or certain portions of it) into the postmodern. Ironically, the latter group is often nagged by the same binarism to which it is opposed. The flawed opposition between modern and postmodern is simply transferred into an unmediated bifurcation within modernism itself. Writers are corralled into rival traditions, each of which possesses a distinct or mutually exclusive set of attributes. Careers of selected writers are cut in half to demonstrate their development from mainline to postmodern modernists (rarely the other way around), and structural complexities that characterize an entire oeuvre are flattened into temporal shifts from one state to another.

These difficulties notwithstanding, the postmodernizing project has provoked a significant reconsideration of modernism. Despite the continued baiting of Eliot and other canonical authors, the entanglement with the postmodern is slowly decoupling modernism from mid-century New Criticism. The scope of the postmodern phenomenon has called forth a new recognition of the international character of modernism and initiated new inquiries into its cultural, social, and political affiliations. At the same time, the postmodern emphasis upon difference, heterogeneity, and multiplicity has heightened awareness of the internal tensions within national traditions and inspired microanalyses of particular individuals, groups, and institutions not always ignored in their own day but largely forgotten ever since.

For more than a generation the conflict over postmodernism has been sustained by the conception of modernism that came to the fore in the decade after World War II. This version of modernism served the polemical interests of both sides in the postmodern debate: for advocates of the new ethos it fenced off a conceptual field for postmodernism to occupy; for adversaries it established a standard by which to measure the degradation of artistic integrity. The remarkable tenacity of this conception of modernism (or, rather, the caricatures that substitute for it) is a function of the polemical needs it continues to serve. But the very changes that have led us away from modernism have also exposed the partial and transient character of its midcentury image and at the same time have begun to alter our understanding of the era we have presumably left behind.

The recent configuration of the modern in light of the postmodern calls into question the antitheses upon which the division between them has been constructed. Nevertheless, in my view this shaking of the foundations points not to the dissolution but, rather, to the complication of the original distinction. Perhaps one lesson to be learned is that we should refrain from the construction of rigid boundaries as well as the demolition of defining difference and activate the full circle of mutual implication, at once logical and temporal, that ties the modern to the postmodern in the very act of distinguishing between them. Or maybe we should simply accept the fact that the process of cultural change involves the double movement of establishing sharp polemical oppositions that simultaneously uphold and undermine the distinction between the old order and the new. That is to say, it may be less a sign of logical failure than a measure of practical success that postmodernism has undercut its constitutive opposition to modernism. In either case we should begin to recognize both the difference that postmodernism has made to modernism and the difference that a revised view of modernism will make to the postmodern as we now conceive it. As a consequence of this process, we may never be in a position to give a definitive name to the difference between the modern and the postmodern, but we may continue to test, qualify, and refine our understanding of each in the ongoing effort to articulate the relationship between them.

NOTES

1. See the elegiac essays on the passing of modernism by Irving Howe, "Mass Society and Post-Modern Fiction," *The Decline of the New* (New York: Harcourt, 1970; reprinted from *Partisan Review,* 1959); and Harry Levin, "What Was Modernism?" *Refractions: Essays in Comparative Literature* (New York: Oxford UP, 1966; reprinted from *Massachusetts Review* [1960]). On the revolt against modernism, see Leslie Fiedler, "The New Mutants," *Partisan Review* 32 (1965); 505–25; Ihab Hassan, "The Dismemberment of Orpheus," *American Scholar* 32 (1963): 463–84; and Susan Sontag, "The Aesthetics of Silence," *Styles of Radical Will* (New York: Dell, 1969; reprinted from *Aspen* 5–6 [1967]): 3–34. See also the retrospective accounts of the 1960s by Andreas Huyssen in *After the Great Divide: Modernism, Mass Culture, Postmodernism* (Bloomington: Indiana UP, 1986) 188–95; and Hans Bertens, *The Idea of the Postmodern: A History* (London: Routledge, 1995) 20–36.

2. The locus classicus of this tendency is Ihab Hassan's celebrated list of thirty-three pairs of antithetical terms in "Postface 1982: Toward a Concept of Postmodernism," *The Dismemberment of Orpheus: Toward a Postmodern Literature,* 2nd ed. (Madison: U of Wisconsin P, 1982) 259–71. Charles Jencks outdoes Hassan with a list of thirty-six distinctions in the preface to *The Post-Modern Reader* (London: St. Martin's Press, 1992) 34. Most of these dyads are binary oppositions, though Hassan reminds us that his distinctions are "equivocal," and Jencks declares that "the post-modern is a complexification, hybridisation and sublation of the modern—not its antithesis" (33). Elsewhere Jencks takes issue with Hassan, arguing that the latter lays out a theory of late-modernism

rather than post-modernism (21). This attempt to sift out counterfeit postmodernisms only compounds the problem of binary logic by replicating it *within* one term of the original opposition.

3. Jean-François Lyotard, *The Postmodern Condition: A Report on Knowledge,* trans. Geoff Bennington and Brian Massumi (Minneapolis: U of Minnesota P, 1984; orig. 1979), xxiv. See also his subsequent work, *The Postmodern Explained,* trans. Don Barry et al. (Minneapolis: U of Minnesota P, 1992; orig. 1988), which suggestively unravels the modern/postmodern divide: "It [the postmodern] is undoubtedly part of the modern. Everything that is received must be suspected, even if it is a day old. . . . The 'generations' flash by at an astonishing rate. A work can become modern only if it is first postmodern. Thus understood, postmodernism is not modernism at its end, but in a nascent state, and this state is recurrent" (12–13). Lyotard's paradox issues from the Baudelairean formulation of *modernité* as the condition that demands perpetual novelty and thereby ensures the superannuation of today's new fashion. The postmodernizing of modernism discussed in this essay proceeds from a different set of assumptions that reflect the particular conditions of the Anglo-American situation.

4. At the risk of sacrificing felicitous ambiguity, I will distinguish between *modernism* in the arts and the epochal notion of "modernity" and, similarly, between *postmodernism* and *postmodernity,* recognizing that elsewhere the two latter terms are sometimes employed interchangeably. My adjectival or substantive use of the terms *modern* and *postmodern* will range more freely across the semantic field. The problem of terminology is tied to a significant issue, since theorists of the postmodern often point to the "modern" propensity to divide human activities into distinct and autonomous spheres, a practice exhibited in the institutional arrangements that have separated the studies of modernism, modernity, and modernization, and masked their profound affiliations.

5. Most studies of postmodernism focus on a specific art or discipline while drawing expedient comparisons to others. Extended efforts to work through and synthesize developments in a broad range of practices include Steven Connor, *Postmodernist Culture: An Introduction to Theories of the Contemporary* (Oxford: Blackwell, 1989); David Harvey, *The Condition of Postmodernity: An Inquiry into the Origins of Cultural Change* (Oxford: Blackwell, 1989); Fredric Jameson, *Postmodernism, or The Cultural Logic of Late Capitalism* (Durham, N.C.: Duke UP, 1991). Jameson's triadic scheme, which situates modernism between realism and postmodernism, overcomes the crudity of most binary theories but perpetuates their tendency to uphold an unmediated (if highly sophisticated) distinction between modernist and postmodernist culture.

6. As persuasive as it seems, the architectural paradigm depends upon a particular formulation of the modernist enterprise that ignores much of its subtlety. For instance, the "black, quasi-Fascist" (Jencks, *Post-Modern Reader,* p.12) glass curtains of the much maligned Mies van der Rohe were often designed to capture the reflection of older buildings of the adjacent cityscape and establish a kind of palimpsestic interplay between the old and the new. Hence, the controversies whenever developers propose to demolish certain

older structures surrounding Mies's Federal Center in Chicago, often regarded as the epitome of modernist indifference to the specificities of time and place. For local residents the center not only broke the monotony of the urban block pattern but also opened a perspective from which to appreciate the city's architectural heritage.

7. Linda Hutcheon, *A Poetics of Postmodernism: History, Theory, Fiction* (London: Routledge, 1988). At points Hutcheon mediates judiciously between critics who defend a sharp modern/postmodern distinction and those who emphasize the mutual imbrication of the concepts and the stylistic continuities they represent. But elsewhere she is so eager to divide modernist formalism and postmodern referentiality that she not only suppresses crucial elements of modernist poetics but also excludes Roland Barthes from the postmodern pantheon for celebrating "repression of reference" in the literary text (144). In the first half of this century the attempt to break with the norms of nineteenth-century realism often drew the charge of "formalism," but, as T.S. Eliot maintains in an early essay on Ben Jonson (1919), the "new worlds" of nonmimetic art suspend referentiality at one level in order to restore it at another: "Jonson's characters conform to the logic of the emotions of their world. It is a world like Lobatchevsky's; the worlds created by artists like Jonson are like systems of non-Euclidean geometry. They are not fancy, because they have a logic of their own; and this logic illuminates the actual world, because it gives us a new point of view from which to inspect it" (*Sacred Wood*, 116–17). The Russian Formalists (so named by their opponents) share this emphasis upon art as a means of redescribing the world as it ordinarily appears. The issue is not referentiality but, rather, the presumption that the artist sees beyond the conventions that organize everyday experience and constructs new forms of thought, feeling, and action.

8. Brain McHale, *Postmodernist Fiction* (London: Methuen, 1987) 3–11.

9. Brian McHale, *Constructing Postmodernism* (London: Routledge, 1992) 1–8.

10. Ibid., 58.

11. William James, *The Will to Believe, and Other Essays in Popular Philosophy* (Cambridge: Harvard UP, 1979; orig. 1896); Hans Vaihinger, *The Philosophy of 'As If,'* trans. C. K. Ogden (London: Routledge, 1924; orig. 1910). On the distinctions between James's position and the one Vaihinger adopts from Nietzsche, see sec. 2 below.

12. Hans Lethen, "Modernism Cut in Half: The Exclusion of the Avantgarde and the Debate on Postmodernism," in *Approaching Postmodernism,* ed. Douwe Fokkema and Hans Bertens (Amsterdam: John Benjamins, 1986) 236. Lethen works with an abbreviated and slightly modified version of Hassan's model (see n. 2).

13. Susan Rubin Suleiman, "Naming and Difference: Reflections on 'Modernism versus Postmodernism' in Literature," in Fokkema and Bertens, *Approaching Postmodernism,* 265. McHale, Lethen, and Suleiman all presented papers at the Workshop on Postmodernism at the University of Utrecht in September 1984.

14. These are also pivotal categories for the principal architects of New Criticism—Ransom, Tate, Brooks, and Warren—and for related critics such as Blackmur and Winters, though their efforts to curb the more dispersive tendencies of early modernism contributed to the domestication of modern literature and literary criticism in the postwar academy. It may be some time before New Criticism begins to recover from the deep freeze of the last few decades, but given the complexity of the movement, its momentous impact, and its affiliations to the critical modes that have replaced it, New Criticism should be in line for the same postmodern reconsideration that modernism is beginning to receive.

It may be worth noting that the theorizing of postmodern poetry often turns on the same distinctions between identity and difference, determinacy and indeterminacy, form and flux. For instance, in his illuminating study *Unending Design: The Forms of Postmodern Poetry* (Ithaca: Cornell UP, 1991) Joseph Conte distinguishes between procedural and serial modes in postmodern verse—the first characterized by the imposition of systematic form, the second by discontinuous and sometimes aleatory sequence.

15. The study of modernism is undergoing a dramatic transformation as a result of the recovery of women in the modernist movement and feminist rereadings of modernist texts. Symptomatic of this change are the essays and selections in Bonnie Kime Scott, ed., *The Gender of Modernism: A Critical Anthology* (Bloomington: Indiana UP, 1990). On the burgeoning study of race, class, and ethnicity in the modernist movement, see, among others Houston Baker, *Modernism and the Harlem Renaissance* (Chicago: U of Chicago P, 1987); Cary Nelson, *Repression and Recovery: Modern American Poetry and the Politics of Cultural Memory, 1910–1945* (Madison: U of Wisconsin P, 1989); and Marcus Klein, *Foreigners: The Making of American Literature, 1900–1940* (Chicago: U of Chicago P, 1981).

16. See, for example, Joseph N. Riddel, "Interpreting Stevens: An Essay on Poetry and Thinking," *boundary 2*, 1 (1972): 79–97; *The Inverted Bell: Modernism and the Counterpoetics of William Carlos Williams* (Baton Rouge: Louisiana State UP, 1974); "Pound and the Decentered Image," *Georgia Review* 29 (1975): 565–91; and J. Hillis Miller, "Stevens' Rock and Criticism as Cure," *Georgia Review* 30 (1976): 5–31, 330–48.

17. Compare, for instance, Cleanth Brooks and A. Walton Litz on *The Waste Land*. Brooks weaves a series of motifs, symbols, and allusions into formal and thematic unity. Litz, writing after the publication of Eliot's drafts in 1971, is wary of the temptation to supply *The Waste Land* "with a spurious plot" and regards the poem as "a museum of verse forms, an experiment with language, the record of a sensibility exposed to the anxieties of a particular culture." Cleanth Brooks, "The Waste Land: Critique of the Myth," *Modern Poetry and the Tradition* (Chapel Hill: U of North Carolina P, 1967; orig. 1939) 136–72; A. Walton Litz, "*The Waste Land* Fifty Years After," in *Eliot in His Time: Essays on the Occasion of the Fiftieth Anniversary of* The Waste Land, ed. A. Walton Litz (Princeton: Princeton UP, 1973) 6–8.

18. Michael Levenson, *A Genealogy of Modernism: A Study of English Liter-*

ary Doctrine 1908–1922 (Cambridge: Cambridge UP, 1984). Some critics contend that Levenson converts enduring structural tensions into a narrative of successive historical phases. In Levenson's case the charge is debatable, but the same problem shadows other studies that presume to track a particular writer's development from modern to postmodern modes.

19. Marjorie Perloff, "Modernist Studies," in *Redrawing the Boundaries: The Transformation of English and American Literary Studies*, ed. Stephen Greenblatt and Giles Gunn (New York: Modern Language Association, 1992) 154–78. Matei Calinescu offers a less nominalist means of pluralizing modernism in *Five Faces of Modernity: Modernism, Avant-Garde, Decadence, Kitsch, Postmodernism*, 2nd ed. (Durham, N.C.: Duke UP, 1987). So does Perloff in some of her own earlier studies (see n. 21).

20. Charles Altieri, "From Symbolist Thought to Immanence: The Ground of Postmodern American Poetics," *Boundary* 2 1 (1973): 605–41.

21. Marjorie Perloff, *The Poetics of Indeterminacy: Rimbaud to Cage* (Princeton: Princeton UP, 1981) 44. See also *The Dance of the Intellect: Studies in the Poetry of the Pound Tradition* (Cambridge: Cambridge UP, 1985).

22. Studies that link the modernist movement to turn-of-the-century philosophy vary considerably in approach. In *William Butler Yeats* (New York: Viking, 1971) Denis Donoghue places Yeats under the sign of Nietzsche, but his is the more traditional (or should we say "modernist") Nietzsche of the Apollonian/Dionysian dialectic and not the deconstructive wizard that informs such studies as Kathryn Lindberg, *Reading Pound Reading* (New York: Oxford UP, 1987) and Michael Beehler *T. S. Eliot, Wallace Stevens, and the Discourses of Difference* (Baton Rouge: Louisiana State UP, 1987), both of which descend from the poststructuralist work of Riddel and Miller.

23. I discuss the relations among turn-of-the-century philosophers in greater detail in *The Matrix of Modernism: Pound, Eliot, and Early Twentieth-Century Thought* (Princeton: Princeton UP, 1985) 40–49, 213–15.

24. See, for example, Anthony Easthope, "Eliot, Pound, and the Postmodern," in *After the Future: Postmodern Times and Places*, ed. Gary Shapiro (Albany: SUNY P, 1990) 53–66, which seems determined to read *The Waste Land* as modernist and *The Cantos* as a postmodernist poem. Such a distinction is defensible, but here it is established through criteria that, with certain adjustments, could yield a postmodern reading of Eliot and a modernist reading of Pound.

25. Richard Rorty, *Consequences of Pragmatism* (Minneapolis: U of Minnesota P, 1982).

26. Alan Wilde proposes a related distinction in discriminating between the *disjunctive* irony of modernism and the *suspensive* irony of postmodernism: the first involves an attempt to project order (somewhat less tentatively than James) upon a world that is "inherently disconnected and fragmented"; in the second "a more radical vision of multiplicity, randomness, contingency, and even absurdity . . . is simply (or not so simply) accepted." *Horizons of Assent: Modernism, Postmodernism, and the Ironic Imagination* (Baltimore: Johns Hopkins UP, 1981) 10. This typological distinction must be qualified by the recognition

that instances of postmodern irony appear in "modernist" literature, and vice versa.

27. Richard Shusterman, *T. S. Eliot and the Philosophy of Criticism* (New York: Columbia UP, 1988).

28. T. S. Eliot, *Knowledge and Experience in the Philosophy of F. H. Bradley* (New York: Farrar, Straus, 1964).

29. The same thing pertains to Eliot's early criticism, which displays not a shift from Bradley's "idealism" to Russell's "realism" but the same oscillation between opposing positions—that is, between the demand to transmute subjective states of emotion into their "objective correlatives" and an equally insistent imperative to transfigure ordinary objects by infusing them, or intensifying them, with human emotion. Eliot applied the first to offset the excessive subjectivism of romantic poetry, the second to counter the excessive objectivism of fictional and dramatic realism.

30. For other narratives of the "breakthrough" to postmodernity in Eliot, Stevens, and Williams, see Stanley J. Scott, *Frontiers of Consciousness: Interdisciplinary Studies in American Philosophy and Poetry* (New York: Fordham UP, 1991).

31. Given that his conception of the postmodern is as hospitable to Gadamer as it is to Derrida, it may be argued that Shusterman slides over significant differences between conservative and radical developments in post-Heideggerean philosophy. Gadamer is the pivotal figure in Shusterman's argument: his position is closest to Eliot's, and, once he is enshrined within the postmodern, the path has been cleared for Eliot's inclusion within it.

32. On the Habermas/Lyotard debate, see Jürgen Habermas, "Modernity versus Postmodernity," *New German Critique* 22 (1981): 3–14; *The Philosophical Discourse of Modernity,* trans. Frederick Lawrence (Cambridge: MIT Press, 1987; orig. 1985); and Richard Rorty, "Habermas and Lyotard on Postmodernity," in *Habermas and Modernity,* ed. Richard Bernstein (Cambridge: MIT Press, 1985) 161–75.

Passing the Time: Modernism versus New Criticism

Jeffrey M. Perl

If modernism—"palaeomodernism" in Frank Kermode's vocabulary, "The Pound Era" in Hugh Kenner's, "The Kenner Canon" in Carolyn Heilbrun's—is to have a future, it will need to be freed from the embrace of loved ones. The New Critics portrayed themselves as friends of the aesthetics and critical theory established by Eliot, Joyce, and Pound; it was thus natural that, when the overdue rebellion against New Critical orthodoxy occurred, academic opinion would turn against modernism. Yet the New Critical reading of modernism was impossibly wrong. Eliot, who appears as founder of New Critical formalism in the Baedekers of the 1990s, was by 1956 annoyed by this presumption. While he held, of course, that the critic must attend to *"poetry as poetry,"* he also wanted it known that "any critic seriously concerned with a man's work should be expected to know something about the man's life," that there is no "reason why biographies of poets should not be written," and that

> I have recently noticed a development, which I suspect has its origin in the classroom methods of Professor [I. A.] Richards, which is, in its way, a healthy reaction against the diversion of attention from poetry to the poet. It is found in a book published not long ago, entitled *Interpretations:* a series of essays by twelve of the younger English critics, each analysing one poem of his own choice. The method is to take a well-known poem . . . without reference to the author or to his other work, analyse it stanza by stanza and line by line, and extract, squeeze, tease, press every

drop of meaning out of it that one can. It might be called the lemon-squeezer school of criticism . . . and, it must be admitted, to study twelve poems each analysed so painstakingly is a very tiring way of passing the time . . . an exercise for pupils.[1]

It would not be easy to miss Eliot's condescension in this lecture to methods of which it was and still is said that he approved—and "missed" is not, in fact, the best way to describe what happened next. F. R. Leavis asked of the volume in which the lecture was collected how it was "possible for a book of criticism to be at once so distinguished and so unimportant."[2] William Wimsatt remarked, in the same spirit, of Eliot's first collection of posthumous prose, that it was "recantatory" and that its author "has not had the right or power to subvert his own image."[3]

In light of Wimsatt and Leavis's resentment of Eliot's resentment, *image* is an interesting piece of diction here—a word en route in 1966 from what Margaret Anderson or Amy Lowell meant by it to its 1990s sense: PR. Eliot's PR was by the 1950s out of his hands; his image was the responsibility of firms in New Haven and in Cambridge (U.K.), firms capable, long before Eliot's late admonitions and recantations, of ignoring his more inconvenient maxims. "Hamlet and His Problems," for example, was a favorite essay of New Critics on both sides of the Atlantic for its insistence that the audience attend to the play—its structure—more than to its central character. But the crucial feature of Eliot's essay was, rather, this assertion:

> *Qua* work of art, the work of art cannot be interpreted; there is nothing to interpret; we can only criticise it according to standards, in comparison to other works of art; and for "interpretation" the chief task is the presentation of relevant historical facts which the reader is not assumed to know. . . . critics have failed in their "interpretation" of *Hamlet* by ignoring what ought to be very obvious; that *Hamlet* is a stratification, that it represents the efforts of a series of men, each making what he could out of the work of his predecessors.[4]

These are, one would think unmistakably, the words of an Old Critic—the word "interpretation" so far outside his parlance, he could use it only in scare quotes. Eliot's description of the critic's job was not

for a Richards, Leavis, or Wimsatt to apply but for someone trained on
E. R. Curtius or Bernard Berenson or W. W. Greg. Eliot's philosophical
papers and dissertation of 1911–16 argue strenuously that meaning is
conceivable only in developed contexts, that no thing has meanings, or
even reality, of itself[5]—and this argument is the basis of Eliot's com-
mendation, in "Hamlet and His Problems," of three non- or antiformal-
ist approaches to literature: that of literary historians (who place works
in intertextual contexts), that of connoisseurs (who place works in the
context of established taste), that of textual scholars (who place texts in
the context of later, coeval, and prior variants). And for interpretation—
for what New Critics meant by criticism—Eliot's contextualist argu-
ment leaves, simply, no room. There is "nothing to interpret."

Why, why on earth, would New Critics take for their mentor a man
who believed interpretation a philosophically naive practice (though
helpful in getting teachers through the day—Eliot once compared
teaching with laboring on a herring trawler), a man who lamented the
decline of Latin and Greek learning, paleography and bibliography,
intertextual study, a man whose longest essay on his favorite English
poet (Herbert) is mostly biographical, a man, in other words, who, if
anyone, had earned the dreaded New Haven epithet "antiquarian"?
Worse: in poems that became New Critical anthology pieces, Eliot por-
trayed as diseased or immature the kind of mind that views the work of
art as independent of society, history, audience, and author. Prufrock
sings his love song to nobody: the epigraph from Dante—which, like
"Alfred" in the title, should have warned *non*-intertextualists to an-
thologize some other poem—suggests that Prufrock would not sing if
he thought a love song implied a lover. This creature ("zone of con-
sciousness," Kenner calls him) prefers poems, were he to write poems,
written not in a social but a private language (a language to which Eliot
in his dissertation denied the possibility). "Shall I say," Prufrock begins
an attempt at verse,

> I have gone at dusk through narrow streets
> And watched the smoke that rises from the pipes
> Of lonely men in shirt-sleeves, leaning out of windows?

Should he, in other words, adapt Baudelairean, urban poetry conven-
tions to the needs and expectations of Anglo-American society? To
which, his response is:

> I should have been a pair of ragged claws
> Scuttling across the floors of silent seas.

Hamlet too—who Prufrock is not ("nor was meant to be")—utters gibberish about a crab, gibberish of such force that an addled philistine gets the message ("Though this be madness, yet there is method in't"). But Prufrock, who identifies with the addled philistine ("Am an attendant lord"), concocts a gibberish expressing, principally, his own disease. His crab is soundless, bodiless, unreachable on the sea floor. Prufrock's solipsism and his aesthetic—aestheti*cism*—are at one.[6]

Even *poésie pure* follows from the mess that is the poet's life. This recognition is where the career of each paleomodern started and where their founder gave up the ghost:

> Those masterful images because complete,
> Grew in pure mind, but out of what began?
> A mound of refuse or the sweepings of a street,
> Old kettles, old bottles, and a broken can,
> Old iron, old bones, old rags, that raving slut
> Who keeps the till. Now that my ladder's gone,
> I must lie down where all the ladders start,
> In the foul rag and bone shop of the heart.

Deliberately near to naturalism (the "raving slut" and "refuse" invoking the Zola milieu), "The Circus Animals' Desertion" identifies the foulness at the heart of Yeatsian symbolism—the escape from loved ones into art:

> Players and painted stage took all my love
> And not those things that they were emblems of.

Yeats's personae emerged from his private life and then, antisocially, replaced it. That Symbolist aestheticism is dangerous to living things is a recognition traceable to Mallarmé; the frozen swan of "Le Vierge, le vivace et le bel aujourd'hui" is a portrait of the failed man who takes refuge in art. Thus, no Symbolist was ever really an aesthete (so Eliot argued in the volume Leavis thought "unimportant"), and the New Critical formalist of my *essai* is something of a strawman (Leavis was a hectoring social moralist).[7]

But my subject here is image, not *what* is seen but when and how. And in the microsaga of how and when modernism and New Criticism are and have been seen together, the decisive turn was taken when scholars of modernism first saw that the application of Old Critical methods to the work of Eliot, Joyce, and Pound would yield a very new image of modernist literature. John Espey was the pioneer. His study of 1955, *Ezra Pound's "Mauberley,"* was, as he said,

> an experiment in criticism, focused on the question of how effective the traditional academic method of attack, with its full panoply of textual collation, identification of sources, and historical method, would prove when used in analysing a piece of contemporary poetry.[8]

Espey's relevant conclusion was that New Critics such as Leavis had misconstrued Pound's assignment of Poundlike interests to Mauberley ("His true Penelope was Flaubert") as a sign that Pound was, like his protagonist, an aesthete. Espey demonstrated how the poem, instead, effects the "separation of Ezra Pound from Hugh Selwyn Mauberley," effects Pound's definitive break from Swinburne and the Pre-Raphaelites, Lionel Johnson, FitzGerald, and Dowson—to which insight Espey added that "such insights into *Mauberley* as these explorations provide are indications of a method that could be profitably used elsewhere."[9]

Similar methods have in fact been used in studying Eliot and Joyce, and evidence has been accumulating for decades that the New Critics should not have liked modernism. I have myself labored in this vineyard, showing, for example, how much intertextual knowledge Eliot's "Portrait of a Lady" presupposes—how much Arnold, Ruskin, Pater—for the reader even to begin to see that the young man of the poem (the closest Eliot came to self-portraiture) is not what New Critics would have had a man of letters be. Eliot's stand-in deems aesthetic talk a tiring way of passing the time, and the "objective correlative," he worries, may be ultimately inferior to discursively direct communication.[10] Were it not for the New Critics' packaging of Eliot's poems as Symbolist monads, organic, subtle, and sophisticated, readers would not have had to wait for publication of *The Waste Land* manuscripts or for Kenner to term *The Waste Land* "a joke" to realize that Eliotic discourse can be direct in the extreme.[11] Written *sous le signe de* Charles Dickens ("I will show you fear in a handful of dust" is spoken, surely, by Jacob Marley),

The Waste Land is didactic, mawkish, and (if I may quote myself) "virtually a piece of journalism"[12]—well-wrought, of course, but not an urn. Noteworthy in this respect is that Philomel, the victim of family violence, shrieks whenever, and only when, someone—an aesthete voice—remarks formal features of the awful or awesome. Appreciation of Verlaine's chanting children, admiration for a picture of the tragic nightingale—each is followed by a twit or jug.[13]

As for the *Four Quartets*, which appears to be the most self-contained, the least intertextual, the most urnlike of Eliot's works, it is, respectively: least, most, and least. Kenner's model for the *Quartets* suggested (1949) that the third of every four-part structure is a false synthesis of the first and second, in some measure shown to be resolvable in the fourth. Donald Davie, reading Kenner, was relieved: "The Dry Salvages," Davie found, was not a bad quartet (he had harbored that belief) but the third of four, a poem "spoken through a mask, spoken *in character*," a poem of Whitman's unlovely century.[14] Davie thus discovered an entry into the historical and intertextual dimension of the *Quartets*. My contribution, rather later, to this conversation was to propose that every movement (every line, I would say now) of each quartet is spoken in character and *in period dress*.[15] The tendency of the poem as a whole is to move from considerations of Time as a timeless category to considerations of History qua specific histories, from explanation out of temporal context to the understanding that explanations are themselves historically placed. Eliot's last major work is so historical, in other words, so contextually and intertextually thick, that there is, I have come to think, scarcely a text there, in the New Critical sense, at all.

A small but tenacious miracle of postmodern criticism has been its capacity for not noticing: not noticing that the New Critical view of modernism was simply that, a view; not noticing that one or two modernists lived past 1945 and had views of their own, negative and condescending views, about the New Criticism; not noticing, above all, that, while Harold Bloom and Geoffrey Hartman were revolutionizing the study of romanticism, the study of modernism was revolutionized by, well, not their students. Eventually, the angel behind the miracle of not noticing will have (in cabalistic idiom) to be named, but there is a last preliminary task to perform. There is a piece of unfinished business from the 1960s, from a moment when the New Critics' ability to render "unimportant" events and monuments inconsistent with their doctrines failed them. It was then that formalist methods failed decisively to expose the moral judgment at the heart of Joyce's *Portrait:* its rejection of formalist aestheticism and of the aesthete personality as immature.

In 1961 Wayne Booth and S. L. Goldberg made good on Kenner's intuition of 1947 that Joyce's first novel is about an aesthete's limitations—"limitations sufficient to make it implausible that an extrapolated Stephen had managed to write" *A Portrait of the Artist as a Young Man.*[16] I was some nine years of age when *The Rhetoric of Fiction* and *The Classical Temper* were published and, from the distance between my generation and that of Booth and Goldberg, they appear as close to New Critics as a critic of prose fiction may be. Goldberg owes "much of his own critical sensibility," as William Chace remarks, "to F. R. Leavis."[17] And Booth has said of himself ("even myself") that he might be included "among the New Critics," were the category broadly defined.[18] Booth identified himself in 1961 with the New Critics ("most modern critics") as preferring "internal rather than external evidence" when interpreting a work of literature—the exception, for him as for Goldberg, was Joyce's *Portrait,* which, Booth argued, could not be understood apart from prior and even later works of Joyce.[19] Booth noted that no critic had observed Joyce's irony against Stephen or against Stephen's aesthetic theorizing until the arrival of *Ulysses* in 1922 and, especially, of the *Stephen Hero* fragment in 1944. But, rather than undertake the labors (which he termed "homework") required to establish what Joyce in 1914 thought of Stephen's aesthetics, Booth, concluding that "the book itself is at fault," despaired of our ever knowing "the pattern of judgments" that Joyce presumably intended.[20]

Still, Goldberg attempted to do exactly what Booth despaired of anyone's accomplishing. Since Stephen Dedalus in *A Portrait* is "obviously not to be identified with [Joyce] as an older man," Goldberg sought "to detect where, and how, Joyce qualifies the attitudes of *the artist as a young man.*"[21] Making use of *Stephen Hero,* "The Day of the Rabblement," "Drama and Life," the 1902 "James Clarence Mangan," the Paris/Pola notebooks, and the evidence of *Ulysses,* Goldberg came to the conclusion that Stephen is the very portrait of "a late nineteenth-century aesthete" and that his aesthetic theory reveals "not so much the nature of art as the nature of Stephen Dedalus":

> Joyce clearly limits Stephen's understanding of art just as he limits
> his understanding of life; what Stephen does not see about the one
> is what he does not know about the other.[22]

Much further than this into Booth's neverland Goldberg did not tread,
except to speculate, without mustering evidence, that Stephen's "rejec-
tion of *kinesis* seems all too like a rejection of emotion . . . it hints at a
fear of reality."[23]

Hints? It is worth additional homework to bring to light what this
disclosure may conceal. First, we must be definite and explicit that, if
Stephen Dedalus was the portrait of a late-nineteenth-century aesthete,
so was James Joyce himself, in the very late nineteenth century (1901–
4). The Stephen of 1914 represents the Joyce of Paris/Pola and of "Rab-
blement," the prig (the "callow youth," in Richard Ellmann's phrase)
who wrote in 1901 that the artist must abhor the multitude and,
"though he may employ the crowd, is very careful to isolate himself."[24]
In the notebooks of 1903–4 Joyce articulated the aesthetic principles
that Dedalus defends in *Stephen Hero* and *A Portrait*: that any theory of
beauty must encompass (à la Baudelaire—though Joyce professed not
to like Baudelaire) the conventionally ugly; that art is neither immoral
nor amoral but beyond conventional morality; that the work of art
should be a wholeness, "selfbounded and selfcontained"; and that the
third of Aquinas's three phases of aesthetic apprehension must be un-
derstood (or changed) to mean not enjoyment but stasis, "the luminous
silent stasis of esthetic pleasure."[25] As a young man, Joyce saw art as ill
favored, supraconventional, independent, and related if at all to an
audience that like itself is static, self-possessed, and cold.

By the time that Joyce was writing *Dubliners*, in 1904–7 (at an age
an American literatus today would be reading Joyce in graduate semi-
nars), he was already showing signs of dissatisfaction with the aesthetic
of adolescent withdrawal. Throughout the stories are characters—
aesthetes at heart but free of talent—who live on fictions that remove
them from the social mainstream. Citing the evidence of Stanislaus
Joyce's reading, A. Walton Litz has proposed that Corley and Lenehan,
in "Two Gallants," reenact in their lives "the stock responses and illu-
sions of romantic fiction," such that their lives are not their own; and
Kenner has described the "fiction in her head" on which Eveline in
"Eveline" subsists as "a daydream of escape," owing "nothing to obser-
vation."[26] The most obvious case is Little Chandler of "A Little Cloud,"

a protopoet of the Celtic Twilight, who relishes the fact that he "would never be popular" (his work will contain "allusions"). Like the fictions of escape on which many Dubliners subsist, Little Chandler's is stilled by a fear of Experience, that foreign place where "rich Jewesses" live.[27] His destiny is Dublin and more Dublin.

Little Chandler is afraid of flying (more than falling), and it is a good idea to remind oneself periodically that Joyce did not name his self-portrait-as-a-young-man Icarus. Even in his *Stephen Hero* incarnation Dedalus is not quite Little Chandler. When Dedalus expounds the Paris/Pola theory, he does so before an audience; an aesthetic valorizing stasis is given a kinetic exposition. Granted, it is unclear whether Joyce intended this as author's irony or character's self-irony. Dedalus-1922 has no recollection of Daedalus-1904 as capable of a joke at his own expense:

> Remember your epiphanies on green oval leaves, deeply deep, copies to be sent if you died to all the great libraries of the world, including Alexandria? Someone was to read them there after a few thousand years, a mahamanvantara. Pico della Mirandola like. Ay, very like a whale.[28]

The Stephen of *Ulysses* remembers *Stephen Hero*'s Stephen as an embarrassing, grandiose, obnoxious child. An even younger Joyce condemned the practice of "setting up a standard of maturity by which to judge" aesthetics, but, clearly, Joyce in his maturity changed his mind about that also.[29]

And the Dedalus of *A Portrait?* There are two. Joyce abandoned *Stephen Hero* for *A Portrait* in large part to resolve whether Stephen was to be self-ironic or the object of the author's irony—a nice problem (in Henry James's sense of "nice"), given that the author signed, for instance, Nora Barnacle's copy of "The Sisters" *Stephen Daedalus.* To be free of this obtuse problem of epistemology (subject/object), Joyce required in *A Portrait* a pair of Stephens. There is the denizen of sections 1 through 5, whom Joyce sentences to Flaubertian justice, and there is the Stephen of the diary coda, who writes like Joyce (at least, like Giacomo Joyce), regains his natural voice (am I alone in hearing echoes of baby tuckoo in the diary?), and exempts himself from authorial irony by directing irony against himself:

Asked me, was I writing poems? About whom? I asked her. This confused her more and I felt sorry and mean. Turned off that valve at once and opened the spiritual-heroic refrigerating apparatus, invented and patented in all countries by Dante Alighieri. Talked rapidly of myself and my plans. In the midst of it unluckily I made a sudden gesture of a revolutionary nature. I must have looked like a fellow throwing a handful of peas into the air.[30]

The self-ironic Dedalus of the diary is substantially the Stephen whom we meet at the opening of *Ulysses*. But Joyce has chosen in *Ulysses* to distribute—aiding readers to observe the change in Stephen—Dedalus's unpleasant *Portrait* qualities to foils: to Mulligan most especially and, in "Scylla," to AE as well. The suitors in the *Odyssey* are fake versions of Odysseus; so Mulligan is a fake Stephen, his function in *Ulysses* to make obvious what Stephen is not (or no longer is). Mulligan absorbs the harsh, mocking, chilly, self-regarding, unsympathetic irony of a prior Stephen; and AE, his ethereal airs. Thus Joyce required only one Stephen in *Ulysses* (though in "Circe" there are briefly two—one Drunk, one Sober) and made Dedalus precisely Joyce's age at the time that Joyce himself began to disavow that "callow youth."

But in *A Portrait of the Artist as a Young Man*, in all but the first two and last seven pages, the author is as distant from his protagonist as Flaubert is from Madame Bovary, and distant for the same reason ("Madame Bovary, c'est moi"). Joyce devotes the greater part of his first novel to showing that the aesthetics and aesthete's life he had abandoned were—in terms of taste, history, and personality—immature (cf. *Prufrock*, cf. *Mauberley*). Stephen Dedalus's aesthetics in *A Portrait* correspond to the shape of his emotional underdevelopment. He describes the work of art as self-bounded, self-contained, a wholeness lacking nothing, and the narrator describes *him* as in "troubled selfcommunion".[31] Stephen Dedalus

was alone. He was unheeded, happy and near to the wild heart of life. He was alone and young and wilful and wildhearted, alone.[32]

The infected-narrator technique that Joyce stole from Emma Bovary's assassin permits the reader to know both the mendacious spin a character puts on her or his life and the verdict of the assize: here "He was alone. . . . He was alone . . . alone" is the narrator's judgment (the rest is adolescence). Stephen, of course, rejects the novel's summary judgment: "Dedalus, you're an antisocial being, wrapped up in yourself."[33]

"Antisocial" is a friendly understatement. Stephen's theory about the purgation of pity from and through art echoes his general lack of fellow feeling in prior chapters and foreshadows his pitiless rebuff of Cranly. Joyce brings to its epiphany Stephen's version of catharsis in a story, produced for Lynch, of a suffering that, in Stephen's view, is neither pitiable nor tragic:

> —A girl got into a hansom a few days ago, he went on, in London. She was on her way to meet her mother whom she had not seen for many years. At the corner of a street the shaft of a lorry shivered the window of the hansom in the shape of a star. A long fine needle of the shivered glass pierced her heart. She died on the instant. The reporter called it a tragic death. It is not. It is remote from terror and pity according to the terms of my definitions.[34]

Stephen and his aesthetic would qualify as, simply, inhuman were it not that Joyce has cast elements of the theory as the alibis of pitiable symptoms. Stephen the intellectual holds that aesthetic emotions must be "more than physical" because Stephen the neurotic stands "in dread . . . of the mystery of his own body."[35] (*"Non serviam"* in this novel means, effectively, "I will not bathe.") The sight of others' "nakedness chill[s] him to the bone," and he is incapable of expressing lust except as language: a prostitute's lips become "the vehicle of a vague speech."[36] "Only those," as Eliot remarked, "who have personality and emotions know what it means to want to escape from these things."[37] Stephen Dedalus's desire to escape—escape from problems for which, at the time, Freud was inventing names—manifests itself in an aesthetic and a metaphysic of transcendent condescension to experience:

> The artist, like the God of the creation, remains within or behind or beyond or above his handiwork, invisible, refined out of existence, indifferent, paring his fingernails.
> —Trying to refine them also out of existence, said Lynch.[38]

A reader of this passage who identifies with Lynch, with his deflation of Stephen Dedalus (and this is the best litmus I know), is an Old

Critic, a neomodernist, or both. The preference of "most modern critics" for "internal rather than external evidence"—these are, again, Booth's words—was not the preference of most modern artists. The modernists had, then outgrew, that preference, outgrew it publicly, in poems and novels that are basically exorcisms. The modernists were born in the nineteenth century, and each came to find, in the first years of the twentieth, that the milieux on offer were "shallow and premature."[39] Joyce's *Portrait*, in a dry run for "Oxen of the Sun," imitates in chronological sequence prose styles that parallel the stages of his protagonist's emotional development: the styles of Stendhal and Dumas translations, George Eliot, the English Symbolists and Decadents, and, finally, the style of *Giacomo Joyce*. The author of *A Portrait* and his allies concluded that those who cling to *l'art pour l'art* and the artwork-as-monad are fixed in the fin-de-siècle, historically, and, developmentally, in the time of adolescence—the time when, without a firm parental hand, a youth will find ways to avoid homework. The conclusion that Booth reached in 1961 was that *A Portrait of the Artist as a Young Man* is not susceptible to New Critical reading, another way of saying (hence, homework) that the novel is unteachable in a seminar and, if taught properly, in biographical and historical and intertextual lectures, would expose both one's students and one's colleagues to the knowledge that Joyce would not, much, have liked them.

The New Critics were teachers, academics; the modernists were artists with small use for the teaching profession. Pound was infamous on the subject: "academic stink" was a favored insult. The most telling of Eliot's many insults to Matthew Arnold was that the Professor of Poetry (*Oxon.*) was an academic poet and an academic critic, and Eliot expressed doubt that English literature should be taught at Anglophone universities.[40] Eliot had good reason for suspecting the motives of contemporary teachers. Their critique of the intentional fallacy, while aiming to direct attention away from the poet's foibles, redirected it not on the poem but on the interpreter's classroom—its needs, its limitations and practices. A sociological explanation of why Joyce scuttled *Stephen Hero* and, in *A Portrait*, made the discussion of poetics more ironic is that he realized that ascribing to art a status independent of history and psychology left one's lifework in the hands of mere nine-to-noon pupils. Booth believes that Joyce's demanding his reader's lifetime for the comprehension of *Ulysses* and *A Portrait* was meant "playfully"—

but I wonder.[41] Joyce was aware that, even before Plato wrote of the poet's irrationality, the Muse Theory implied that the poet's is not the last (or best) word on his own work. The idea that the real significance of a work is unavailable to its author—a notion held by New Critics and other formalists, Marxists, Freudians, feminists, structuralists, deconstructionists, New Historicists, by definition every one of us in the academy—is a difficult idea to hold in the face of *Ulysses,* out of the question when we are lying prostrate before *Finnegans Wake.*

The new academic schools of criticism, by enforcing a division between author and work, mandate for literature an entrepreneurial economy in which the critic/teacher is the intermediary. The Old Critical intermediary was, primarily, a linguist and archivist, on the monastic or (in the true sense) the humanist model. To join the severe order of Old Critics required an education in classics, history, and bibliography that had been traditional at European aristocratic universities since the humanist Renaissance. The newer critical approaches—the New Criticisms, one might term them—have been united, whatever their apparent disputes, in doing away with old mandarin learning and with the disciplines that it sanctioned. As for the New Criticism proper, it was (I quote Edward Said),

> for all its elitism . . . strangely populist in intention. The idea behind the pedagogy, and of course the preaching, of Brooks and Robert Penn Warren was that everyone properly instructed could feel, perhaps even act, like an educated gentleman . . . the New Critics aimed at nothing less than the removal of *all* of what they considered the specialized rubbish—put there, they presumed, by professors of literature—standing between the reader of a poem and the poem.[42]

"Like an educated gentleman"—as a definition of the bourgeois—is the trope by which power has, since the Renaissance, been wrested from aristocrats. Claiming to be disciples ("the sincerest form of flattery is imitation"—another useful trope), when in fact they were the opposite, the New Critics proper, to the benefit of all the academic New Criticisms, read Eliot, Joyce, and Pound out of existence. The passing of the New Critics has had small effect on this result, which after all serves the interest of academics (as teachers, democrats, and nonantiquarians). Each attempt to recover the modernists' view of themselves has been rendered, if distinguished, unimportant; and, if workmanlike, imperceptible. It will exact a traumatic disinterest, and a new Booth (or *Booth*), to bring the New Criticisms to take notice.

NOTES

1. T. S. Eliot, "The Frontiers of Criticism," *On Poetry and Poets* (New York: Noonday Press, 1957) 123–26. Rehearsed as a talk before the Authors' Club, London, "The Frontiers of Criticism" was delivered as a lecture at the University of Minnesota, 30 April 1956, published by U of Minnesota P then reprinted, interestingly, in the *Sewanee Review* 64:4 (Autumn 1956): 525–43.

2. F. R. Leavis, "T. S. Eliot's Stature as a Critic," *Commentary* 26 (October 1958): 399.

3. William Wimsatt, "Eliot's Weary Gestures of Dismissal," review of *To Criticize the Critic, Massachusetts Review* 7 (Summer 1966): 589.

4. T. S. Eliot, "Hamlet and His Problems," *Selected Essays* (1932; New York: Harcourt, Brace, Jovanovich, 1978) 122.

5. For the arguments of Eliot's philosophical papers, see Jeffrey M. Perl, *Skepticism and Modern Enmity: Before and After Eliot* (Baltimore: Johns Hopkins UP, 1989) chaps. 3–5.

6. On Prufrock and solipsism, see Jeffrey M. Perl, *The Tradition of Return: The Implicit History of Modern Literature* (Princeton: Princeton UP, 1989) 90–93.

7. All Western poetics, Eliot was arguing by 1944, uphold the doctrine of "edification," even the Symbolist poetic, which appears to contradict it: "'art for art's sake' is only a variation under the guise of a protest" (T. S. Eliot, "Johnson as Critic and Poet," *On Poetry and Poets*, 211).

8. John Espey, *Ezra Pound's "Mauberley"* (Berkeley and Los Angeles: U of California P, 1974), preface.

9. Ibid.: "separation," 21; "insights," preface.

10. Perl, *Tradition*, 92–94.

11. Hugh Kenner, *The Pound Era* (Berkeley and Los Angeles: U of California P, 1972) 440.

12. Jeffrey M. Perl, "Penelope without Ulysses," *Southwest Review* (Autumn 1991): 551.

13. Verlaine: "The Fire Sermon," 202–6. Nightingale: "A Game of Chess," 96–103.

14. Hugh Kenner, *The Invisible Poet: T. S. Eliot* (New York: Harcourt, Brace and World, 1959) 289–323. Donald Davie, "T. S. Eliot: The End of an Era," *Twentieth Century* (April 1956): 350–62. Kenner's argument concerning *Four Quartets* appeared first in an article of 1949 ("Eliot's Moral Dialectic"), to which Davie's article refers.

15. Perl, *Tradition*, 94–108; *Skepticism*, 61–62.

16. Hugh Kenner, *Dublin's Joyce* (1956; rpt., New York: Columbia UP, 1987)

preface to the Morningside ed., xii. Kenner's evaluation of Stephen Dedalus first appeared in a 1947 essay in the *Kenyon Review*.

17. See William M. Chace, ed., *Joyce: A Collection of Critical Essays* (Englewood Cliffs, N.J.: Prentice-Hall, 1974) intro., 5–6.

18. Wayne C. Booth, *Critical Understanding* (Chicago: U of Chicago P, 1979) 78.

19. Wayne C. Booth, *The Rhetoric of Fiction* (Chicago: U of Chicago P, 1961) 330.

20. Ibid., 335.

21. S. L. Goldberg, *The Classical Temper* (London: Chatto and Windus, 1961) 43, 42.

22. Ibid., 43, 63.

23. Ibid., 64.

24. "The Day of the Rabblement," in *The Critical Writings of James Joyce*, ed. Ellsworth Mason and Richard Ellmann (New York: Viking, 1959) 69.

25. Baudelaire: Joyce, "James Clarence Mangan" (1902), in *Critical Writings*, 75. "Selfbounded": *A Portrait of the Artist as a Young Man* (1916; rpt., New York: Viking, 1962) 212. "Stasis": *Portrait*, 213. On Joyce's revision of Aquinas's *usus* (enjoyment), see Jacques Aubert, *The Aesthetics of James Joyce* (1973; rpt., Baltimore: Johns Hopkins UP, 1992) 106.

26. A. Walton Litz, "Two Gallants," as reprinted in *"Dubliners": Text, Criticism, and Notes*, ed. Robert Scholes and A. Walton Litz (New York: Viking, 1969) 372; Kenner, *Pound Era*, 34–35.

27. *Dubliners*, ed. Scholes and Litz, 74, 83.

28. James Joyce, *Ulysses* (1922; rpt., New York: Random House, 1986) 34.

29. Joyce, "James Clarence Mangan" (1902), in *Critical Writings*, 74.

30. Joyce, *Portrait*, 252.

31. Ibid., 160.

32. Ibid., 171.

33. Ibid., 177.

34. Ibid., 205.

35. Ibid., 206.

36. Ibid., 168, 101.

37. Eliot, "Tradition and the Individual Talent" (1919), *Selected Essays*, 10–11.

38. Joyce, *Portrait*, 215.

39. T. S. Eliot, *The Use of Poetry and the Use of Criticism* (London: Faber, 1933) 81.

40. Ibid., 108, 36.

41. Booth, *Rhetoric of Fiction*, 336.

42. Edward Said, "Opponents, Audiences, Constituencies and Community" (1982), in *The Anti-Aesthetic: Essays on Postmodern Culture*, ed. Hal Foster (Port Townsend, Wash.: Bay Press, 1983) 138–39.

James Joyce, Eleanor Marx, and the Future of Modernism

Ronald Bush

Modernity and Modernism, 1718–1898

According to his brother Stanislaus, the young James Joyce more than anything else prized "extraordinary moral courage—courage so great that I have hopes that he will one day become the Rousseau of Ireland."[1] Yet Stanislaus's hopes, which James instigated and shared, were every bit as ambiguous as Rousseau's significance—which is to say, as ambiguous as European modernity itself. On the one hand, having the moral courage to "become the Rousseau of Ireland" implied a will to lead Ireland toward enlightened social change into the modern world, and the young James Joyce was ferociously intent on "uprooting" all the "feudal principles" of Irish society (*DD* 54). Joyce, however, also desired to fashion out of his own life an Irish version of the *Confessions* and to expose rather than advance the pretense of Western rational conviction. In *Stephen Hero*, the early version of *A Portrait of the Artist as a Young Man*, Joyce calls attention to the way the *Confessions*, confounding the puzzlement of Rousseau's English biographer,[2] dares to acknowledge "the young [Rousseau's] stealing his mistress's spoons and allowing a servant-girl to be accused of the theft at the very moment when he was beginning his struggle for Truth and Liberty."[3]

Joyce became Joyce when he began to value the second of these kinds of "moral courage" over the first. At that point he did not end his commitment to "being modern" (*DD* 54)—enlightened, modernizing, and progressive—but he did increasingly devote himself to examining

49

the buried and conflicted motives behind modernity's two-centuries-old search for "Truth and Liberty." Inclined by temper to social critique, his modernity came to fix itself irrevocably on art, an activity that not long before his adolescence Nietzsche had pronounced more "enlightened" than philosophy.

Then, as now, not everyone approved. By the time of Joyce's youth Nietzsche's insight had been echoed in the aesthetic movement, and the respectable middle classes in Britain had attacked Pater's and Wilde's claims to seriousness like hounds after prey. Their fury was repeated in Joyce's maturity by Marxists and then after Joyce's death by Marxicizing pundits of various stripes. To such intellectuals so-called pure, or modernist, art is an interesting game or a distraction—from this point of view, a distinction without a difference. "Enlightenment" philosophers, sociologists of "modernity," and political economists studying "modernization" tend to read the snowballing difficulties of the nineteenth and twentieth centuries as preludes to a better time. Yet one distressing feature of Western experience has been that those intent on advancing modernity have all too frequently been undone by complexities that lie waiting, like the hidden folds of Leviathan, within the rational curatives that bid so fair in their studies and their drawing rooms.

Although it has been the object of no small ridicule, Joyce's fixation on art allowed him narrowly to escape the usual fate. Proceeding headlong toward an inevitable confrontation with the intellectual contradictions of his age, he sensed where he was heading and fashioned a self-portraiture to reflect on his (representative) dilemma. He converted his early life into critical allegory and set a pattern for his generation. To come to terms with his achievement and to appreciate its futurity at a time when we are used to relegating the phenomenon of "modernism" to a historical curiosity, I propose to approach him in an unusual manner—by way of a near contemporary he never knew. Though slightly older than Joyce and living in a more privileged niche of British intellectual life, Eleanor Marx shared with Joyce a remarkably precise set of political, literary, intellectual, and moral convictions—convictions that gathered up the passions of a half-century of European thought. Yet the way she fashioned her life out of these materials led to an untimely death that frames the central issues of Joyce's career with brutal clarity.

**Being Modern in 1886: The *Annus Mirabilis* of
Eleanor Marx**

In the 1880s Eleanor Marx quite reasonably felt that she had mastered the demons of the past. The daughter of Karl Marx and a member of London's intellectual elite, she would not be out of place in today's London or New York. Holding with her friend Bernard Shaw that "progress must involve the repudiation of an established duty at every step," she committed her life to what she saw as the last stages of transforming traditional duty into rational choice.[4] Above all, convinced that the obstructions to a better future had been theoretically solved by her father's work, she gave herself up to what she regarded as the largest remaining difficulty of modernity, the "Woman Question." In 1886, in a pamphlet of that title, she argued that the terrible problem of women's lives in Western Europe "rests, as everything in our complex modern society rests, on an economic basis." "The excellent and hardworking folk who agitate for . . . woman suffrage . . . for the higher education of women; for the opening to them of . . . the learned professions, and all callings, from that of teacher to that of bagman" fail to reach "bed-rock." "The truth, not fully recognised even by those anxious to do good to woman, is that she, like the labour-classes, is in an oppressed condition; that her position, like theirs, is one of merciless degradation"; and that marriage itself is "based on commercialism."[5]

The feminist who wrote these words was convinced that she personally, at least, had solved such problems. Two years earlier she had, in her late twenties, become the common-law wife of the sometimes socialist, sometimes playwright and dramatic critic Edward Aveling, with whom she coauthored *The Woman Question*. Believing that the alternative to bourgeois marriage she had chosen was a step toward overcoming the last hurdle of socialist change, she shared her wealth with Aveling and eventually made him the chief beneficiary of her father's estate.

Feeling ever more sure of her choice, in 1886 she undertook to consolidate and explain her commitment by sponsoring translations of what seemed (then as now) two of the most significant literary documents of modern life, Gustave Flaubert's *Madame Bovary* (1856) and Henrik Ibsen's *Et Dukkehjem* (1879). The latter had briefly appeared on the London stage as *Nora* in 1882 but would not be properly translated into English as *A Doll's House* until 1889. Eleanor staged the original translation in her drawing room, incidentally introducing Shaw to his first production of Ibsen. She played Nora Helmer and cast her husband, Edward, as Nora's husband, Torvald. Only a supremely confident woman would have dared the dramatic irony of discovering that her husband secretly resembled the cowardly Torvald, but Eleanor had no hesitation.

Both "translations" proved minor landmarks in the history of English culture. Yet neither helped Eleanor Marx ensure the future she assumed had already begun. Within a decade her "marriage" ran spectacularly aground, and the way she had idealized her modern identity began to look like a monument to Enlightenment blindness.

Translating *Madame Bovary*

Eleanor Marx's version of *Madame Bovary* was the first and for years remained the only English translation. Encouraged by the Irish novelist George Moore, who guaranteed publication despite certain scandalized resistance at the firm of Vizetelly, the text was preserved with Marx's introduction until recently in the Everyman's Library edition and forms the basis of Paul de Man's subsequent Norton version, in which its pathos has been augmented.[6] Looking back from the perspective of a "modern" woman who believed she had been spared the plight of Emma Bovary because socialism had encouraged her to pursue her own work and create a more rational model of domestic relations, Eleanor Marx introduces Flaubert's story with a mixture of superiority and horror. In her eyes the novel portrays a "strong woman" who "finds nothing to do; there is nothing actually depending upon her." Emma's life is "idle, useless," and her pathos is that she tries so hard (having nowhere else to expend her effort) to "make herself in love" (xv).

In Eleanor's Marx's account Flaubert becomes a master of socialist and feminist critique. As scientist, he shows "infinite patience in observing" and "quick power of analysis" (viii). His signature, in fact, is the surgeon's: spurning "fig-leaf morality," he "speaks frankly, honestly, with the calm of a doctor describing a disease" (xii). And the disease he describes is social. "But for her surroundings, [Emma Bovary] would be a monster and an impossibility." Because of those surroundings, she is neither. Her economic and social inequality have conspired to leave her so "ignorant of life" that she allows bourgeois circumstances and bourgeois lovers to turn her into "something utterly corrupt and base." In Eleanor Marx's eyes "Emma is in search of an ideal. She has intellectuality, not mere sensuality. It is part of the irony of her fate that she is punished for her virtues as much as for her vices" (xv). The implication of her story is that one need only change woman's "surroundings"—change the relations of property on which bourgeois European marriages are built and destroy the fig-leaf morality of the nineteenth century that effectively masks those relations—to ensure that Emma's successors will live more productive and happier lives.

A hundred years later it is clear that Eleanor Marx got a number of things wrong about *Madame Bovary* and about the life and times of Flaubert. Not only does her introduction simplify the novel; it also ignores the tricks the nineteenth century had played on a Flaubert more self-conscious than the one Eleanor had imagined. But, just as clearly, Marx got a number of things right. As the latest generation of Flaubert's commentators has emphasized, *Madame Bovary* does indeed chronicle the course of modernization in early-nineteenth-century France.[7] Stephen Heath observes, for example, that Flaubert makes the social setting of *Madame Bovary* "money on the move." A relentless hunger for money drives the "economic and social transformation" of a story that takes place at the moment a new road joins the sleepy market town of Yonville to the Amiens highway. The most fundamental and sweeping aspect of Flaubert's transformation can be found in the buried narrative of five financial failures on which he constructed his plot: the decline of Charles Bovary's father; the financial disappointment of Charles's first wife; the worsening fortunes of Emma's father, "who loses money every year on his farm and finishes up paralysed"; the collapse of the *Café Français*, "engineered by Lheureux and beyond which lies the foreseeable collapse" of the *Lion d'or*; and the ruin of the Bovary household by Lheureux and Homais. Indeed, the entire plot can be framed by the fate of Charles's family line: "Charles's father had speculated in the manufacture of cotton goods, his daughter ends as a worker in a cotton-mill" (Heath 56–57).

In *Madame Bovary*, no less than in *The Communist Manifesto*, the forces of modernization—the efficiencies of industrialism, the reduction of value to cash exchange, and the breakdown of traditional social relations—transfigure every facet of social life. As Flaubert himself summed it up in a letter to Louise Colet (29 January 1854), while composing *Madame Bovary*, a "mediocrity" synonymous with modernity is creeping in everywhere; the very stones under our feet are be-coming dull, and our highways are boring beyond words. Perish though we may (and perish we shall in any case), we must employ every means to stem the flood of trash [*merde*] invading us. We must take flight in the ideal. . . . And so we must raise our voices against gloves made of shoddy, against office chairs, the mackin-tosh, cheap stoves, against imitation cloth, imitation luxury, imita-tion pride. Thanks to Industrialism, ugliness has assumed gigantic proportions. How many good people who a century ago could have lived perfectly well without Beaux Arts now cannot do with-out mini-statues, mini-music, and mini-literature! . . . We are all fakes and charlatans. Pretense, affectation, humbug everywhere—the crinoline has falsified the buttocks. Our century is a century of whores, and so far what is least prostituted is the prostitute.[8]

Mediocrity signifies an imitation, made cheaply to sell, and Flaubert wonders, here as in *Madame Bovary,* whether anything in French society can withstand the ineluctable forces of money, materialism, and char-latanry that contribute to the psychology of the marketplace, where things are valued not because they are real but because people condi-tioned by their "surroundings" live and dream about marketplace sim-ulations of reality. Those who hated *Madame Bovary* when it was pub-lished recognized Flaubert's social animus immediately and held it most abhorrent that the book shows every one of the institutional pil-lars of French moral judgment to be thus undermined and on the point of collapse. In the words of the state prosecutor who tried to censor the novel, translated into English in Eleanor Marx's introduction, the argu-ment that *Madame Bovary* condemns Emma's adultery is difficult to accept because "in the book there is not one person who could condemn her. . . . Could it be in the name of conjugal honour. . . . Why, conjugal honour is represented by an idiotic husband. . . . Could it be in the name of religious sentiment? But this sentiment is personified in the Curé Bournisien, a priest . . . believing only in physical sufferings" (xiii).

Most shocking of all in the prosecutor's eyes was the personifica-tion of "public opinion" in the "grotesque" chemist Homais (xiii). In fact (the reason for the prosecutor's shock), what Flaubert questions is not simply public opinion but the rational, scientific, liberal world of nineteenth-century French thought. For, as a more recent commentator has pointed out, Flaubert satirizes not just superstitious traditional culture nor a caricatured version of rational modernity, but the Enlightenment itself. Flaubert's portrait of Homais is not "the contempt of Aristophanes, or Molière, or Shakespeare, directed at the usual human foibles. Homais is not the standard, sly, self-serving buffoon. He is made to mouth the rhetoric of the Revolution as if he represents the Revolution and not its perversion; he identifies himself as a 'modern,'" and should be understood as a figure of "social modernization."[9]

Flaubert's skewering of modernizing cant—what prompted Eleanor Marx to compare his style to the frankness and honesty of "a doctor describing a disease"—finds its reflection in *Madame Bovary* in connection with the doctor Larivière, who attends Emma's deathbed and who

> belonged to that great school of surgeons [and] that generation, now extinct, of philosophical practitioners, who, cherishing their art with a fanatical love, exercised it with enthusiasm and wisdom. . . . Disdainful of honors, of titles, and of academies, hospitable, generous, fatherly to the poor, and practicing virtue without believing in it, he would almost have passed for a saint if the keenness of his intellect had not caused him to be feared as a demon. His glance, more penetrating than his scalpels, looked straight into your soul, and would detect any lie, regardless how well hidden. (233–34)

But the art that Flaubert himself "cherished" goes well beyond either rational critique or his disdain for fig-leaf morality, as *Madame Bovary* acknowledges by permitting Dr. Larivière an entrance so belated that his intervention can only be futile.[10] Though acutely sensitive to social and economic life, the primary focus of the novel was not (in the sense Eleanor Marx emphasized) social and economic, nor were its sympathies principally with an emerging class of workers. Though Flaubert shared Karl Marx's dislike of the bourgeoisie, he puts no faith in an eventual triumph of the oppressed (in contemporary French terms, the people). His reading of nineteenth-century France was in this respect especially bleak: "'89 demolished royalty and the nobility, '48 the bourgeoisie and '51 *the people*. Now there is *nothing*, only a rascally and imbecile rabble. We are all sunk at the same level in a common mediocrity. . . . Social equality has entered the sphere of the Mind."[11]

No, it is not primarily through scientific precision that *Madame Bovary* interrogates modernization but, rather, via a radical skepticism whose target is not cant but reason itself. Flaubert's only "scalpel" is art. Not the artistic or romantic temperament, which can be contaminated by marketplace clichés, but a discipline that, Flaubert wrote in a letter, "in the precision of its assemblages, the rarity of its elements, the polish of its surface, the harmony of the whole" exhibits "an intrinsic virtue"[12]—what Flaubert, in another, more famous letter, calls "a second nature":

> An author in his book should be like God in the universe, present everywhere and visible nowhere. Art being a second nature, the creator of that nature must behave similarly. In all its atoms, in all its aspects, let there be sensed a hidden, infinite impassivity. The effect on the spectator must be a kind of amazement. "How is all that done?"[13]

This is the basis for the famous Flaubertian "style," less a thing in itself than a thousand coordinated ways to hold the forces of modernization at a distance:

> What seems beautiful to me, what I should like to write, is a book about nothing, a book dependent on nothing external, which would be held together by the internal strength of its style, just as the earth, suspended in the void, depends on nothing external for its support; a book which would have almost no subject, or at least in which the subject would be almost invisible. . . . I believe that the future of Art lies in this direction. I see it, as it has developed from its beginnings, growing progressively more ethereal.[14]

In other words, since the tools to change the world are within the world and contaminated by its mediocrity, the sole remaining resistance to modernity has been reduced to a stubborn belief in art valued for its own sake. Only this kind of disinterested and, indeed, absurd authenticity, Flaubert implies, can withstand the general dishonesty. In modern life the writer is "either commercial agent, meeting the demands of the mass culture, or self-conscious artist, split between the necessity of writing and its impossibility . . . what can it mean to write in this world with this language? . . . writing in opposition to industrial literature and its world, outside its parameters of production and consumption."[15]

The ultimate futility of even artistic discipline would be inevitably impressed even on Flaubert. But it is important to understand that Flaubert's "stubbornness" was no more a matter of empty formalism than it was a matter of rational dissent. More than simply an escape into art for art's sake, *Madame Bovary* enacts, through a rigorous philosophical skepticism, the successive moves of the Enlightenment's analysis of its own contradictions, concerning which the critique of liberal hypocrisy that Eleanor Marx noted was only the first step.

As a writer of fiction, Flaubert's fundamental decision was to reject an omniscient narrator, so that no speech acquires authority outside his fictional dialectic. Flaubert's fashioning of *le style indirect libre*, his great contribution to the European novel, serves to root the characters of *Madame Bovary* in the particularities of individual experience and to suspend each of them in an open dialectic of fictional discourse. The prime beneficiary of the first function is Emma herself, whose concrete realization surpasses anything heretofore accomplished in psychological fiction. But the negative thrust of *le style indirect libre* is to strip the speech of all Flaubert's characters of an implied moral authority and place every utterance within implied double quotes, making us conscious of each instance as something distanced, ironized, framed. This is the effect of philosophical "aestheticization": every speech, and at a deeper level every social, political, or moral statement, is entertained rather than asserted, with special animus against the more "intellectual" or "advanced" instances of rational discourse. As the state prosecutor lamented, there is no prime, or ur-, discourse in the novel. All are equally suspect.

Flaubert's practice anticipates the main line of modern philosophy. As Robert Pippin argues in a book called *Modernism as a Philosophical Problem,* the development of "modern" thought from Descartes to Kant, Hegel, Nietzsche, and Heidegger has been precisely toward a self-conscious, or "aestheticized," acknowledgment of contingency. In Pippin's words, in every attempt to assess modernity from Kant to Nietzsche and Heidegger, philosophy has arrived at the conclusion that "the 'official' or Enlightenment, bourgeois notion of modernity" had

not been "modern" enough, that the restless, perpetually self-transforming, anomic, transient spirit of [modern reality] had to be

affirmed much more honestly and consistently, and not qualified
by . . . [a] typically modern [trust in] the public authority of phi-
losophy and science in culture as a whole. For many of these
writers, [only] an "aestheticization" of the modern spirit . . . would
fulfill its premise.[16]

Ultimately, the philosophical imperative to aestheticize, to reduce, as
Nietzsche would have it, all notions of tradition, nature, biology, his-
tory, and logic to the status of fictions, to hold life at the distance of
"as-if," would displace philosophy itself from its position as the queen
of the intellectual disciplines and replace it with literature, or what
Richard Rorty has called "ironism."[17]

Flaubert's modernism, plumbing the problematic depths of En-
lightenment individualism, inevitably calls his own illusion of psycho-
logical depth into question. The last generation of Flaubert's critics has
also discovered that Flaubert's *style indirect libre* is surprisingly unreli-
able and necessarily involves (to quote the title of a book by Jonathan
Culler) *The Uses of Uncertainty*.[18] That is, Flaubert creates enough ambi-
guity about his narrative point of view to make it impossible to trust his
realistic conventions. He establishes "an indeterminacy of narrative
voice that unsettles the moral security of the reader and renders de-
cisive judgment about characters or story difficult to attain."[19] Flau-
bert undermines his own representation and subjects his own surgical
rigor to the same critique he applies to Emma's secondhand romantic
dreams. Both are aesthetic conventions, and relying on them endorses
that which art cannot give—a rock of stability or value that might serve
in the world as substitute for Homais's degraded science or Bourni-
sien's degraded religion.

Implicitly claiming a more advanced modernity than positivist sci-
ence, liberal politics, practical philosophy, or rational religion, in the
mid-nineteenth century self-conscious modernism focused on its own
futility, on the conviction that aesthetic discourse can be trusted only as
a negative or oppositional force and never as replacement science or
philosophy or religion. As Flaubert wrote in April 1853:

At the present moment I believe that a thinker (and what is an artist
if not a triple thinker?) should have neither religion, country, nor
even any social conviction. Absolute doubt now seems to me so

completely substantiated that it would be almost silly to seek to formulate it.[20]

In Stephen Heath's words, Flaubert's conception of impersonality

has nothing to do with . . . some voice of knowledge *à la Balzac,* a sort of witness to things who guides our reading and decrees meanings. . . . It is not a question of an "objective" position *in* the work but of a play of visions, perspectives, perceptions across the characters and their doings and their world, of a tissue of discourses, ideas, orderings of meaning; leaving the reader deprived of any given grounds as to "what to think," not taken in hand by some privileged voice. Impersonality is accompanied by uncertainty, nothing is sure, nothing definitive. Flaubert's truth is that there is no concluding truth other than the conclusion that there is no such truth, and art is true as the recognition of that; with impersonality as its mode of recognition, against *bêtise,* the stupidity of conclusions. *Tout mentait,* "it was all lies": this is Emma's fundamental discovery one day after leaving Léon." (106)

"All lies." Even art—for Flaubert's "aestheticism" necessarily concludes in self-critique. Nothing is more painful in *Madame Bovary* than the paradox that the heroine of the most perfect work of nineteenth-century literature is destroyed for subjecting the world to the energies of the aesthetic imagination. Henry James's criticism of Flaubert (that Emma's sensibility is far too limited) is in this sense beside the point; even a much more intelligent center of consciousness would in the terms of Flaubert's modernism have come to the same end, since it would remain vulnerable to that implied self-critique of an unironized vision of art that runs through every nerve of the novel. One of the intuitions inscribed in Emma's fall is how quickly art turns into idolatry, anticipating the way that, in Pippin's words, after disillusionment with political and social forms of independence and self-determination, "everywhere pursued . . . by modern men and women, but nowhere truly realized,"

modernist suspicions about social and intellectual pretensions to autonomy (or bourgeois optimism in general) helped generate at the same time (and somewhat paradoxically) the hope that art itself (for its own sake, as non-representational, *sui generis,* self-defining) would both be, and in dress, taste, personal style, be a model for, a renewed modern view of self-definition. (118)

Ultimately and inevitably, even modernist art, approached in any way but sustained irony, becomes a fad of modern life, a symptom of the disease it would diagnose. It is to Flaubert's credit that he saw this far (which is to say, very far indeed) into the philosophical and social foundation of his writing. But, having said that, one must also say that he came fully to understand as much only after he had finished his book, in response to a near tragedy of his own.

The prosecution of *Madame Bovary* has become legend. In April 1856 Flaubert sold the manuscript of the novel to his friend Maxime du Camp, coeditor of the liberal *Revue de Paris,* for two thousand francs. But du Camp demanded that Flaubert cut it, both because he feared prosecution over the passages that dealt with sex and religion and because he did not understand the purpose of its literary indirection.[21] Flaubert was enraged but eventually worn down. He cut out offending passages but insisted that the review publish a disclaimer that the author no longer considered the work his own. In the end the cuts and the disclaimer made no difference. The book and the review provoked prosecution for corrupting public morals, with a potential sentence for Flaubert of a year in prison. The trial, in January 1857, centered around whether the novel celebrated or censured Emma's adultery. As previously observed, the imperial prosecutor, Pinard, perceptively argued that Flaubert had so hollowed out the institutions of French life that not one was left strong enough to condemn her. But the judges were less subtle and, like most of Flaubert's subsequent critics, agreed with the defense counsel, Sénard, that Emma's fate would incline young readers to turn away from adultery and that, "if anything, Flaubert had been too harsh in his punishment of Emma" (Bart 361). Flaubert and the journal were acquitted, but, inevitably, the *Revue* was shut down shortly thereafter in a similar action. Still, with a perverse poetic justice, more than twenty years later, the prosecuting lawyer was publicly unmasked as the author of pornographic verses.[22]

What came next, if by now predictable, caught Flaubert utterly off guard and constituted the most painful irony of all. If his good friend's revisions and the resistance of the state had compelled Flaubert to realize that no nineteenth-century fiction could be "dependent on nothing external," publishing now forced him to realize how difficult it was to avoid the social forces he loathed. With his name well-publicized by the trial, he suffered something worse than censorship. He acquired immense popularity as the author of a dirty book. The sales were immediate and very large. Flaubert was appalled at his success, won for all the wrong reasons amid praise of the kind Homais himself might have coined. Swept into stunning celebrity by the forces of the marketplace, he never really recovered. More misanthropic than ever, for the remainder of his life he published, and he fumed.

Nor, if we listen to Jean-Paul Sartre, did the irony stop there. In the thesis of Sartre's unfinished but monumental three-volume biography, *L'Idiot de la famille,* this rage, which had driven the writing of *Madame Bovary* from the beginning, reinforced, instead of weakened, the bourgeois system that Flaubert despised. Intended to undermine the reality of French life, Flaubert's fiction in Sartre's view helped late-nineteenth-century France to resign itself to the way things were: it strengthened both the futile self-hatred of the French middle class and a generalized resignation to the political status quo. In Dominick La Capra's paraphrase of Sartre, it performs "the predominantly symptomatic function of reinforcing capitalism and justifying alienation. But it is not simply symptomatic. It actually aggravated conditions that informed it and to which it responded."[23]

And so, having been convinced that he had worked through the problems of modernity and that his masterpiece would be protected by its calculated sophistication from the literal-minded stupidities of the practical world and from the weak misreading of the dandy, Flaubert discovered that he was still part of the problem. He had insisted that the work of art lies beyond social utility, with "its own intrinsic value." But he could not prevent society from assigning the work a value of its own. Nor could he prevent meretricious value being assigned to his own rejection of social utility: in the upper echelons of the market his art would become, "by virtue of its uselessness, a luxury of decoration, a fetishism of style" (Heath 43).

A hundred years later the issues are not very different. In Robert Pippin's words,

> The idea that modern art can maintain an independent, critical, "negative" perspective on modern social existence (the kind of thing [Theodor] Adorno tried to promote as a defense of modern

art) [has turned] out to be a grotesquely self-serving illusion. Modernist art [now seems] simply the deepest expression of the modern crisis, understood either as paradigmatically "bourgeois art," or ultimately as nihilistic, self-consuming and as much a historical dead-end as bourgeois civilization itself. . . . [It is only] the last game played by Western bourgeois high culture, an elitist code designed only to preserve and celebrate the "subjectivist" point of view of an exhausted but still immensely powerful upper middle class.

At best it has created an "exhausted, co-opted, everywhere displayed and commercialized 'culture of rupture'" (Pippin 41, 119).

But what are the alternatives?

Interpreting *A Doll's House*

Translating *Madame Bovary* in 1886, Eleanor Marx remained innocent of these dynamics. For her Emma's "surroundings" were the focus of Flaubert's writing, and the point of the novel was to provoke social change. In her introduction she praises but admits to not being "overwhelmed" by Flaubert's prose, and she says she does not regret having undertaken her English version in the spirit of "the conscientious worker" (xxi). Someone had to do the job—the future of too many women depended on it.

The obvious alternative to the tragedy of Emma Bovary for her and for an entire generation of British progressives was represented by the refusal of Ibsen's Nora Helmer to continue to live in *A Doll's House*. In the same year that Eleanor Marx translated Flaubert she and Edward Aveling finished their account of *The Woman Question* with a vision of the future couched in Ibsen's terms. In "a society in which all the means of production are the property of the community, a society which recognises the full equality of all without distinction of sex," they predicted, "there will no longer be one law for the woman and one for the man . . . nor will there be the hideous disguise, the constant lying, that makes the domestic life of almost all our English homes an organized hypocrisy" (14–16).

To readers familiar with *A Doll's House* it was clear that the last of these predictions is but a précis of Ibsen's plot, the penultimate an explicit reference to one of Nora's speeches in its last act. It was logical, then, for Eleanor and Edward Aveling to supplement their feminist

manifesto by making sure that "people understand our Ibsen a little
more than they do."[24] In January 1886 they arranged to stage Ibsen's
play in their drawing room in Great Russell Street. Ibsen had published
Et Dukkehjem in 1879, but, although it had created a furor on the Conti-
nent, by 1886 it had yet to make a real British impact. Translated in 1882
by Frances Lord as *Nora*, it attracted little attention outside a small
circle, and, when adapted by Henry Arthur Jones and Henry Herman
in 1884 as *Breaking a Butterfly*, it was reconstructed as an inoffensive
domestic comedy (Kapp 161). With increasing frustration Eleanor per-
suaded her friend George Bernard Shaw to take part in a drawing room
production of Mrs. Lord's translation. For Shaw it was "his first ex-
posure to Ibsen in performance" and may well have sparked some of
the enthusiasm that would turn him into the foremost proponent of
Ibsen in English.[25] But he was only one player in an intellectually stellar
cast. Eleanor played Nora, Aveling Helmer, Shaw the blackmailer
Krogstad, and William Morris's daughter May Kristina Linde.[26] The
presentation was the most important predecessor of the blockbuster
June 1889 production of the play newly translated as *A Doll's House* that
was produced by Charles Charrington and starred his wife, Janet
Achurch (both prominent socialists). This production revolutionized
British drama and established Ibsen's reputation as (so William Archer
claimed in the July 1889 *Fortnightly Review*) the most famous man in the
English literary world.[27]

Yet the Avelings' production, crucial to Ibsen's transmission as a
"socialist" writer, carried a frame of reference very much of their own
making and apparent from the way they wrote about *A Doll's House* in
The Woman Question. Not only do they make no allusion to the fact that
Nora leaves her family in the play; they end the essay with an image of
socialized domestic bliss: "Husband and wife," they prophesy, "will be
able to do that which but few can do now—look clear through one
another's eyes into one another's hearts. For ourselves, we believe that
the cleaving of one man to one woman will be best for all, and that these
will find each in the heart of the other, that which is in the eyes, their
own image" (16).

The Avelings' domestic utopia is completely consistent with the
sequel (*A Doll's House Repaired*) that Eleanor penned with Israel Zang-
will in 1891, in which Nora is portrayed as a "repentant woman listen-
ing obediently to her husband's exhortations on ideal womanliness,
and Helmer as a considerate husband."[28] It is also consistent with Elea-

nor's conception of her relationship: she and Edward, she believed, were two of the "but few" who had already achieved a rational substitute for marriage. (Or, in a less optimistic reading, that they were a couple held together by the courage and will of a liberated woman: Aveling was a man with a reputation for being "irresponsible and unscrupulous" about money and promises; Eleanor often felt estranged but "felt she was bound to Aveling by her own free will" [Tsuzuki 165].)

When *A Doll's House* finally created its English sensation three years later, ordinary reviewers understood neither the Avelings' interpretation nor their enthusiasm. They dismissed the play as immoral, morbid, and dreary, which only made the Avelings' circle more eager to take up Ibsen's claim. Overnight he became "the dramatist of the avant-garde [and] the spokesman of liberal values in Europe . . . a reputation he retained for decades" (Durbach 20). Thus, although he was admired for his writing by George Moore, Henry James, Thomas Hardy, and Yeats, "the strongest and most conspicuous signs of interest in Ibsen's work" were to be found in radical circles (Britain 24). And, although Shaw, in "The Quintessence of Ibsenism" (1891), played down Ibsen's socialist affiliations, more enthusiastic admirers were not so fastidious. They adopted Ibsen for his skepticism toward bourgeois conventions and his support of feminism—what Ibsen himself called "the transformation of social conditions . . . in Europe [that] is very largely concerned with the future status of the workers and of women" (Britain 25–31).

Yet serious socialists and feminists had reservations, nor was there always a unity of purpose between them. The socialist Beatrice Webb considered Ibsen's endorsement of "Truth and Freedom and the Emancipation of Women" "old fashioned stuff" that distracted energy from economic issues. And feminists such as Havelock Ellis's wife, Edith Lees, considered Ibsen an equivocal ally and wrote that Ibsen's importance was largely that it "drove thinking women *further together* towards their emancipation" (Britain 32–33). Both were suspicious of Ibsen's flashes of anarchism and individualism, which were as difficult to reconcile with socialism as with feminism, although they could appear more radical than either. As Ibsen told his Danish disciple Georg Brandes in 1871, "undermine the concept of the state, set up free choice and spiritual kinship as the one decisive factor for union, and that is the beginning of a liberty that is worth something. Changing the form of government is nothing more than tinkering with degrees . . . rotten, all of it" (Britain 40).

Eleanor Marx especially seems to have harbored doubts about Ibsen's individualism and in *The Woman Question* slighted such attitudes as they appeared in *An Enemy of the People* (Britain 36). But she continued her fervent support, going so far as to learn Norwegian to translate *The Lady from the Sea,* because for her *A Doll's House* demonstrated once and for all that, as she had argued in her introduction to *Madame Bovary,* once women are liberated from restricting custom, they will see the world as it is. On that day, she wrote, citing Nora Helmer's words, "there will no longer be one law for the woman and one for the man."

Swayed by Enlightenment optimism, however, Marx had gotten her Ibsen wrong. In his first jottings toward the play that became *A Doll's House,* entitled "Notes for a Modern Tragedy," Ibsen had asserted that there are indeed

> two kinds of moral laws, two kinds of conscience, one for men and one, quite different, for women. They don't understand each other; but in practical life, woman is judged by masculine law, as though she weren't a woman but a man. . . .
>
> A woman cannot be herself in modern society. It is an exclusively male society, with laws made by men and with prosecutors and judges who assess feminine conduct from a masculine standpoint.
>
> [My heroine] has committed forgery, and is proud of it; for she has done it out of love for her husband, to save his life. But this husband of hers takes his standpoint, conventionally honourable, on the side of the law, and sees the situation with male eyes.[29]

Far from advancing a universalist feminism and a common law for men and women, then, Ibsen began *A Doll's House* to explore the reality of opposing moral conventions. Nor does *A Doll's House* suggest that it is likely they will be harmonized. In fact, the action turns on just the opposite. Nora, having argued, when Krogstad proposes to blackmail her for forgery in act 1, that she does not believe in a law not concerned with love ("Hasn't a daughter the right to protect her dying father from worry and anxiety? Hasn't a wife the right to save her husband's life? I don't know much about the law, but I'm quite certain that it must say somewhere that things like that are allowed"),[30] reasserts these beliefs more vociferously to her husband, Torvald (who holds her accountable by the same logic) in act 3 (228). Then, as part of the illumination that drives her departure, she insists on the authority of her own values. (When Torvald admonishes her that "no man would sacrifice his *honour* for the one he loves," Nora replies, "Thousands of women have" [230].)

The strongest current readings of *A Doll's House* with Eleanor Marx acknowledge the subversive force of its feminist critique but also affirm the play's stress on what Ibsen's biographer Michael Meyer has called "the need of every individual to find out the kind of person he or she really is."[31] It is a work, in other words, that portrays opposing spheres of value and portrays them with full understanding that they are incompatible. No less than *Madame Bovary*, *A Doll's House* subtly suggests that the choice between perspectives turns on interests rather than truths and that any choice between them is ultimately arbitrary. No less aestheticizing than Flaubert's practice, this technique is offered not in the key of Flaubert's horror of the bourgeois world but, rather, with a sense of Kierkegaardian existential choice. As she is about to slam the door, Nora tells Torvald, "we must both be perfectly free" (231); her departure does not solve her problems so much as begin a step into the unknown, since she "can't be satisfied any longer with what most people say, and with what's in books" (228). As a rejection of accepted truths, *A Doll's House* presents yet another variation of skeptical aestheticism, an ironic reduction of all truth to the status of as-if and an unequivocal rejection of assumptions such as Eleanor Marx's about universalist progress.

This philosophical aestheticism lies at the heart of Ibsen's dialectical procedure, not only in individual plays but also in the logic of succeeding compositions. Indeed, an open dialectic such as Ibsen's is only possible within an aesthetic structure, both in the limited sense of a work of art and in the larger philosophical sense of a discourse fashioned to distance the truth value of propositions. As Errol Durbach has pointed out, Ibsen's dying word was *Tvertimod*—"on the contrary"; it was the last expression of a willingness "to entertain an idea and its opposite in a single visionary moment" and a fundamentally "dialectical frame of mind" (Durbach 6).

A Doll's House especially needs to be read as a struggle between opposites, a dialectic rather than a manifesto. Throughout, Nora, reacting against a life of hypocrisy, is opposed to her friend Kristina Linde, who has been living without a family in the darkness of separation and purposelessness. In the progress of the play Nora is impelled out into the cold, while Kristina seeks to reenter a domestic world. At the end they cross, but, although Nora commands our attention, *A Doll's House* is deliberately constructed so that each woman's choice questions the other's, and so there is no easy way for us to decide between their opposing claims. In Durbach's words, "Nora's slamming the door on the doll's house must be seen in the dramatic context of Mrs. Linde's motives for reentering that secure domestic world, and to see the play as recommending domestic revolution is to miss its surprising *tvertimod*" (92). The value of either choice is relative, dialectical. There is no question of improving things simply by changing surroundings. And, although it was vital, as Ibsen said later in his life, to solve the "problem of women," that was not the "whole object" of *A Doll's House* or his other work.[32]

It was almost inevitable that the open ending of *A Doll's House* would prove unacceptable. Its shock generated a number of sequels of the kind Eleanor Marx Aveling produced, nor was Ibsen displeased. Every rewriting underlined the distinction between a kind of philosophical aestheticism that forces us to encounter the painful contradictions of life and a safer kind of composition that insulates us from such contradictions. Nevertheless, the distinction was in constant danger of blurring. The contradictory choices of a Nora Helmer and a Kristina Linde were, despite Ibsen's dramatic revolution, only elements of a play, and, as everyone knows, plays are meant to satisfy our need for order and pleasure.

For Ibsen the inevitability of this kind of reduction was a constant worry. Aestheticizing his own experience, in the end he might succeed only in derealizing everything he loved. Such broodings, we have seen, had led Flaubert into more and more advanced forms of unhappiness a generation before, and the same was to prove true of Ibsen. Exile from his native Norway, recurring estrangements from his wife, and an inevitable alienation from the women and workers whose rights he had so vehemently defended[33] were the equivalent in Ibsen's life to Flaubert's misanthropy. And yet, like Flaubert, Ibsen came to incorporate his frustration into his work and, most important, into the increasing self-consciousness of aesthetic self-critique.

Michael Meyer comments on the extent of Ibsen's self-consciousness in an account of Ibsen's career focused on his last play, *When We Dead Awaken* (1899):

> Ibsen had been planning to write an autobiographical book which would relate his life to his work. Did he perhaps, before starting *When We Dead Awaken*, decide to write that book in dramatic form? For the play certainly covers that ground; it is Ibsen's final account with himself. He had portrayed different facets of himself in most of his plays: the unsatisfactory husband preoccupied with his work (Tesman in *Hedda Gabler*, Allmers in *Little Eyolf*), the uncompromising idealist who brings unhappiness to those he loves most (Brand, Gregers Were, Dr Stockmann), the egotistic artist (Ejnar in *Brand*, Hjalmar Ekdal, Lyngstrand in *The Lady from the Sea*), the ruthless old man who despises the world and neglects his wife (Solness, Borkman). But nowhere do we find so complete and merciless a self-portrait as the character of Arnold Rubek. The aging artist [is] restless in his married life, restless in the homeland to which he has returned after a long sojourn abroad, restless in his art. (830)

Meyer neglects to say that in *When We Dead Awaken* Ibsen, while criticizing the consequences of mere aestheticism, makes a heroic attempt to reaffirm the kind of aestheticization that involves a philosophical cycle of existential unmooring and recommitment. In the play Ibsen's alter ego Rubek is forced to encounter a living emblem of his alienation in the person of his former sculptor's model, who left him in horror when she realized he had taken their spiritual collaboration and turned it into something trivial. The play turns not upon the issue of art versus love but, rather, upon a realization that art in a real sense is not just composition but a terrifying leap into a future enabled by the opening of aesthetic detachment. The artist in this sense possesses an existential obligation to follow where the work leads. Irena, the returned model, forces Rubek to realize that in his caution he had betrayed not only her and their sculpture (called *Resurrection Day* because in a generic sense this kind of art necessarily requires the resurrection of the artist) but his own life as well. He has ceased to be an artist or a human being and has turned himself into what she derisively calls a "poet,"[34] a "weak" artist whose cowardice is excused by "self-forgiveness for your lifetime of sins both of thought and deed." For her his cowardice resulted in a "self-murder"—a "mortal sin against myself." But, had he instead accepted the freedom to grow, her "death" would have been a rebirth into a new life initiated by a living work of art, the existential equivalent of a child. She and the work were "hidden away in tombs" (271), but she returns to bring him back to a moment of renewed crisis and genuine freedom. (A moment that James Joyce, reviewing the play the year it was first produced, called a "soul crisis"—a recognition at the heart of the play that "life is not to be criticised, but to be faced and lived.")[35]

In *When We Dead Awaken* Ibsen is careful to distinguish this kind of proto-existential openness from the nihilism that it so resembles. The counterparts to Rubek and Irena in the play are a hunter named Ulfheim and Rubek's wife, Maia. They too are released into a dizzying freedom but, with no future purpose in sight, must choose between the destruction of the void and a safe and simulated freedom. The final counterpoint to Rubek's and Irena's plunge into the future is Maia's nursery rhyme insistence that

> I am free, I am free, I am free!
> No longer the prison I'll see!
> I am free as a bird, I am free!

(p. 290)

Compared with Flaubert's, Ibsen's can seem a less socially engaged and more optimistic response to modernity. And yet it proceeds by the same dialectic of suspicion, self-conscious of its own peculiar variety of bad faith. For Ibsen's Nora Helmer modern love guarantees no prosperity or continuity and involves high and inevitable costs. And for Arnold Rubek modern art can be nothing more and nothing less than recurrently betting one's existence on a step into the void.

Eleanor Marx, James Joyce, and the Future of Modernism

Eleanor Marx Aveling did not live long enough to read Ibsen's last play. In 1898 she discovered that her common-law husband, using one of his pen names, Nelson, had legally married an actress he had been secretly living with for some time. Though she had been convinced "that her union with Aveling was a true marriage 'just as if a dozen registrars had officiated,'" she found herself being regarded as a "mistress" not only by her newfound rival but also by the law. She confronted Edward, whom she had understood for years to be untrustworthy and irresponsible but whom she had sincerely believed had been straightened out by the seriousness of her commitment and the inspiration of the socialist cause. She announced her intention to kill herself. Edward offered to commit suicide with her and sent Eleanor's maid to the pharmacist with a note that read, "Please give bearer chloroform and small quantity prussic acid for dog, [signed] E.A." (Tsuzuki 317). Edward reneged; Eleanor did not. She was found, dressed in white, dead by the time the doctor arrived. Edward became sole executor of her estate, and the property he inherited from her (potentially, it was at first feared, including the considerable mass of Karl Marx's unpublished writings) eventually went to "Mrs. Nelson."

With or without premeditation Eleanor Marx literalized (substituting only chloroform for the agonies of arsenic) the fictional death of Emma Bovary. But, then, her readings had already literalized *Madame Bovary* and *A Doll's House,* and she had replicated the innocence of those readings in her own life. Lacking Flaubert's or Ibsen's self-consciousness about the arbitrariness of human truths, overlooking their lives, which had been darkened by social repercussions they had failed to anticipate, overlooking the methods they had developed to negotiate the void, she, like Emma Bovary, had allowed herself to take lies for truths when there were no truths, about money, about love, or about art. A more modernist reading of Emma's or Nora's encounter with modernity might have sensitized her to the difference between Ibsen's caustic questioning of all values in the pursuit of existentialist engagement and its dark twin, nihilism, and might have promoted a reflex sense of the fundamental arbitrariness of human action, a reflex suspicion about the outcome of rational choice. But in 1886 such readings were hardly common. (Even Oscar Wilde, one of Britain's pioneering modernist sensibilities, would founder on similar contradictions ten years later.)

Instead, Eleanor Marx constructed expectations of her domestic future based on Emma Bovary's limitless potential (restricted, Eleanor had written, only by her surroundings) and on her progressivist readings of Nora Helmer's marital equality. She had written and she herself apparently believed that a time had begun when "the woman will no longer be the man's slave" and "for divorce there will be no need" (*Woman Question* 16). Ultimately, she confused Edward Aveling's cynicism with modern heroism. Conditioned by her idealism, she was crushed by the depths of Edward's falsehood, and she despaired.

Eleanor Marx's suicide suggests the perils of modern idealism in the year, 1898, that James Joyce began his modernist career. That year, in a progressive, feminist drawing room belonging to the Sheehy family of Dublin and much like Eleanor's own, James Joyce found himself acting in the same kind of amateur theatricals and discussing the same schemes of Enlightenment progress Marx had so recently sponsored. It was the year (at age sixteen) he entered University College Dublin, itself a recent testimony to the modernizing hopes of Irish nationalism, and began to profess strong socialist beliefs that would guide his life and work for a decade and more. About socialism, about marriage, he was as modern as Marx: he remained a socialist until 1907 and probably longer; he refused to marry; he wrote the first two versions ("A Portrait of the Artist" and *Stephen Hero*) of his autobiographical novel, *A Portrait of the Artist as a Young Man,* as documents of socialist defiance.[36]

Most strikingly, he formed himself on precisely the texts Eleanor Marx had championed in 1886: *Madame Bovary* and *A Doll's House.* He would tell anyone who asked that he had "read every line" of Flaubert, the best of "the great nineteenth century masters of fiction,"[37] but without need: the lineaments of Flaubert's style in *Madame Bovary* are inscribed in everything he wrote through *Ulysses.*[38] As for *A Doll's House,* he informed his friend Arthur Power that the only way to understand Ibsen (who "had been the greatest influence on the present generation; in fact you can say that he formed it to a great extent") was to start from "the purpose of *The Doll's House* . . . the emancipation of women, which has caused the greatest revolution in our time in the most important relationship there is—that between men and women; the revolt of women against the idea that they are the mere instruments of men."[39]

The difference between Joyce and so many other turn-of-the-century moderns, including Eleanor Marx, had less to do with the divergence of their interests (they, in fact, diverged very little) than with his understanding of the social dynamics of modern art. Attending not to the "message" of Flaubert and Ibsen but, rather, to the way the form of their work engaged with nineteenth-century society, he understood the social pressures on oppositional art to degrade into formal aestheticism, social engineering, or nihilism. Joyce, moreover, heeded not only the lesson of the work but the lesson of the lives of those who produced it. He did not invent modernism, which was by the turn of the century a sophisticated reaction to modern life already fifty years old. He did, however, absorb it and modify it for the twentieth century. It was the example of Joyce's struggle to publish *Dubliners* and then *Ulysses* that taught us to read the paradoxes of Flaubert and modern art in the marketplace. And it was Joyce's awareness of the way Ibsen registered the "cross-purposes and contradictions of life," placed at the center of an essay in the 1900 *Fortnightly Review* on *When We Dead Awaken,* that launched his career at the age of eighteen and kept Ibsen's focus on the relations between men and women at the center of the avant-garde agenda ("Ibsen's New Drama" 66). Seven years later, in "The Dead," Joyce went back to *A Doll's House* and used it as the basis of the first masterpiece of twentieth-century literature. For, as Margot Norris has perceptively observed, "The Dead" is first and foremost a "husband's version of Ibsen's plot of a [Christmas] party that ends in a ruinous marital exchange."[40]

By the time "The Dead" was written, however, there were other modern tragedies to heed. That of Oscar Wilde, for example, whose philosophical assault on gender roles and on gender itself had pushed the dialectic of modernity well beyond the different laws of *A Doll's House* and had established the limits of society's tolerance of aesthetic skepticism. And that of Charles Stuart Parnell, who for a while miraculously squared the demons of nationalism by launching a politics of liberation that depended neither upon race nor religion, only to be destroyed by the demons he could no longer contain.

Joyce's response in all of these cases was cumulative and consistent: he attempted not, as Eleanor Marx had done, to find a core problem and then derive the rational principle on which it could be solved but, rather, as Ibsen had in *When We Dead Awaken,* to illuminate the contradictions of modernity by exploring his own implication in them. He began to write modernity by inscribing the histories of his predecessors into the writing of his own life. Neither "The Dead" nor *Ulysses* nor *Finnegans Wake* can be said to resolve any of the problems of modernity, but they encounter them in a progressively more self-conscious fashion. At the heart of Joyce's project one can find his original progressive politics articulated in a philosophical and ironic frame. His work maintains an oppositional stance toward traditional values but also maintains a thoroughgoing suspicion of its own idealism.

There were those at the beginning of the century, of course, as there are those now who would argue that the ethical neutrality of such irony is an evasion of the first responsibility of the philosopher. (As Eleanor Marx's father famously wrote, it is the duty of the philosopher not to understand history but to change it.) For them modernism is a moment of cultural transition and, more likely, an unfortunate detour. Social criticism of modernism in the 1890's reaction against aestheticism, in the Marxist criticism of the 1920s and 1930s, and in neo-Marxist social criticism of the 1980s and 1990s, would have it that modernism has no future, having already been superseded by the progress of modernity.

To take only one very recent example, Edward Said, in an essay entitled "Representing the Colonized: Anthropology's Interlocutors," argues from the perspective of postcolonialism that modernism repre-sents a kind of halfway house—a stage of cultural understanding rooted in a situation in which "Europe and the West" were for the first time forced "to take the Other seriously" but which proceeded no far-ther than the "formal irony of a culture unable either to say yes, we should give up control, or no, we shall hold on regardless"—that is, with "paralyzed gestures of aestheticized powerlessness." For Said that stage of understanding is dead, and he foresees an era of postcolonial resolution of modernity's problems based on a postmodern hybridity that goes beyond modernism's ironies and establishes a better world "on the idea of a collective as well as a plural destiny for mankind, Western and non-Western alike."[41] His assurance is currently echoed by many others—by Marianna Torgovnick, for example, the author of an enthusiastically received study of modernist primitivism, who la-ments the colonialism, racism, and sexism implied in the ambiguities of modernism's encounters with the Other and who aspires to an affirma-tion beyond irony, to what she calls "a neutral, politically acceptable vocabulary" of non-Western culture that would acknowledge the col-lective destiny of postcolonial hybridity in a postmodern world.[42]

Yet, as Marjorie Perloff inquires in a response to Torgovnick, what idiom have we developed to transcend the sophistication of that irony? What "neutral" vocabulary might we now employ to supersede the dialogism that is the self-reflexive heart both of the ethnographic en-counter and of modernist irony—the kind of formalized self-ques-tioning that, if it opens itself to the charge of ethical fence sitting, at least acknowledges the phenomenological structure of the dilemma. Don't we, Perloff continues, when we fantasize we are enlightened beings "who live at the end of the twentieth century [and] can see the hidden and not-so-hidden colonialism, racism, and sexism of the early twentieth century as in themselves they really were," expose exactly the same kind of hubris that undermined the righteous efforts of the imperialists whom modernist writers fixed in their ambiguous gaze?[43] And do we not, I would add, in the terms of the history outlined here, then increase the likelihood of repeating the tragic irony of Enlightenment optimism? As with nineteenth-century Orientalists or Eleanor Marx, might we not, as idealistic reformers, look forward once more to finding ourselves not part of the solution but part of the problem?

Modernism, then, after a hundred years of obituaries, may still have some prospects left (even if we insist on calling it postmodernism). After the Enlightenment optimism of the Fabians, of the 1930s, and of the rosier versions of postcolonialism have faded, we may wish to keep a line open to the way Joyce transferred the combination of idealism and skepticism embodied in the histories of *Madame Bovary* and *A Doll's House* into the present. Despite the heated misgivings of his more "progressive" contemporaries, after all, starting in 1900 James Joyce extended the future of modernism for forty years.

NOTES

1. Stanislaus Joyce, *The Complete Dublin Diary*, ed. George H. Healey (Ithaca: Cornell UP, 1971) 30. Subsequent citations will be indicated parenthetically in the text using the abbreviation *DD*.

2. Most probably John Viscount Morley, *Rousseau and His Era* (1873). For the embarrassment Joyce refers to, see, for example, Morley, vol. 2 (rpt., London: Macmillan, 1923) 142: "But Rousseau's egotism manifested itself perversely. This is true to a certain small extent, and one or two of the disclosures in the Confessions are in nauseous matter, and are made, moreover, in a nauseous manner."

3. James Joyce, *Stephen Hero*, edited from the manuscript in the Harvard College Library by Theodore Spencer (1944; rpt. and rev., New York: New Directions, 1963) 40. Joyce here confuses spoons with ribbon and misremembers the incident near the beginning of the *Confessions* in which Rousseau blames the cook, Marion, for stealing a little pink and silver ribbon that he had himself taken. See the *Confessions*, trans. J. M. Cohen (London: Penguin, 1958) 86.3.

4. The standard biographies of Eleanor Marx are Chushichi Tsuzuki, *The Life of Eleanor Marx, 1855–1898: A Socialist Tragedy* (Oxford: Oxford UP, 1967), in which the quote from Shaw's *The Quintessence of Ibsenism* (1891) appears on 327;

and Yvonne Kapp's *Eleanor Marx*, 2 vols. (London: Lawrence and Wishart, 1972–76).

5. *The Woman Question*, by Edward and Eleanor Marx Aveling (London: Swansonnenschein, Le Bas and Lowrey, 1886) 4–6, 9. The pamphlet was issued to promote the publication of the translation into English of August Babel's "Die Frau in der Vergangenheit, Gegenwart, and Zukunft."

6. Marx's translation was published in London by Vizetelly and Company in 1886 as *Madame Bovary: Provincial Manners*, by Gustave Flaubert. Trans. from the French Edition Definitive by Eleanor Marx-Aveling. (All quotations from Marx's introduction are from this edition.) In 1965, at the beginning of de Man's career, W. W. Norton brought out his "Substantially New Translation Based on the Version by Eleanor Marx Aveling" and made it the basis of *Madame Bovary: A Norton Critical Edition* (New York: Norton, 1965). Subsequent citations from the novel will be from this text, unless otherwise indicated.

7. See, for example, Stephen Heath, *"Madame Bovary"* (Cambridge: Cambridge UP, 1992); and Dominick La Capra, *"Madame Bovary" on Trial* (Ithaca: Cornell UP, 1982) esp. chap. 4.

8. See Francis Steegmuller, trans., *The Letters of Gustave Flaubert*, 2 vols. (Cambridge: Harvard UP, 1980) 1:212. The letter is cited in La Capra (67).

9. Robert Pippin, *Modernism as a Philosophical Problem: On the Dissatisfactions of European High Culture* (London: Basil Blackwell, 1991) 40.

10. See La Capra 186. La Capra, however, goes too far in suggesting that Larivière's futility marks him as a "false model" like one of Emma's "romantic novels" ("or at least a model that is used falsely").

11. Letter of 22 September 1853 to Louise Colet, trans. Heath, 14.

12. Letter of 13 April 1876, trans. La Capra 77.

13. Letter of 9 December 1852 to Louise Colet. See *Letters* 1:173; cited in Heath 104–5.

14. Letter to Louise Colet of 16 January 1852, trans. in *Letters* 1:154; cited in Heath 7.

15. Heath 145.

16. Pippin 6–7. Subsequent citations are indicated parenthetically in the text.

17. Richard Rorty, *Contingency, Irony, and Solidarity* (Cambridge: Cambridge UP, 1987). See esp. chapter 4, "Private Irony and Ritual Hope."

18. Jonathan Culler, *Flaubert: The Uses of Uncertainty* (Ithaca: Cornell UP, 1974; rev. ed., 1985).

19. La Capra 60.

20. Letter of 26 April 1853 to Louis Colet, trans. in *Letters* 1:185; cited in La Capra 70.

21. The full transcript of the trial can be found in the Pléiade Flaubert, ed. Albert Thibaudet and René Dumesnil, *Oeuvres* vol. 1 (Paris: Gallimard, 1951). For a good, brief account of the resistance, negotiations, and trial, see Benjamin Bart, *Flaubert* (Syracuse: Syracuse UP, 1967) 354–66. A more tendentious account of the trial can be found in La Capra, *Madame Bovary on Trial* chap. 2, 30–52.

22. See Bart 356, 362.

23. Jean-Paul Sartre, *L'Idiot de la famille*, 3 vols. (Paris: Gallimard, 1971–72). See 3:325. Cited, trans., and explicated in La Capra, *Madame Bovary on Trial* 88. On Sartre and Flaubert, see esp. 81–99.

24. Letter from Eleanor Marx to Havelock Ellis, December 1885, cited in Kapp, *Eleanor Marx* 103.

25. Ian Britain, "A Transplanted Doll's House: Ibsenism, Feminism and Socialism in Late-Victorian and Edwardian England," in *Transformations in Modern European Drama*, ed. Ian Donaldson (London: Macmillan, 1983) 17. Subsequent citations will be indicated parenthetically in the text.

26. For accounts of the productions, see Tsuzuki 164 ff.; Kapp 103 ff.; and Britain 16–17.

27. For the reception of the 1889 production, see Errol Durbach, *A Doll's House: Ibsen's Myth of Transformation* (Boston: Twayne, 1991) 19–20. Subsequent citations will be indicated parenthetically in the text. Durbach notes that the production was also reviewed (anonymously) by Shaw and by Harley Granville Barker, who called it "the most dramatic event of the decade."

28. Tsuzuki, *The Life of Eleanor Marx* 182. See also Kapp, *Eleanor Marx* 2:517.

29. Michael Meyer, *Ibsen* (1967; rpt., London: Cardinal Books, 1988) 466.

30. Henrik Ibsen, *A Doll's House and Other Plays*, trans. Peter Watts (London: Penguin, 1965) 175–76. Subsequent citations will be indicated parenthetically in the text.

31. See Meyer's reading in *Ibsen:* "its theme is the need of every individual to find out the kind of person he or she really is and to strive to become that person. Ibsen knew . . . that liberation can only come from within; which is why he had expressed to Georg Brandes his lack of interest in 'special revolutions, revolutions in externals'" (478).

32. See Meyer, *Ibsen* 817. These words, from an 1898 speech to the Norwegian Society for Women's Rights, in which Ibsen was resisting the kind of narrow reading imposed upon him by those only interested in the cause of feminism, have often been cited (as they are by Meyer and Durbach) as a reason to discount the real feminist sympathies of the play. To do so is itself a simplification, however, as Joan Templeton demonstrates in "The *Doll House* Backlash: Criticism, Feminism, and Ibsen," *PMLA* 104.1 (1989): 28–40.

33. For Ibsen's class alienation, see Britain, "Transplanted Doll's House" 44 ff.

34. Henrik Ibsen, "When We Dead Wake," trans. Peter Watts in *Ghosts and Other Plays* (London: Penguin, 1964) 271. Subsequent citations of this translation will be indicated parenthetically in the text.

35. James Joyce, "Ibsen's New Drama," first published in the *Fortnightly Review* (1 April 1900), and reprinted in *The Critical Writings of James Joyce*, ed. Ellsworth Mason and Richard Ellmann (New York: Viking, 1959) 47–67; see 50, 67. Subsequent citations will be indicated parenthetically in the text.

36. On the seriousness and tenacity of Joyce's socialism, see Dominic Mangiello, *Joyce's Politics* (London: Routledge and Kegan Paul, 1980) esp. chap. 3.

37. See Frank Budgen, *James Joyce and the Making of 'Ulysses' and Other Writings* (1934; rpt., Oxford: Oxford UP, 1972) 186, 184.

38. See Richard K. Cross, *Flaubert and Joyce: The Rite of Fiction* (Princeton: Princeton University Press, 1971).

39. Arthur Power, *Conversations with James Joyce*, ed. Clive Hart (1974; rpt., Chicago: U of Chicago P, 1982) 35.

40. Margot Norris, *Joyce's Web: The Social Unraveling of Modernism* (Austin: U of Texas P, 1992) 99.

41. Edward Said, "Representing the Colonized: Anthropology's Interlocutors," *Critical Inquiry* 15 (Winter 1989): 224, 222–23.

42. Marianna Torgovnick, *Gone Primitive: Savage Intellects, Modern Lives* (Chicago: U of Chicago P, 1990) 21.

43. Marjorie Perloff, "Tolerance and Taboo: Modernist Primitivisms and Postmodernist Pieties," in *Prehistories of the Future: The Primitivist Project and the Culture of Modernism*, ed. by Elazar Barkan and Ronald Bush (Stanford: Stanford UP, 1995) 339.

Laughter and Nonsense in the Making and (Postmodern) Remaking of Modernism

Holly Laird

The high seriousness of criticism's endeavor to make sense of literary modernism—whether in making the modernist canon or, more recently, revising it—has often smothered its laughter.[1] From widely taught works such as *The Waste Land*, at one point more risibly called *He Do the Police in Different Voices*, to nearly forgotten works such as Edith Sitwell's *Façade*, examples abound of books that emerged amid and through laughter. In Sitwell's swipes at "the Laureate's feet," in Eliot's caricatures of scribbling Fresca, in Hurston's signifying on the brink between black and white, the modernist "revolution," the "making of the new," the cross-cultural "Harlem Renaissance," were begotten and grew.[2] In part the laughter of these modernists exhibits a new willingness to break the boundaries between sense and nonsense.[3] But their jokes also mark contested sites of literary production, where writers collaborated to surpass others or empower themselves, not merely to make something new. The various shapes and sounds of nonsense had varying targets, and, far from being whimsically spontaneous, the laughter was learned—acquired not only through long practice but (since laughter springs from, as well as at, its opposites) through over-seriousness and disillusionment. And, insofar as modernist poetry undertook the social arbitration that had been overtly embraced by Victorian poetry, it did so partly by showing its readers what to laugh at. In the canonization of modernism, modernist nonsense eventually came to seem inseparable from the sense that was made of it and from the ways it could be allegorized as social critique, and this is as true of postmodern readings of modernism as of modernist ones. Postmodern thought and writing are less different from modernism than early proponents of postmodernism believed, and, in the remaking of modernism, the contentious use of laughter is something that postmodernists share with their precursors. Mocking nonsense and the laughing destabilization of meaning have developed a marketable and oddly canonical life of their own.

This essay will consider the role of polemical laughter and nonsense in relation to the canonical status of two women writers: Zora Neale Hurston, who is now widely read and taught in courses on modern literature, and Edith Sitwell, who is not. Sitwell, whom I will discuss first, possesses a particularly vexed relation to the processes of twentieth-century canon making; her writing exhibits modernist humor at its funniest and bravest, but the writing was obscured by the spectacle of her public rivalries and by the successful self-canonizations of male modernists. In returning to her poetry, one discovers an engagement with the female figure and with sexuality that has gone nearly unmentioned in previous accounts of Sitwell and that ally her, I will argue, with recent feminist postmodern thought. This essay then turns to the turbulent history behind Hurston's more firmly established reputation and explores her critical reception in order, first, to suggest how canonical the concepts of mocking nonsense and destabilizing laughter have become in contemporary theory and, second, to warn against one result of this: a false polarization that sets modernist and postmodernist writing at one extreme and "naturalist" and "sentimentalist" writing at another. Modernist and postmodernist writers do not own laughter, nor are they sole possessors of strategies to destabilize meaning. As Susan Stewart puts it, in her book-length study of nonsense:

> it seems that it is difficult to have one of these universes [of common sense and of nonsense] without the other. . . . common sense [is not] a stable ground for social process, but . . . an ongoing accomplishment of that process—acts of common sense will shape acts of nonsense and acts of nonsense will shape acts of common sense. (vii)

I

The balancing act between seriousness and nonsense in modernist and postmodern writing and the pattern of a contentious, alternately debunking and canonizing laughter—of laughter first as resistance, then as normalization, then again as resistance, and again as normalization—may be witnessed in the ways in which Eliot and Sitwell contended with the spectacle of women (with the spectacle of herself in Sitwell's case) as successful writers. Sitwell moved beyond gender hierarchy (and gender slander) even while prodding male egos and evoking powerful females in her poems; her pioneering modernist poems celebrate a carnival of scandalous women yet also poke fun at matriarchal and patriarchal figures alike. But her extended and polemical struggle for recognition and, eventually, for a place among the "great" writers of her day had mixed results.

I turn to Sitwell here rather than to Woolf, H.D., or Stein (or even Richardson, Barnes, Loy, or Moore) because, in the ongoing business of opening, reforming, and possibly even transforming the canon, it is essential to remind ourselves of the seemingly incessant resubmergence of so-called minority writers. None of these other women writers had a longer or more public career than Sitwell, yet they are all more widely discussed now. Sitwell presents a particularly curious case. Surely one cannot call uncanonical a writer who appears with clocklike regularity in the *Norton Anthology of English Literature* and who was for years considered the grande dame of British verse, yet analysis of her work by critics and theorists is almost nonexistent.[4] Despite the biography by Victoria Glendinning that appeared in 1981 and a revisionary study by Cyrena Pondrom of Sitwell's relation to Stein in 1991, Sitwell's work is virtually ignored by both feminists and nonfeminists. How could someone so apparently mainstream be so routinely overlooked? To explore all the possible reasons would take me beyond the scope of this essay, but both Sitwell's nonsensicality and her contentiousness are major culprits. Much of Sitwell's groundbreaking early poetry has been considered, then and now, too nonsensical, too silly, and too exclusively concerned with technique—with "facades"—to merit (or even permit) serious exegesis. Meanwhile, the controversy that swirled around Sitwell, which she fostered, attracted attention to her eccentricity and has continued to divert it from her poems.

Sitwell was, as David Perkins stresses in his book *A History of Modern Poetry*, the first British poet to create "a distinctively Modernist movement" (428); her aim was to mock the (to her eye and ear) rigidly polite poeticisms of the Georgians. With some success Sitwell countered the staid English countrysides of Edward Marsh and John Squire's periodical *Georgian Poetry* anthologies with six cycles of modernist

Wheels. Wheels also made one or two women poets more visible, for, though it was by no means explicitly dedicated to making women's writing more prominent, these anthologies were the aggressive, joint production of Nancy Cunard and Sitwell, and Sitwell edited them from their initiation in 1916 to their end in 1921.[5] As Glendinning notes, the name was taken from a poem by Cunard: "I sometimes think that all our thoughts are wheels / Rolling forever through the painted world, / Moved by the cunning of a thousand clowns" (58). These semifuturist, semi-French symbolist figures of unthinking thought demarcate an antihumanist vision, turning something serious into something frivolous, mechanical, and random.

More obvious to Sitwell's early readers than her interest in new poetic themes were her experiments with new poetic techniques. She was praised for the "verbal and rhythmic virtuosity" of the poems published in *Wheels* and later in *Façade* (*Norton* 2132). But explication of her experimental work has remained practically at a standstill, so that she is to an unusual degree associated with technique rather than with meaning.[6] Even Perkins, who devotes a short section to her work in his extensive history of literature and who sees *Façade* as "a gay, witty, and gallant harlequinade, gallant because the antics of the harlequin both expressed and masked a fundamental despair," finds this book "more important as a fascinating experiment in technique rather than in any other way" (430–31). Perkins describes not only Sitwell's methods but also her own exotic technical explanations. He thus follows Sitwell's lead in emphasizing technique.

Exaggerated attention to technique allies Sitwell, of course, with other modernists. From the outset their technical innovations functioned in ambiguous, potentially contradictory ways: as an attention-grabbing form of mockery of previous poetic conventions, as a convenient source of shock effects to tease the "bourgeoisie," but also as a dramatic way to associate themselves with technological "modernity" and as an effective way to take the high road in their own proto–New Critical discussions of verse, to make their own criticism sound rigorous, even scientific. Their success in this is measured by the extent to which literary critics of modernism today take for granted the Paterian principle that the message dwells within the method. But Sitwell's technical innovations have tended to be viewed as merely technical, shocking once upon a time but now a historical curiosity.[7]

In efforts to bring Sitwell into the canon most scholars (including the Norton editors, though not Perkins) follow Sitwell in stressing her technical experimentation and then go on to demonstrate meaning in her nonsense:[8] "But Edith Sitwell was more than a juggler of colored balls," say the Norton editors. "There is always a human meaning hinted at, sometimes with mocking laughter, sometimes with anguish" (2132). It is the "anguish" that these scholars stress.[9] Arguing for the "architectonic interest in the order and design" of her poetry, James D. Brophy, author in 1968 of the only book-length critical study of her poetry, offers "shadow" as the "unifying" symbol of her poetry. Again, this choice exemplifies the tendency among modernist scholars—and the poets themselves in their later criticism—to ennoble, and render serious, modernist nonsense by discovering shadows at its heart. In her own defense of her poetry, published in 1949 as the introduction to her *Collected Poems*, Sitwell, too, stresses a darker side to the verse:

> Many years ago, Villiers de l'Isle Adam wrote of his own work, *Tribulat Bonhommet*, that it was "an enormous and somber clowning, the color of the century." "Words and thoughts," said Arthur Symons of this work, "never brought together since Babel, clash into a protesting combination." This might also be said of certain poems in *Façade*.
> . . . The gaiety of some masks darkness—the see-saw world in which giant and dwarf take it in turns to rush into the glaring light, the sight of the crowds, then, with a terrifying swiftness, go down to the yawning dark. An example is "Said King Pompey"—a poem about the triumphant dust. (xvii, xviii)

All of this would make her a convenient example of what many postmodern writers and theorists most dislike and find self-contradictory in modernism (if postmodern scholars took her seriously enough to discuss it): the avant-gardism; the contempt for "philistines," as opposed to the conscious postmodern adoption of popular cultural forms; the modernist technological obsession with its invocation of mechanical images of the industrial revolution, as opposed to the postmodern critique of the brutal consequences of industrialization; and yet also the modernist vision of loss of meaning, crisis, the overwhelming despair in and retreat from modern life, as opposed to the buoyant, if ironically tinged, postmodern embrace of the oddities of modernity.[10]

Yet even a superficial reconsideration of her work discloses a more complex Sitwell than the arrogant aristocrat/technocrat of the stereotypes. For one thing, though she joined the chorus of laughter at philistinism, hers was a rovingly skeptical eye, dissecting social stratification as well as bourgeois complacency; for another, her "technical" experiments turn out to be combinations (as Perkins says) of "nursery rhymes and jazz syncopation" (431)—projects in parodic juxtaposition of popular cultural sounds; and, finally, as the sound recordings of her memorable performances reveal, her modernist poems are exceedingly funny, not sad—witty and silly in their mockery even of "the triumphant dust."

Admittedly, it may be thanks to disillusionment (at least in part) that Sitwell came, with her brothers, to specialize in the "twentieth-century harlequinade"—the phrase that Osbert and she used as a title for their first joint modernist production. (The strong allegiance among the three Sitwells made them appear to others a "new school" in themselves and did much to help each of them in turn establish a career.)[11] Some of her first published poems featured a dreamy, romantic, early Yeatsian style, but she moved quickly on from this to develop startlingly experimental methods—the harsh catachresis, impersonal metaphorics, and dry wit for which she is best known—and this development in her work occurred more rapidly than comparable transformations in the poetry of others (Pound or Lawrence, e.g.). If despair were necessary to lead her from romanticism to mockery, dreamlike love scenes to hellish cityscapes, and personal lyricism to impersonal performance, she had plenty to be miserable about. The oft-told story of her unwanted birth, of her frequently unhappy, discordant childhood, and of the disastrous break in her family's fortunes that led to her mother's imprisonment and her own impoverished but independent establishment in Bayswater may well lie behind a poetry full of grandiosity abruptly deflated.

The distanced yet clear relation of this deflated grandiosity to her own experience is characteristic of the mock-heroic mode in which much of her work is written. As Roger B. Salomon has argued, writers adopt the mock-heroic mode to preserve, yet hold at a distance, their earlier hopes for something more heroic. Treating writers from Cervantes to Bellow and focusing particularly on the modernist mock-heroism of Joyce, Williams, and Stevens, Salomon does not mention Sitwell (or indeed any female writer). Sitwell would belong on such a list—except that she found mockery a congenial mode almost from the start, a style in which she could be brazen without writing about herself.

Yet linking anguish to mock-heroism in Sitwell's poetry does not entail the conclusion that the true or final meaning of her writing (or that of Nabokov and Joyce, for that matter) is despair. The coupling of the serious and the unserious is as tight as the hyphen (as Salomon argues) between the "mock" and the "heroic" in these writers' writing, and their work does not "mean" one attitude more than the other (6). More particularly, it is a mistake to take literally, or entirely seriously, Sitwell's "Defense" of her poetry as technical innovation in the *Collected Poems* introduction (xv). Even while invoking apologetic writings by Sidney, Jonson, and Campion to frame her elaborate explanations of her poems' sound effects, this defense, like the poems, makes light of traditional poetics, and her explanations belabor the obvious: that Sitwell would sit still for no one else's trivialization or explanations but, instead, preemptively invented her own self-parody and self-ennoblement as she went along.

Meanwhile, what she does not reveal in this introduction is the extent to which onlookers were taken aback not only by the technically precocious poems but also by the self-advertisements of a woman poet. Feminist scholars such as Marianne DeKoven and Sydney Kaplan have shown that modernist women writers became anxiously self-protective in their self-disclosures and ambivalently both sought attention and sought to divert it from themselves as women in their writing. Sitwell called attention to herself as a public figure, but her writing is also self-concealing. Her defense avoids mention not only of the gender politics in which she was enmeshed but also, on the one hand, her own deliberate, attention-grabbing exploitation of the image of herself as a "strange" woman and, on the other, the unforgettable, outrageous female figures and sexual suggestions in her poems.

Making an astonishing spectacle of herself, she became, as Sandra Gilbert and Susan Gubar name her, along with a number of other women writers, a "female female impersonator," "ascend[ing] lecture platforms as exuberantly as [she] gave readings in private salons" (3:65).[12] Sitwell engaged, with every weapon in her arsenal, in literary battle with other writers and critics of her day, criticizing other writers and countering criticism of herself with everything from ridicule to lawsuits, so that perceptions of her, even today, are intensely polarized.

She is seen as either brilliantly funny and accomplished or hideously self-assertive and absurd. She is reviled by some, admired by others, for example, for having crowned herself "Queen Edith" (deposing Queen Victoria in her poems only to crown herself). But, again, to take her entirely seriously is as great a mistake as not to take her seriously at all; she aimed, and succeeded, at confusing the boundaries between the silly and the serious.

The polemics of Eliot, Pound, Wyndham Lewis, and other male modernists have appeared to critics as far more substantial, more coherent, and (as perhaps they should) more earnest than Sitwell's. But we should remember that the polemics became increasingly serious as these poets invested themselves in the long process of self-canonization: as Michael Levenson has shown, their modernism "was individualist before it was anti-individualist, anti-traditional before it was traditional, inclined to anarchism before it was inclined to authoritarianism" (79). Levenson hints in passing that Pound and Eliot were also inclined to discover allegiances with women before their polemics became antifemale.[13] These male writers' polemics, and their antifemale bias, have almost entirely crowded out Sitwell, leaving little trace of her in current histories of modernist poetics—and even less trace of her attention to sexual politics.[14] With *Waste Land*–like poems such as "Clowns' Houses" (published in the *Times Literary Supplement* in 1918) Sitwell did her part for the modern movement, invading the prim, friendly Georgian skies with laughter: "Beneath the flat and paper sky / The sun, a demon's eye, / Glowed through," and sounds "Seemed out of tune, as if the light / Were fiddle-strings pulled tight" (112). Far more famous is Eliot's Unreal City of 1922, in which "A woman drew her long black hair out tight / And fiddled whisper music on those strings" (145). Could that overstrung, out-of-tune woman, whom Eliot condemns to a wasteland of towers "upside down . . . Tolling reminiscent bells," be partly Sitwell (whom Eliot knew)?[15] Sitwell had already published comparable nightmare images—"The market-square with spire and bell / Clanged out the hour in Hell"—and had placed herself rather than some Other in this scene: "When once I ventured in, / Chill Silence, like a surging sea, / Slowly enveloped me" (112–113). Whether or not Eliot's woman fiddling with her hair is Sitwell, Eliot and Pound (as other critics have shown) joined to combat the threat of scribbling women in much the same mocking way they dealt with the Georgians.[16]

Eliot registered his opinion about the successes of women writers in his ridicule in *The Waste Land* (deleted by Pound) of Fresca's "Unreal emotions": "She scribbles verse of such a gloomy tone / That cautious critics say, her style is quite her own"; "She may as well write poetry, as count sheep." Like Fresca, Sitwell was "baptised" in water of Swinburne and Baudelaire and was "thrilled" by Russians; she may well also have been immersed in "Symonds—Walter Pater—Vernon Lee." She would even make sense out of Eliot's "sort of can-can salonnière," which might be thought to mock her mixture of the popular with the elite. Eliot sees the scribbling woman as driven by sexual lust, a "strolling slattern in a tawdry gown": "The same eternal and consuming itch / Can make a martyr [Magdalene], or plain simple bitch" (41). No need to draw distinctions between the woman who suffers or desires and the artist who creates; here once again a male writer sexualizes his stereotype of the professional woman.[17]

Sitwell was well placed to resist such caricatures of popular women writers, resembling other women modernists here again—as Gilbert and Gubar also point out—in her ambivalence about popular scribbling women, among whom Sitwell feared to be lost and against whom she endeavored to establish a countertradition of a few "great" women writers (Sappho, Rossetti, Stein, and herself) (1:206). In the struggle to achieve recognition for herself she endeavored anxiously to surpass other women writers. Pondrom argues that what makes Sitwell worthy of consideration by the side of Stein is precisely Sitwell's dual achievement in simultaneously promoting and transforming a contemporary woman writer's work in her own. Pondrom notes that Sitwell has too often been stereotyped "in terms of female rivalry"; Sitwell herself combatted this stereotype by making "a nearly unprecedented attribution of influence to one of her contemporaries," thereby positioning herself as Stein's advocate at a time when Stein was reaching only "a limited public audience" (206–7).

Moreover, the imagery of Eliot's phobic slander is anticipated and resisted by its counterpart in Sitwell's imagery of women's sexuality. The poetry itself, with its numerous satiric portraits of Victorian gender relations, provides a bold vision of women, often frankly wicked, yet not unironic, such as "that shady lady," the "new-arisen Madam Venus," who shocks Queen Victoria ("Hornpipe" 153); or the flaming "queans," quarrelsome Hattie and Mattie, who "blow up like boxes," forcing Pluto to turn as "red as George / The Fourth" ("Mazurka" 140);

or "the tall Spanish jade" who with a "Tee-hee!" announces "our Pa-phian vocation" to Il Capitaneo, "Swaggart braggadocio / Sword and mustachio" ("Trio for Two Cats and a Trombone" 119).

In "En Famille" (128–29) the joke at first is on patriarch Sir Joshua Jebb, "An admiral red" who escorts his daughters Jemima, Jocasta, Dinah, and Deb prudently through the country fields in the spring, but to whom the daughters complain: if only "Papa, you would once say 'Damn'— / Instead of merely roaring 'Avast' . . . / We should now stand in the street of Hell," where they could enjoy a siesta and let their eyes "glide" over to Myrrhina at her toilette. The admiral replies not merely that "it would not do at all" but that "her scandalous reputa-tion" for forgetting to say please or her prayers "Has shocked the whole of the Hellish nation . . . / For Hell is just as properly proper / As Greenwich, or as Bath, or Joppa!" These are poems that acknowledge that propriety constitutes a slippery slope yet also suggest the ease with which one hierarchy—say, that of Heaven and Hell—may be reversed or replaced by yet another.

After witnessing the notorious performance of *Façade* at the Aeolian Hall in 1923 (where the poems were intoned by Sitwell through a "sengerphone"—a type of megaphone—projecting out of a painted curtain, accompanied by William Walton's music), a satiric gossip col-umnist announced that Sitwell was working on publication of new books to be called *Gilded Sluts and Garbage*,[18] thus deploying (as do all "angels," to use Milan Kundera's term for the guardians of sober mean-ing [55–76]) Sitwell's laughter against her. With four words Sitwell's funny, exciting "gilded sluts" were snatched away and hurled back at her as a mean obscenity. The many people who knew of her but did not read her poems would not even have known that she wrote about prostitutes; they might have seen this as a parody of her extravagant language effects rather than of her own imagery, but they might also have seen it as a description of her (a gilded slut) and her art (garbage): Sitwell as Fresca again and a familiar slur against a too-assertive woman. Noël Coward produced a send-up of the Sitwells, the revue *London Calling*, which was enormously popular and made the Sit-wells—Edith, in particular—still better known as objects of a good joke. The jokes against the Sitwells are remembered when her own cunning, deconstructive humor is not.

Coward's ridicule also had a more intensely personal effect, for it stirred up a hornet's nest of latent anxiety in Sitwell; she never went to see his skit, but the gossip about it made her think that she had been turned by Maisie Gay—the actress who played "Miss Hernia Whittlebot"—into an "obscene" figure and a lesbian (Glendinning 81). Withdrawing to her room, she fell ill from her distress at this public exposure. What had started out as a lively dance of sexually vivid female figures was, for a time, abruptly silenced by the imagined stereotype of herself as sexual pariah. Sitwell eventually returned to the fray, however, and willingly made a spectacle of herself, if not as radical lesbian, nonetheless as a self-publicizing female eccentric—perpetually off center and decentering others' norms for women.[19]

It is not far from Sitwell's "gilded sluts" or Sitwell herself with her frequent changes of eccentric costume to Donna Haraway's feminist cyborg. (Sitwell dressed for excess rather as Madonna does.) Haraway's well-known postmodern "manifesto" seeks to establish "an ironic political myth," for, she argues,

> Irony is about contradictions that do not resolve into larger wholes. . . . Irony is about humor and serious play. It is also a rhetorical strategy and a political method. . . . At the center of my ironic faith, my blasphemy, is the image of the cyborg. (190–91)

Sitwell professed herself, and all women, indifferent to politics, including gender politics, while simultaneously protesting nuclear armament. This in itself was a political statement about women, men, and politics as usual.[20] Her clowning "shadows, or ghosts, moving, not in my country world, but in a highly mechanized universe" and her gay "butterflies" or "spivs" who mask "the see-saw world" are deployed similarly as ironic, contradictory myths (xviii)—participants in a strategically destabilizing social "blasphemy."

Why a cyborg? Because it is not "whole" but, rather, hybrid, like Sitwell's harlequins, "a creature of social reality as well as a creature of fiction" (191). In a curious echo of Cunard as well, Haraway continues: in "our time, a mythic time, we are all chimeras, theorized and fabricated hybrids of machine and organism" (191). But, if we are "fabricated," we may take responsibility for our "construction" and change our fabrications. The kind of change Haraway evokes and endorses is ceaseless change of old identity categories and continual erosion of hierarchical power structures; so also in Sitwell's modernist poems, "Said King Pompey the emperor's ape / . . . 'The dust is everything'"

(116). "Faith" in Haraway's polemical nonsense figure of the cyborg produces a liberating "confusion of boundaries" between man and machine, emperor and ape, high and low, woman and man—and between the serious and the unserious.

II

Having risen on the strength of her own wits and guts and then fallen again, Zora Neale Hurston has re-arisen and is now a far more familiar figure in literary studies than Sitwell. I wish to look next not at Hurston's writing (which has received readings too numerous to list) but briefly, and more broadly, at her canonization. In considering Hurston, I am not selecting a writer who wrote much nonsense, in the strictest sense of that term, but both laughter and the destabilization of meaning are defining features of her writing.

"Twenty years ago," Henry Louis Gates Jr. reminds us, "Hurston's work was largely out of print, her literary legacy alive only to a tiny, devoted band of readers," but "today" (in 1993) "her works are central to the canon of African-American, American, and Women's literatures." In fact, as he further explains in his introduction to the criticism collected in the Armistad Series edition, her fiction "was well received by mainstream American reviewers" during her own time (xi, xii)—that is, in the late 1930s and 1940s, when Anglo-American modernism had achieved some respectability and stature. What I wish to consider in Hurston's career is not how and why she fell from view after this propitious start but, rather, what is entailed in her reemergence. Along with countless other African-American writers she lost her readership in the 1950s and 1960s, only to become, in the 1970s and 1980s, institutionalized in an alternative tradition of African-American literature and established, according to Gates in *The Signifying Monkey,* as "the first writer that our generation of black and feminist critics has brought into the canon, or perhaps I should say, canons" of white anthologies and syllabi (180).

Hurston's reemergence and eminence are fascinating, for the purposes of this essay, because she offered different groups as many reasons as Sitwell to distrust her example. Hurston provoked controversy—analogously to Sitwell—for her opportunistic love of publicity, for her interest in intraracial relations, and for her choice of modernist methods. While Sitwell, with only partial success, patronized younger male (rarely female) writers in order to ally herself with the insurgent modern movement, Hurston, with equally mixed results, eagerly sought the patronage of her wealthy white "godmother," Charlotte Osgood Mason, for the sake of a secure career. And, while Sitwell was writing not only about "gilded sluts" and "Il Capitaneo" but about "allegro Negros" (rather than hyacinth girls and fisher kings), Hurston was writing about black/black and female/male tensions as well as black/white racial divisions.

In addition, Hurston was severely criticized in her day by, Gates explains, "a few prominent black male writers . . . for her 'African-Americanization' of modernism. In the thirties, at least, both Wright and Ellison were more interested in the resources of naturalism as a literary mode than they were in the sort of lyrical symbolism that Hurston would develop" (*Hurston* xii). Gates implies that this criticism by "black male" writers was tinged with sexism, but, as Gates also points out, Hurston gained greater acclaim from white audiences in her own time than any other African-American writer, and this must have seemed in itself proof of Wright and Ellison's suspicions, which were partly suspicions that Hurston did not challenge white racism directly enough—that she was not serious, by this criterion. The many-headed challenge of Hurston's writing was, not entirely without reason, difficult for other African-American writers to embrace.

Readers of the 1970s were understandably more tolerant of Hurston's earlier mainstream successes and eager to read the works of a forgotten black woman; her rediscovery was an exciting process, as students and teachers passed one another her texts (as Gates and Mary Helen Washington indicate) in the "underground network" of photocopy rooms (*Hurston* xi). But the still more recent flood of scholarship on Hurston—predominantly sober in tone and serious in approach—may have done something to subdue the challenge of Hurston's writings while promoting them. Christine Levecq sees even the most recent criticism of Hurston as prone to stereotyping Hurston with its interpretive categories and thus rendering her docile, and she argues for an interpretation of laughter in *Their Eyes Were Watching God* that is unremitting in its deferral of meaning:

> The name of Zora Neale Hurston has come to evoke originality and ebullience, sassy behavior, and colorful taletelling, intelligence and wit. Yet it is precisely the humor, the flamboyance, the celebratory

impulse in her works that have created much controversy in academic circles, where they have been repeatedly held against her as utopian and stereotypical. I want to argue that Hurston puts humor in the service of complexity, that the laughter, the humor, the comic voices, rather than producing a stereotypical representation of (black) identity, on the contrary keep destabilizing it. (87)

Levecq's argument for Hurston's laughing indeterminacy, and criticism's unlaughing determinacy, permits us, if not fully to retrieve, at least to recapture glimpses of the laughter in Hurston's "signifyin(g)" (*Signifying* xxi). But, given its own status as serious critical argumentation, Levecq's essay may remind us also of the ways in which its endorsement of laughter is itself a well-known critical gesture, both in general and (as Levecq shows in her numerous acknowledgments) in 1980s criticism of Hurston.

Have the radical, polemical ideas of modernism—tamed by early modernist scholars, who defended them as expressive of disillusionment, as nostalgia for a past order, and as hints toward new forms of unity, new engagements with tradition—resurfaced as postmodernism's clichés? Have modernist methods themselves become (in Kundera's terms) angelic? Haraway's essay, first published in 1985, is, for example, standard reading, at least among students of contemporary culture, postmodernism, and feminism. Her influence is surely due less to any revolutionary impact her essay can have in 1997 than to the vivid shape it gives to what are now extremely familiar ideas. Contradiction, irony, play, identity-as-construction, irresolution—all of these have become critical commonplaces; they enjoy the status of canonical ideas in contemporary culture. The canonization of postmodernist thought operates, moreover, to exclude or diminish some forms of writing while elevating others, to single out certain writers at the expense of the larger intertextual matrices in which they were originally embedded, and also, paradoxically, to mute the impact of some writers, such as Sitwell, who might benefit most from this shift in expectations.[21]

But it is not against these ideas in themselves that I would argue; on the contrary, concepts such as these remain among the most controversial ideas today (when we look beyond the academic scene of cultural studies) and, to my mind, among the most promising that cultural studies have to offer. To move these ideas from theory to social practice, moreover, remains an unresolved challenge. I would argue, rather, for a continued vigilance to the hidden polemics, the concealed divisions, that haunt postmodern writing and thought, even as they haunted the modernists. Among such divisions are, as many critics have shown, differences of gender, race, and class. Of less obvious social centrality, but not unrelated and equally influential in the construction and reconstruction of canons, is that between postmodernist writing and what Gates terms "naturalism" in his study of Hurston. Today's cultural polemics continue to depend upon unexamined assumptions about what counts as sense and what does not.

Historically, the division between modernism and naturalism has been closely linked to differences of gender, race, and class.[22] Many more twentieth-century women writers have chosen to write within traditions of "realist" narrative or, as Suzanne Clark has demonstrated, of sentimentalism than have chosen the modernist and postmodernist metafictional novel or antinovel, while still challenging social norms and without necessarily losing a sense of humor. This work can't be construed as nonsense or as pastiche; for the sake, in part, of accessibility to wide audiences, it goes against the grain of New Critical and new (cultural) critical aesthetic criteria, which favor, respectively, modernism and postmodernism. No such writing is going to be included in the charismatic lists and anthologies of experimental twentieth-century literature. Still more worrisome is the moat between the free-standing Great Halls of postmodernist canons and the busy "streets" of African-American writing.[23] It is with the "style" war, then—a war that involves far more than style—that I would like to conclude.

Langston Hughes and Hurston are important beneficiaries of the post-1940s taste for mocking irony, language play, and other modernist stratagems, but they are also exceptions. Gates registers his own amazement at Hurston's new clout in this example: "Last year at Yale alone, seventeen courses taught *Their Eyes Were Watching God!*" (*Hurston* xi). Gates does not comment in the Armistad introduction on what other African-American writers might have been left out of these courses in favor of Hurston, but it is not unusual to discover courses at other universities in which she is the token African-American writer, perhaps especially in smaller institutions seeking through a small array of courses to develop a "multicultural" curriculum. James De Jongh titles his recent study of the Harlem Renaissance *Vicious Modernism,* since it charts the developments of "a century marked by the vicious dynamics of the color line" (1); modernism itself changes color in this study to include Harlem as a complex, feisty, and rivalrous literary environment, and the dominant figures at the start of this movement dipped again and again into "the resources of naturalism." These writers' naturalism did not draw criticism, however, during the Harlem Renaissance; rather, the association of Hughes with the popular forms of jazz and blues, which, as De Jongh says, "now seems so natural—perhaps even a bit trite—was severely criticized by black authority figures and rejected in its own time" (24). These authorities could not afford either the potential backlash of irony or the proliferation of innuendo in Hughes's writing:

> The initial negative reaction to *The Weary Blues* objected as much to Hughes's using jazz and blues as literary material as to the flexible sexual morality of the cabarets. The spirituals had come to be accepted by the Negro elite as dignified and ennobling folk forms, but blues and jazz were embarrassing reminders of a status they were trying to escape. (24)

Hughes's portrayal of Harlem was completely "overshadowed" by the "two sensational, best-selling novels about Harlem," Carl Van Vechten's *Nigger Heaven* and Claude McKay's *Home to Harlem* (26).

The ultimate success of the "vicious modernism" of writers such as Hughes and Hurston, however, leads De Jongh, despite his sensitivity to historical textures and nuance, to undervalue writers unlike Hurston, including, for example, the black women writers Jesse Redmon Fauset and Nella Larsen, whose work, among others, he sums up as "effect[ing] a generic Harlem novel, focused thematically on dispiriting topics of passing, intraracial color prejudice and class divisions, concentrated stylistically on the atavistic and exotic local color of the Harlem cabarets" (47). In so readily typing *Plum Bun, Passing,* and *Quicksand*— and the themes themselves—as "generic" and "dispiriting,"[24] De Jongh takes one side in the contest between styles that Gates details in *The Signifying Monkey* between Wright's concern with naturalism in the 1930s and Hurston's modernism. None of these naturalist novelists are "modernist" by any stretch of the imagination, but their texts are not unironic, not humorless, not without destabilizing effects. Indeed, critics such as Deborah McDowell have already begun to apply postmodern readings to these nonpostmodern novels, with intriguing results, particularly for *Passing*—uncovering their parodistic, ironic, and sexually illicit subtexts and indeterminacies.[25]

Too much has been made of the gap between modernism and its literary surroundings, too little of how one method may refer to, recontextualize, even replicate the effects of the other. Too much is made of the gaps, wherever these are said to occur, between period concepts, aesthetic styles, alternative ways to make (and unmake) sense. My own central choices of Sitwell, Eliot, and Hurston as representative modernists result in unusual juxtapositions, and, though each of these writers in turn has frequently and for good reason been defined as modernist, their combination here may serve to remind us of how notoriously mobile such categories are.

Modernism unsettled apparently settled meanings and did so in part by making those meanings into things to be laughed at. But, in so doing, modernists were not opening up a space in which laughter, destabilization, and freedom would dominate. They were, in fact, eager to establish not only the laughability of their rivals but also their own seriousness and the importance of the structures of meaning to which their work gave access. But this also means that their relation to laughter, and to nonsense, is unstable over time. Whether, as readers of a later generation that many call postmodern, we wish to invest modernist writing with serious meaning or to remind ourselves of its instabilities, we too will be engaged in a contest of ideas in which there can probably be no final winner, only a process of successive upheavals. If we are critics, we are always already engaged in argument with others, and, if those opponents begin to seem ridiculously one-dimensional, they have probably become mirrors only of ourselves. But there is also nearly always something seriously at stake beyond the ideational in such contests. While cultivating a sense of the limits of the power of writers to affix final meanings or determine final judgments, we should also recognize, so I believe, that it would be a mistake (indeed not possible) to avoid meaning or judgment.

NOTES

1. Lillian Robinson reminds us that the term *canon* itself began as "a mild, self-deprecatory joke," but "use of the term has expanded with the increasing challenges to tradition and consequent demonization of the challengers, assur-

ing that it has had no chance to become a dead metaphor" (21); the term now is taken quite seriously, while becoming itself the target of many punning jokes.

2. For "the Laureate's feet," see Sitwell, "Sir Beelzebub" 156:

> When
> Sir
> Beelzebub called for his syllabub in the hotel in Hell
>   Where Proserpine first fell . . .
>
> Nobody comes to give him his rum but the
> Rim of the sky hippopotamus-glum
> Enhances the chances to bless with a benison
> Alfred Lord Tennyson crossing the bar laid
> With cold vegetation from pale deputations
> Of temperance workers (all signed In Memoriam)
> Hoping with glory to trip up the Laureate's feet
>
>   (Moving in classical metres) . . .

For "scribbling Fresca," see Eliot, *The Waste Land: A Facsimile and Transcript* 27:

> But women intellectual grow dull,
> And lose the mother wit of natural trull.
> Fresca was born upon a soapy sea
> Of Symonds—Walter Pater—Vernon Lee.
> The Scandinavians bemused her wits,
> The Russians thrilled her to hysteric fits.
> From such chaotic misch-masch potpourri
> What are we to expect but poetry?
> When restless nights distract her brain from sleep
> She may as well write poetry, as count sheep.

3. Since this essay is an exploration of the status of nonsense in the politics of modernist canon making rather than a formalist analysis, nonsense is defined broadly to include both texts that disturb syntactical and semantic norms, as parts of *Ulysses* do or initially seemed to do and as *Finnegans Wake* is still perceived to do, and texts that are thought of as nonserious, silly, or light, such as Lewis Carroll's humorous verse.

4. MLA on-line for 1981 to February 1996 lists the publication in 1987 of the Twayne book on all three Sitwells and two essays in which she is compared to Gertrude Stein and Charlotte Mew, respectively; otherwise, there is one essay on her letters, one reminiscence, one bibliographical note, one recovery of previously unpublished poems, two articles that focus either on her reading performances or on the musical adaptation of *Façade*, five dissertations (one of which deals with her work in the context of British women writers during the two world wars), two Spanish-language articles, one generalist essay (a reconsideration published in a poetry journal), and one short review essay of Glendin-

ning's biography. Brophy's 1968 book remains the sole full-length study of her work.

5. Iris Tree's poetry and Helen Rootham's translations also appeared regularly in *Wheels*.

6. The woman writer most analogous to Sitwell is, of course, Stein, who, in contrast to Sitwell, has received a small avalanche of attention in the last decade.

7. Indeed, Sitwell's experiments can now be seen as too orderly, too governed—as Perloff argues—by "a fixed set of rules," to deserve consideration alongside other modernist poetry that "allows for free play" and "indeterminacy" (85). See Pondrom's interesting rebuttal of this argument (esp. 204, 215, 217).

8. Most critics who have given her prolonged attention turn quickly from the spectacle of technique to various arguments for the meaningfulness of her poetry: see Brophy, Cevasco, and Glendinning. An important and complex exception occurs in Pondrom's study, which points suggestively toward thematic readings of several poems even while focusing on Sitwell's experimentalism as a distinctive contribution to modernist innovation. Pondrom argues that Sitwell needs to be "appreciated as one thread in the polymorphous fabric of female modernism" (216).

9. See, however, the provocative chapter on Sitwell's writing in Williams.

10. For a general description of postmodernism that, in summarizing its various aims and sketching its contours a decade ago, also suggests how canonical it—and the writers and theorists associated with it—have become, see Calinescu 265–312. (The long lists, however, of postmodernists in Calinescu's 1987 summary of postmodernism include only two women writers, Christine Brooke-Rose and Iris Murdoch, and hark back to only one woman modernist, Gertrude Stein [297–98, 301].)

11. Some recent scholars have as a result favored discussing them as a group, a tendency that also contributes to submerging Sitwell's distinctive career: see Pearson's group biography and Cevasco's Twayne overview.

12. Gilbert and Gubar discuss Sitwell's poetry only in passing in their three-volume survey of twentieth-century women's writing, singling out some of Sitwell's war-related poems for commentary (3:5, 225–26).

13. Levenson does not include women writers (such as H.D., who influenced Pound even as he influenced her) as central objects of his study, but he mentions in passing, for example, Pound's gradual "assumption" of "control of the literary side" of Dora Marsden's journal the *New Freewoman* and his change of its title to the *Egoist*, his attempt to "bully" Harriet Monroe into "altering the policy" of *Poetry* (70), and his conflict with Amy Lowell over her "threatened appropriation of the *name*" of imagism (147).

14. Perkins's placement of Sitwell in his history of modern verse emblematizes this crowding out of her career, since she is discussed in just one small section among several unrelated authors in a chapter called "British Poetry after the War, 1918–1928," in contrast to the pervasive references and separate chapters devoted to, for example, Eliot, Pound, and Yeats.

15. Eliot and Sitwell first met at a poetry reading in December 1917, where he read "Hippopotamus" (Glendinning 55).

16. See, for example, Koestenbaum 112–29.

17. Sitwell read *The Waste Land* in 1924 and made a point of following Eliot's work from then on, continually recommending it to others (Glendinning 100); it is lucky that she did not see this piece of it, for in other respects their methods and aims had much in common.

18. Probably this was Noël Coward himself; as Philip Hoare records in his biography of Coward, the joke appeared in Coward's gossip column: "Hernia is busy preparing for publication of her new books, *Gilded Sluts and Garbage*. She breakfasts on onions and Vichy water" (120).

19. My secondhand copy of Sitwell's autobiography contains a newspaper clipping from the *San Jose Mercury* of 10 December 1964 (an AP, UPI story) with an obituary headlined "English Eccentric: Poetry's Dame Edith Is Dead," which focuses on "eccentricities" such as her "medieval-style clothes, and huge rings and brooches" (2).

20. For example, the AP, UPI story quotes her, saying, "Women know nothing about politics. . . . And I don't wish to make men so irritated with my interference that they will start bombing everything to bits" ("English Eccentric").

21. I was recently persuaded still more deeply of this by the arguments of one of my graduate students, Kerri Shaw, against abstraction of Joanna Russ's *The Female Man* from its context in radical lesbian science fiction and transportation of it into a postmodern milieu—something that I did in a course on "Gender in Modernism and Postmodernism" and that a few other critics are doing (see, e.g., Haraway, 215, 220). Something may be gained for postmodernism but some things lost also for comprehension of *The Female Man*.

22. The "working-class novel" is another important example: see Hawthorn.

23. See, for example, West and hooks on the vexed relations between postmodernism and African-American artists and thinkers.

24. De Jongh does not intend to suggest that these novels focus on the cabaret scene, though other writers' novels do; the themes of passing, intraracial color prejudice, and class divisions, however, are all central to these three novels.

25. See also Blackmore, Caughie, Rabinowitz, on *Passing*.

WORKS CITED

Blackmore, David L. "'That Unreasonable Restless Feeling': The Homosexual Subtexts of Nella Larsen's *Passing*." *African-American Review* 26.3 (1992): 475–84.

Brophy, James D. *Edith Sitwell: The Symbolist Order*. Carbondale: Southern Illinois UP, 1968.

Calinescu, Matei. *Five Faces of Modernity*. Durham: Duke UP, 1987.

Caughie, Pamela L. "'Not Entirely Strange, . . . Not Entirely Friendly': *Passing and Pedagogy*." *College English* 54.7 (1992): 775–93.

Cevasco, G. A. *The Sitwells: Edith, Osbert, and Sacheverell*. Boston: Twayne, 1987.

Clark, Suzanne. *Sentimental Modernism: Women Writers and the Revolution of the Word*. Bloomington: Indiana UP, 1991.

De Jongh, James. *Vicious Modernism: Black Harlem and the Literary Imagination*. Cambridge: Cambridge UP, 1990.

DeKoven, Marianne. *Rich and Strange: Gender, History, Modernism*. Princeton: Princeton UP, 1991.

Eliot, T. S. *The Waste Land: A Facsimile and Transcript of the Original Drafts Including the Annotations of Ezra Pound*, ed. Valerie Eliot. New York: Harcourt Brace Jovanovich, 1971.

"English Eccentric: Poetry's Dame Edith Is Dead." *San Jose Mercury*, 10 December 1964, 2.

Gates, Henry Louis, Jr. *The Signifying Monkey: A Theory of African-American Criticism*. Oxford: Oxford UP, 1988.

Gates, Henry Louis, Jr., and K. A. Appiah, eds. *Zora Neale Hurston: Critical Perspectives Past and Present*. New York: Armistad, 1993.

Gilbert, Sandra M., and Susan Gubar. *No Man's Land: The Place of the Woman Writer in the Twentieth Century*. Vol. 1: *The War of the Words*; Vol. 2: *Sexchanges*; and Vol. 3: *Letters from the Front*. New Haven: Yale UP, 1988, 1989, and 1994.

Glendinning, Victoria. *Edith Sitwell: A Unicorn among Lions*. London: Weidenfeld and Nicolson, 1981.

Haraway, Donna. "A Manifesto for Cyborgs: Science, Technology, and Socialist Feminism in the 1980s." In *Feminism/Postmodernism*, ed. Linda J. Nicholson. New York: Routledge, 1990. 190–233.

Hawthorn, Jeremy, ed. *The British Working-Class Novel in the Twentieth Century*. London: Edward Arnold, 1984.

Hoare, Philip. *Noël Coward: A Biography*. New York: Simon and Schuster, 1995.

hooks, bell. *Yearning: Race, Gender, and Cultural Politics*. Boston: South End P, 1990.

Kaplan, Sydney Janet. *Katherine Mansfield and the Origins of Modernist Fiction*. Ithaca: Cornell UP, 1991.

Koestenbaum, Wayne. *Double Talk: The Erotics of Male Literary Collaboration*. New York: Routledge, 1989.

Kundera, Milan. *The Book of Laughter and Forgetting*. Trans. Michael Henry Heim. New York: Penguin, 1981.

Levenson, Michael. *A Genealogy of Modernism: A Study of English Literary Doctrine, 1908–1922*. Cambridge: Cambridge UP, 1984.

Levecq, Christine. "'You Heard Her, You Ain't Blind': Subversive Shifts in Zora Neale Hurston's *Their Eyes Were Watching God*." *Tulsa Studies in Women's Literature* 13.1 (1994): 87–111.

McDowell, Deborah E., ed. Introduction. *Plum Bun: A Novel without a Moral*. By Jesse Redmon Fauset. Boston: Beacon, 1990. ix–xxxiii.

————, ed. Introduction. *Quicksand and Passing*. By Nella Larsen. New Brunswick: Rutgers UP, 1986. ix–xxxv.

The Norton Anthology of English Literature. 6th ed. Vol. 2. Ed. M. H. Abrams, et al. New York: Norton, 1993.

Pearson, John. *Façades: Edith, Osbert and Sacheverell*. London: Macmillan, 1989.

Perkins, David. *A History of Modern Poetry: From the 1890s to the High Modernist Mode*. Cambridge: Belknap, 1976.

Perloff, Marjorie. *The Poetics of Indeterminacy: Rimbaud to Cage*. Princeton: Princeton UP, 1981.

Pondrom, Cyrena N. "Influence? or Intertextuality? The Complicated Connection of Edith Sitwell with Gertrude Stein." In *Influence and Intertextuality in Literary History*, ed. Jay Clayton and Eric Rothstein. Madison: U of Wisconsin P, 1991. 204–18.

Rabinowitz, Peter J. "'Betraying the Sender': The Rhetoric and Ethics of Fragile Texts." *Narrative* 2.3 (1994): 201–13.

Robinson, Lillian. "Firing the Literary Canons." *Insight* (18 July 1994): 20–22.

Salomon, Roger B. *Desperate Storytelling: Post-Romantic Elaborations of the Mock-Heroic Mode*. Athens: U of Georgia P, 1987.

Sitwell, Edith. *The Collected Poems*. New York: Vanguard, 1968.

Stewart, Susan. *Nonsense: Aspects of Intertextuality in Folklore and Literature*. Baltimore: Johns Hopkins UP, 1978.

West, Cornel. "Black Culture and Postmodernism." In *Remaking History*, ed. Barbara Kruger and Phil Mariani. Seattle: Bay P, 1989. 87–96.

Williams, Amelia. "'Venus' Hand: Laughter and the Language of Children's Culture in the Poetry of Christina Rossetti, Edith Sitwell, Edna St. Vincent Millay and Stevie Smith." Ph.D. diss., University of Virginia, 1993.

Heirs of Yeats: Eire as Female Poets Revise Her

Vicki Mahaffey

To launch into a discussion of the future of modernism is perhaps to beg the question of what modernism *was*, a question that grows increasingly vexed as the century that initiated the movement draws to a close. In some respects modernism, like nationalism, has a different meaning when viewed retrospectively than it had in the grip of the social forces that provoked it. Viewed retrospectively, the different streams of modernist experimentation produced during a period of seismic global change are not seen as diverse, complex, often agonized responses to historical disaster, but, instead, are seen as a mighty river, a unified ideology, an oversimplified "tradition." In recent years that tradition has also been identified with specifically, almost exclusively, male interpretive power and privilege. Comparatively speaking, men as a category had many more freedoms than their female counterparts, but that does not mean that they were powerful or privileged in relation to the society in which they lived. In retrospect, the so-called high modernists have been lionized and belittled in succession, although more and more frequently what is being attacked in the name of modernism is not the various and elastic strands of modernist practice but, rather, the dominant critical theory of the time—the New Criticism—so often confused with it. The "modernism" we hear decried in the 1990s is represented as ideologically self-consistent, the product of a group of intellectual elitists whose relation to one another is at best clubbish and at worst conspiratorial.

What is most disturbing about such a misconstruction of modernism is its refusal to interrogate the premise that licenses it: the assumption that modernism was powerful, successful, and culturally central, an institution rather than a diverse synchrony of movements. What gets left out is the penury of its practitioners, the status of many of them as colonized and disenfranchised subjects, as well as the diversity of the supporting cast of socialists, communists, lesbians, and feminists who struggled alongside men with aristocratic, fascist, or misogynistic leanings to envision possible new orders that might be assembled from the shards of cultural collapse. To assume (and resist) an ideologically unified modernism is to deny the most important historical force behind the movement: what Eavan Boland calls a "wounded history"[1] and the volatile responses such a history provokes.

Modernist writers such as James Joyce, William Butler Yeats, Virginia Woolf, T. S. Eliot, and even Ezra Pound were united across their differences in what Boland elsewhere calls (in another context) "a community of grief" ("A Kind of Scar," *A Dozen Lips*, 89). The various writers grieved for different losses, some national, some artistic and personal, some international, but the fact that Virginia Woolf is very much a part of this group shows that the grief of women over the uncompromising constriction of their social, intellectual, and sexual freedoms is fully comparable to the grief produced by colonial oppression (as in Ireland) or the grief occasioned by World War I. Boland, although writing about the nationalist tendency to mask a history of defeat with nostalgic and self-congratulatory assertions of moral triumph, pinpoints the danger of rewriting suffering as mastery, which is what we have been doing for the past decade in "postmodernist" critiques of modernism:

> There is a recurring temptation for any nation [read: tradition], and for any writer who operates within its field of force, to make an ornament of the past; to turn the losses to victories and to restate humiliations as triumphs. In every age language holds out narcosis and amnesia for this purpose. But such triumphs in the end are unsustaining and may, in fact, be corrupt.
>
> If a poet [or critic] does not tell the truth about time, her or his work will not survive it. Past or present, there is a human dimension to time, human voices within it and human griefs ordained by it. Our present will become the past of other men and women. We depend on them to remember it with the complexity with which it was suffered. As others, once, depended on us. ("A Kind of Scar," 92)

What, then, are the truths about modernism, and how are contemporary writers like Boland bringing them—in transfigured forms—into the future? Although one truth is that the majority of influential modernist writers were male, those writers were also, in different ways, dispossessed and were therefore vocal participants in a "community of grief" that also includes large numbers of women and the poor. Second, many high modernist writers were committed not to the transmission of the past but to its revision, so that the critique of modernist male privilege becomes part of the ongoing (modernist) project of revisionist thought.

Modernism as a collection of experiments can almost be defined by its obsessive commitment to revision (and to revisionism), not only in the stylistic sense of correcting or improving written expressions but also in a more literal sense, the determination to "look at again." Modernism was neither a "reversion" nor a "revirescence" but, rather, a carefully revisionist account of, or re-spect for, the past. Eavan Boland uses Adrienne Rich's poem "Diving into the Wreck" to illustrate the compulsion to revise, or re-spect, the legacies of the dead: "Like the swimmer in . . . 'Diving into the Wreck', I needed to find out 'the damage that was done and the treasures that prevail'" ("A Kind of Scar," 87). When Pound, Joyce, Yeats, and Woolf spend years writing and revising their visions of the past, what is at stake on an ideological level is not egotistical perfectionism; it is, rather, the social and ethical value of a determination to disinter, with respect and without undue simplification, the damage and treasure of history.

With Boland's caveats against the cheap triumph of simplifying the past to glorify the present in mind, I propose that part of the future of Irish modernism is already unfolding in the work of several contemporary Irish women poets. My particular focus is on the tradition of personifying Ireland as a woman, beginning with the myth that the invading Milesians named the country after a woman at her request (the De Danaan goddess Eire) and proceeding through the *aisling* tradition of the Middle Ages, which was politicized during the Jacobite period, producing the legacies of Cathleen Ni Houlihan, the Shan van Vocht, and Dark Rosaleen, among others.[2] My subject, then, is a literal re-vision: the current revision by Irish women writers of the *aisling* vision of Ireland as a woman and their critical analysis of what Boland calls "that old potent blurring of feminine and national" ("A Kind of Scar," 88).

In Ireland national politics has long been closely bound up with gender politics. In part the designation of the Irish as female (or, alternatively, as animalistic) is a product of colonization by an empire that troped itself as dominant and masculine; in the nineteenth century, however, even someone like Ernest Renan, who was sympathetic to the Celts as the epitome of creativity (in contrast to the "barbaric" Teutons), described them as "an essentially feminine race."[3] It is not controversial to claim that the Irish have long occupied what we would now call the female subject position,[4] but the implications of occupying such a position, especially for *real* women, are complex and interesting. As Boland explains:

> Womanhood and Irishness are metaphors for one another. There are resonances of humiliation, oppression and silence in both of them and I think you can understand one better by experiencing the other. . . . A woman poet is part of Irish history. She is, first, part of the ordeal, and second, part of the meaning. And that society has to argue out the ordeal and the meaning in terms of poetry by women, just as much as poetry by men.[5]

This is my project: to argue out the ordeal and the meaning of womanhood *and* Irish history, of nationalism *and* feminism, by considering how both men and women poets have differently embodied the nation as female. What I propose to do here is to counterpoint Yeats's early symbolist representations of the female nation with the more fractured and realistic metaphors of Irish womanhood in the works of contemporary Irish women poets.[6] The operative contrasts are not only between male and female representations of womanhood but also between an undivided and a divided Ireland and between nineteenth-century fin de siècle and the end of the twentieth century. Frank O'Connor once described the literature of the Irish literary Renaissance as a "peculiarly masculine affair." The question that drives the comparison I am making is a relatively simple one: what happens to the romance of idealism when the Sovereignty, the Shan van Vocht, Dark Rosaleen, and Cathleen Ni Houlihan begin to speak for themselves, in a voice that is individual and poetic rather than rhetorical and collective?[7] What happens when women themselves begin to ask, with the legendary "long tongue" of the ancient Irish poets, what Anne Hartigan questions:

Do I carry dark blame
   And sorrow double deep,
Because I sing a woman's song,
   So therefore, must I weep?

(Sleeping with Monsters, 207)

Yeats famously personified Ireland as Dark Rosaleen and as Eire, one of the three sisters after whom the country was named, in "The Rose" (1895) and in *The Wind among the Reeds* (1899), respectively. The symbolist meanings that gather around the image of the Rose as the volume unfolds are remarkably various, designed to span the usually unspeakable distance between the sexual and the divine. The Rose is a female muse, the personification of Ireland, an idealized vision of a real woman—Maud Gonne, a shadow of Dante's image of God in the *Paradiso,* and a representation of physical female sexuality. As the rose upon the rood of time, she is Christ on the cross (who also a*rose*), the Celtic cross, the heart in the body, an image of the violent, even apocalyptic conjunction of male and female principles, both spiritual and sexual (the rose female, the Cross male), and a Blakean image of eternity in love with the productions of time. The Rose is alternately flushed with passion and white from a brush with the Godhead.

Particularly revealing is the way Yeats represents the sexuality of the Rose and her relation to myth and religion. As an image of femaleness, the Rose is graphically and botanically sexual, a transplanted version of Blake's "The Sick Rose," its "bed of crimson joy" infected by "the invisible worm that flies through the night," a phallic force that in its new setting is also English. Yeats's way of evoking the sexuality of the Rose in the poems themselves is more delicate, euphemistic; the rose has been displaced upward onto facial lips, as in "The Rose of the World," in which the poet encapsulates the beauty and sorrow of the rose through the synecdoche of "these red lips." The image is more unmistakably apparent in "The Sorrow of Love," in which Yeats famously puns on the verb *arose* as a noun, *a rose:* "A girl arose that had red mournful lips."

Equally interesting is how Yeats positions the Rose in relation to religion and myth. The volume begins with "To the Rose upon the Rood of Time," which links the Rose with Christ not only by the allusion to the cross but also by the implied allusion to the vision that Christ arose from the dead. The final poem, "To Ireland in the Coming Times," is, in contrast, a nationalist clarion call:

> *Know, that I would accounted be*
> *True brother of a company*
> *That sang, to sweeten Ireland's wrong.*

In this poem the Rose is a fitting consort and complement to God—both are gigantic figures of whom we see or hear only the lowest part—her *"red-rose-bordered hem,"* His *"white footfall."* Whereas God is white and grave, the Rose is red and dancing, the muse of Ireland and of poetry: *"The measure of her flying feet / Made Ireland's heart begin to beat."* Her feet, in alternation with God's footfall, beat out the rhythm of Yeats's poetic feet, a rhythm also represented as a heartbeat, the heartbeat of both Ireland and the poet.

> *I cast my heart into my rhymes,*
> *That you, in the dim coming times,*
> *May know how my heart went with them*
> *After the red-rose-bordered hem.*

The association between the Rose and Christ is supplemented by a parallel and contrast from Greek and Irish myth: in addition to being Christ, the Rose is also Helen of Troy and Deirdre of the Sorrows. What is most arresting about this juxtaposition is Yeats's insistence on balance—a balance not only between religion and myth but also between male and female catalysts, between Christ's suffering in his own person for others and the suffering of others for Helen/Deirdre. By juxtaposing Christ and Helen/Deirdre, he equates their significance even while registering their structural oppositions, much as in *The Tower* he will juxtapose the Virgin Mary and Leda (mother of Helen), and as he here puts the Rose on an equal footing with God. If God is the principle of "truth's consuming ecstasy," the Rose is the emblem of the mortal and eternal beauty of the world—"the greatness of the world in tears, / Doomed like Odysseus and the laboring ships / And proud as Priam murdered with his peers." Before God created the Angels, He lived with the Rose, weary and kind; "He made the world to be a grassy road / Before her wandering feet."

Before I go on to discuss the female personification of Eire, I should note that, despite the dazzling comprehensiveness of the Rose in theory and her revolutionary status as a counterpart and equal to God, she—like God—exists primarily in the imaginary and the symbolic registers but not in the real. Despite the fact that she is an emblem of the heart, she herself has no feelings, and, although she is also microcosmically represented by the lips, she does not speak.[8]

When Yeats turns at the very end of the century to *The Wind among the Reeds* he reapplies many of the same symbolist techniques that he used in *The Rose*, although he uses them in more complex, local, and specifically Irish ways. Again, the muse of the volume is a female figure animated by puns: the wind is the *sidhe*, the fairies, but it is also a *she* (in English), and this she is *Eire* (air), an imperfect English/Irish pun reinforced by the pun on *Gael/gale*. (Gaelic, as Yeats was quick to apprehend, is the language of Eire [air], in which the fairies are felt in the wind.) Eire is also, of course, the woman from Irish mythology after whom Ireland was named; Yeats evokes her explicitly in "Into the Twilight" when he reminds the worn-out heart that "Your mother Eire is always young."

Like the Rose, who is a poetic muse as well as a national one, the image of wind among reeds also evokes the music of poetry. If the Rose's dancing produces a combined image of poetic feet and a beating heart, the wind among reeds calls up not only the pastoral associations of a shepherd's pipe superimposed onto a waterscape but also the act of speech itself, the wind passing through the vocal cords, and the literal meaning of inspiration. (As Yeats writes in "He Thinks of Those who have spoken Evil of His Beloved," I made this song "out of a mouthful of air.") Breath is here divine as well as passionate, an evocation of the Holy Spirit ("blessedness goes where the wind goes"), which in local mythological terms is equivalent to the *sidhe*, but the wind is also, like the rose, sexual as well as divine: it is the wind of desire in which the spirits of Paolo and Francesca perpetually blow in *The Inferno*. Finally, Eire is literally the land, a lake edge or shore in Sligo: her breast is the surface of lake or sea, which encloses her heart; her hair is reeds (as is clearly apparent in "The Host of the Air"); and what blows through her is not only the animating wind of desire, inspiration, music, poetry, myth, and nation but also the wailing of the banshee, harbinger of destruction. As Yeats represents her, Eire, like the Rose, is complex and powerful, a brilliant riposte to English degradations of Ireland's image; but, despite her kinship to an idealized Maud Gonne, who presents herself in *A Servant of the Queen* as the "woman of the Sidhe," Eire is neither real nor individual. Although she represents the conditions of speech, she herself never speaks but is spoken through.

It is precisely the symbolic, decorative function of a female Ireland that changes when women such as Nuala Ní Dhomhnaill, Eavan Boland, Anne Hartigan, Deirdre Brennan, Sara Berkeley, Mary E. O'Donnell, Paula Meehan, Eithne Strong, Roz Cowman, and Medbh McGuckian begin to write poetry. These women register and resist what Boland refers to as "the power of nationhood to edit the realities of woman-hood."[9] Many of these women definitively dissociate themselves from nationalism (see Eithne Strong, *Wildish Things*, 113), from the old ideal of political martyrdom, from Yeats's Rose Tree watered in the Christian tradition with human blood, which flowered into the Easter Rising. As Paula Meehan relates in "Don't Speak to Me of Martyrs," listening to a political speech brings her back to the nationalist propaganda of her childhood in which nine- and ten-year-old children recited nationalist verse in school:

> I wind up in the ghost place
> the language rocks me to,
> a cobwebby state, chilled vault
> littered with our totems;
>
> a tattered Plough and Stars,
> a bloodstained Proclamation,
> Connolly strapped wounded to a chair,
> Mayblossom in Inchicore.

In contrast to the "Rose," with its twin connotations of sexuality and death, Meehan evokes a different image, of the swollen genitalia of the Sheila-na-Gig in the national museum, her "yoni made luscious in stone," and the peace and touch of her mother. She concludes by reject-ing the male fantasy of violent and secret martyrdom:

> Don't speak to me of Stephen the Martyr
> the host snug in his palm
> slipping through the wounded streets
> to keep his secret safe.

> *(Wildish Things, 74–75)*

Roz Cowman, too, indicts the church as well as nationalism for its erasure of women. In "Medea Ireland" she suggests that the snake that Saint Patrick drove out of Ireland when he Christianized the country was the mother, who would then no longer mate and breed with him, with his hell thunderings and madness, and so, Medea-like, she killed her children: "The rime of death on children's bodies still / delays his pursuit of her flight through time."[10] Cowman's image of Ireland as Medea, enraged by Saint Patrick's denaturing of her, puts some of the burden of Ireland's violent self-division on Saint Patrick and the church, redrawing Stephen Dedalus's misogynist image of Ireland as "the old sow who eats her farrow."

When women poets begin depicting their own mythology, their own experience, and their own bodies (in relation to the once invisible sexuality of men), the result seems, when generalized, rather predictable: women become more real, more ordinary, more flawed, and threatening in new ways. But the whole point of the female poetic enterprise is to avoid generalizations about women, thereby unveiling the hidden complexities that the dominant stereotypes had, in the interests of national and personal pride, resolutely disguised.[11] As Eavan Boland argues, "There are certain areas that are degraded because they are silent. They need to be re-experienced and re-examined. Their darker energies need to be looked at" (*Sleeping with Monsters*, 82).

Boland voices the difficulty of being a woman poet "in a nation whose poetry on women consistently simplifies them . . . [through] powerful, simplifying fusions of the feminine and the national" (*Sleeping with Monsters*, 86–87). Her goal is to complicate that field of force. She explains:

> Irish poets of the 19th Century, and indeed their heirs in this century, coped with their sense of historical injury by writing of Ireland as an abandoned queen or an old mother. My objections to this are ethical. If you consistently simplify women by making them national icons in poetry or drama you silence a great deal of the actual women in that past, whose sufferings and complexities are part of that past, who intimately depend on us, as writers, not to simplify them in this present. (87)

Boland proclaims her position on women and nationalism most movingly in "Mise Eire" ("I Am Ireland," *Sleeping with Monsters*, 89–90):

I won't go back to it—

my nation displaced
into old dactyls,
oaths made
by the animal tallows
of the candle—

land of the Gulf Stream,
the small farm,
the scalded memory,
the songs
that bandage up the history,
the words
that make a rhythm of the crime
where time is time past.
A palsy of regrets.
No. I won't go back.
My roots are brutal:

∽

I am the woman
in the gansy-coat
on board the "Mary Belle,"
in the huddling cold,

holding her half-dead baby to her
as the wind shifts East
and North over the dirty
water of the wharf

mingling the immigrant
guttural with the vowels
of homesickness who neither
knows nor cares that

a new language
is a kind of scar
and heals after a while
into a passable imitation
of what went before.

What I'd like to do now is briefly show what has happened to the Rose, to female sexuality, to the muse, to religion and myth, and to Cathleen Ni Houlihan and the Shan van Vocht in these poets' "new language." The rose is still apparent as an image of female sexuality and poetic inspiration, but it is no longer a prescriptive image: the diversity of femaleness is represented by the many flowers that now figure female sexuality and its potential productivity. For McGuckian woman is a begonia (Medbh McGuckian, "Collusion"),[12] "a garden escape in her unconscious / Solidarity with darkness, clove-scented / As an orchid taking fifteen years to bloom" ("The Flitting," *Monsters*, 7), a fertile sunflower, filled with "decorous seeds" that lie "in wait" ("Death of a Ceiling").[13] Sara Berkeley, in "Seeding," describes woman as a splitting pea pod awaiting "the tiny explosion / Of ripe, tense seeds . . . The floating time seeds of the dandelion" (*Pillars of the House*, 168). In "Learning to Count" she describes the sound in a mother's throat as "the music of blossom" (*Bitter Harvest*, 201); she describes the female child, who "sleeps through the shrouded night," as blooming

> with such pretty grace, snapping in my hand
> Like the daffodil, dusting my fingers with the dry powder of her
>   lust
> Curving from earth as she will,
> Neither drooping nor withered.
>
> (*Bitter Harvest*, 202)

Deirdre Brennan presents herself as an aging flower in a pot, "Compressed in a web of roots / The seasons gone astray / In the damp press of peat." She asks:

> When will I break
> My binding pots? . . .
> I will suck the rain
> That will run dry in me
> Until great summer daisies sprout
> From the seedbed of my heart.
> I will toss out the petals of my hair
> In every wind that blows

> And in icy winter clay
> I will cover resurrection seeds.
>
> (*Wildish Things*, 81)

Mary E. O'Donnell describes the modern woman poet as a starving reader of fat, yellow, fertile sunflowers, a genderless reincarnation of Christ:

> She reads sunflowers daily,
> the spindles of her fingers reach out,
> stroke yellow ellipses
> as if each petal were a sign.
> What really holds her are the seeds,
> Tucked tight like critical reviews
> within a yellow convention.
> They swell and separate while autumn
> seems to idle . . .
>
> She is bent on hers,
> knows what she creates will have it all—
> the Word made genderless.
>
> (*Wildish Things*, 95)

It is McGuckian, though, who, in addition to diversifying female sexuality as a variety of flowers, constructing men as the root (*Sleeping with Monsters*, 3), takes on the image of the rose explicitly, appropriating it for private use, making it an image not of national but of highly personal poetic inspiration. She turns the Rose into Rosalind, the girl who can play the boy at will, in "The Unplayed Rosalind," proclaiming in a kind of dialogue with Yeats, "I have been the poet of women and consequently / Of the young." She explains:

> The room which I thought the most beautiful
> In the world, and never showed to anyone,
> Is a rose-red room, a roseate chamber.
> It lacks two windowpanes and has no waterjug.
> There is red ink in the inkwell.

Yet this poet in the roseate chamber has a double who accepts a lover; the double prefers to read

. . . the fire-red rip down heaven
As a saucer of iced water where she could
Dip her hands, as in the reciprocal blue
Ashes of his eyes.

By so doing, "She remove[s] the rose from" the speaker's mouth, be-traying the man in her with another.[14]

McGuckian's matter-of-fact assumption that the woman speaker also contains a man in her is replicated in the ways that the various female poets gender their muse. Yeats's muse was female, although at another level it was divided between male and female (if we see the Muse of "The Rose" as double, encompassing both the Rose and Christ/God, as in "To the Rose upon the Rood of Time"). Interestingly, both McGuckian and Ní Dhomhnaill also choose a double muse that is partly or sometimes *male*. McGuckian writes that she "wouldn't have been a poet . . . if she had lived anywhere [other than Belfast]," that the conflict in the North gave her "a sense of dislocation, a sense of being two people or a divided personality" (*Sleeping with Monsters*, 2). This divided personality is "as much male as female"—and she describes her poems as arguments between the male and female sides of experi-ence, and Irishness as "something [she doesn't] understand" (4). McGuckian again takes up the issue of the composition of the poetic self and the limitation of being "merely female," an "open rose," in "Open Rose" (*Marconi's Cottage*, 80). She depicts the gradual loss of the man in her as a diminishment, comparing her femaleness to a partly empty house or to the fetal confinement of an open rose, unborn within a womb of nurturing words, a rose that can only say so much:

His head is there when I work,
It signs my letters with a question-mark;
His hands reach for me like rationed air.
Day by day I let him go

Till I become a woman, or even less,
An incompletely furnished house
That came from a different century
Where I am a guest at my own childhood.

I have grown inside words
Into a state of unbornness,

An open rose on all sides
Has spoken as far as it can.

Ní Dhomhnaill, too, consciously alternates between several
muses—one male and black; another a destructive old woman whom
she calls the Tooth Mother; and, of course, Eire herself, the country, "the
whole sovereignty of Ireland" (*Sleeping with Monsters*, 153). She argues
that, although the male poets always said that the muse was female,
when they were really "talking about their inner woman and projecting
it onto us," "women have had a male muse" who is "ferociously
dangerous" because: (1) "being a man, he's inclined to all or nothing
action"; and (2) "he's allied with society against you, against your
deeper levels of femininity, because he's male" (150). She argues that
her female muse is, as a rule, much softer, having to do with the joy of
being (which is not goal directed), although she has also felt the
cailleach, the hag—the female and ugly spirit at the corner of every road.
She cherishes the energy of Negative Femininity, too, considering her-
self lucky to be writing in Irish, which, she argues, "wasn't indus-
trialized or patriarchalized. . . . Irish in the Irish context is the language
of the Mothers, because everything that has been done to women has
been done to Irish." Ní Dhomhnaill is most like Yeats in her sense that
the land is "the muse . . . and an echo of an inner landscape" (154), but
for her that inner landscape is not only mythical and linguistic; it is also
female and subconscious. She describes her goal as a poet as bringing
things up from the *lios,* or faery fort, of which there are sixteen hundred
in Ireland (149), and as an attempt to reclaim a lost continent, a new
psychic land. She writes:

> What women find when they go in there [to the deeper levels of
> consciousness] is very different from what men have written
> about. That's the really exciting thing. Lots of women's poetry has
> so much to reclaim: there's so much psychic land, a whole conti-
> nent, a whole Atlantis under the water to reclaim. It's like this
> island . . . in Irish folklore, which surfaces from under the water
> every seven years, and if somebody can go out to it and light a fire,
> or do something, it will stay up forever. (152)

Ní Dhomhnaill is impatient with old idealizations: compare her
version of the Shan van Vocht and Cathleen Ni Houlihan with Yeats's
Rose. She dismisses the Shan van Vocht as a cranky, cantankerous and

cancered woman, "locked into self-pity," and she would do "anything at all / To get this old bitch to shut the fuck up."[15] Cathleen Ni Houlihan is placed, cursing, in a "secret room at the top of the stairs" of the poet's household; she is ignored, the madwoman in the attic who once said her real name was Grace Poole ("Mo Theaghlach," trans. Eiléan Ní Chuilleánain as "Household," *Pharaoh's Daughter,* 153). The wind, unlike Yeats's Eire, is an indifferent, rapacious housewife as she-wolf who "hasn't the slightest interest / In you or your sore throat: / The solar system is all hers / To scrub like a floor if she pleases" ("An Casadh," trans. Medbh McGuckian as "Nine Little Goats," *Pharaoh's Daughter,* 111). What Ní Dhomhnaill evokes, instead, is a "dark mother, cave of wonders," to whom the race spins on its violent course, whose "kiss is sweeter than Spanish wine, Greek honey, or the golden mead of the Norse" ("An Ras," trans. Derek Mahon as "The Race," *Pharaoh's Daughter,* 97). The land is a terrifying giantess: "O, Mam, I'm scared stiff, / I thought I saw the mountains heaving / like a giantess, with her breasts swaying, / about to loom over, and gobble me up" ("Cailleach," trans. John Montague as "Hag," *Pharaoh's Daughter,* 137).

The Rose has moved inward, and what has replaced her is a mighty mother, a formidable hag, a personified fault, who, as Sara Berkeley writes, some day "will burst her corset of rock / And take the air" ("Valley Poem I," *Wildish Things,* 127). The earth is moving, transforming the old female and national icons into what Anne Hartigan calls "the new political force" (*Sleeping with Monsters,* 206). And this powerful, earthy mother who is not virgin has a new promise for the *daughter* that unto her "was given" ("Mac Airt," trans. Tom Mac Intyre, *Pharaoh's Daughter,* 79), because, as McGuckian writes, "Between every two moments stands a daughter" ("The Horse Fair," *Wildish Things,* 141). That promise is voiced in Ní Dhomhnaill's "Poem for Melissa":

> O white daughter here's your mother's word:
> I will put in your hand the sun and the moon
> I will stand my body between the millstones
> in God's mills so you are not totally ground.
>
> (*Bitter Harvest,* 169)

Not to be ground—not background nor dirt nor wheat totally ground into flour/flower—this is the determination with which contemporary Irish women poets would imbue their daughters, and this is their answer to the early Yeats. They have punningly revised the red rose into ground flour, and they have replaced the roseate chamber with a profusion of wilder blooms. Their response to the Eire of *The Wind among the Reeds* is to become Yeats's heirs, to reproduce the discourse of nationalism as an unstable and complex cacophony of desires and, instead of figuring the nation through the image of a beautiful woman, to tell the future of modernism with a woman's breaking voice.

NOTES

1. Eavan Boland, "A Kind of Scar: The Woman Poet in a National Tradition" (1989), *A Dozen Lips* (Dublin: Attic Press, 1994) 75.

2. See, for example, Yeats's account of Hanrahan's patriotic poems in the 1897 edition of *The Secret Rose:* "Others again [of Hanrahan's poems] were poems disguising a passionate patriotism under the form of a love-song addressed to the Little Black Rose or Kathleen the Daughter of Hoolihan or some other personification of Ireland." "Kathleen the Daughter of Hoolihan and Hanrahan the Red," *The Secret Rose* (New York: Dodd, Mead, 1897) 159.

For a dramatically different transfiguration of Cathleen Ni Houlihan as a post-1968 image of anorexia (realized by hunger strikers and by Irish women themselves), see Edna Longley, "From Cathleen to Anorexia: The Breakdown of Irelands" (1990), *A Dozen Lips,* 162–87. Longley locates the breakdown of nationalist ideology at the "juncture where the image women-Ireland-muse meets contemporary Irish women" (176).

3. David Cairns and Shawn Richards, *Writing Ireland: Colonialism, Nationalism, and Culture* (Manchester: Manchester UP, 1988) 46.

4. See Richard Kearney, "Myth and Motherland" (1983 and 1984), *Ireland's Field Day,* for a theory of when and why the "feminization" of Ireland began (Notre Dame: U of Notre Dame P, 1986) 61–82.

5. "Eavan Boland," in *Sleeping with Monsters: Conversations with Scottish and Irish Women Poets,* ed. Gillean Somerville-Arjat and Rebecca E. Wilson (Edinburgh: Polygon, 1990) 86.

6. It is important not to simplify Yeats's own changing attitudes in the process of making such a comparison. I agree with Boland when, in "A Kind of Scar," she remarks that the later Yeats is a "rare exception" to the tendency among male Irish poets to feminize the national and to nationalize the feminine (86).

7. What I am posing as a question is what Boland refers to as the "central premise" of her argument in "A Kind of Scar," that "over a relatively short time—certainly no more than a generation or so—women have moved from being the subjects and objects of Irish poems to being the authors of them." She continues:

It is a momentous transit. It is also a disruptive one. It raises questions of identity, issues of poetic motive and ethical direction which can seem almost impossibly complex. What is more, such a transit—like the slow course of a star of the shifts in a constellation—is almost invisible to the naked eye. Critics may well miss it or map it inaccurately. Yet such a transit inevitably changes our idea of measurement, of distance, of the past as well as the future. Most importantly, it changes our idea of the Irish poem; of its composition and authority, of its right to appropriate certain themes and make certain fiats. And, since poetry is never local for long, that in turn widens out into further implications. (75)

8. Compare Boland's critique of poems that blend the feminine and the national, in which the "real woman" behind the image is, like the narrator of Ralph Ellison's novel *Invisible Man*, "never even seen" ("A Kind of Scar," 88).

9. *Wildish Things: An Anthology of New Irish Women's Writing*, ed. Ailbhe Smyth (Dublin: Attic Press, 1989) 8.

10. *Pillars of the House: An Anthology of Verse by Irish Women from 1690 to the Present*, ed. A. A. Kelly (Dublin: Wolfhound Press, 1987) 134.

11. The strength of the imperative to maintain an idealized vision of Irish womanhood is apparent in the otherwise bizarre controversy over Yeats's play *The Countess Cathleen* and later in the riots that erupted over the use of the word *shifts* in Synge's drama *The Playboy of the Western World*.

12. *Bitter Harvest: An Anthology of Contemporary Irish Verse*, sel. John Montague (New York: Charles Scribner's Sons, 1989) 145.

13. Medbh McGuckian, *On Ballycastle Beach* (Winston-Salem, NC: Wake Forest UP, 1988) 26.

14. Medbh McGuckian, *Marconi's Cottage* (Winston-Salem, NC: Wake Forest UP, 1991) 59–61.

15. In the translation, "The Shan Van Vocht" by Ciaran Carson. Nuala Ní Dhomhnaill, *Pharaoh's Daughter*, rev. ed. (Winston-Salem, NC: Wake Forest UP, 1993) 131.

"Caresses—Withheld": William Carlos Williams's Dialogue with the Future

Christopher MacGowan

Ezra Pound, defining "Dr. Williams' Position" as he saw it in a 1928 essay in the *Dial*, argued that this position was one of an outside observer of America and its culture. A major strength of Williams as a writer, for Pound, was his lack of that "porous" quality characteristic of so many American writers, a quality that brought them to absorb every current faddish idea and fashion. "He starts where an European would start," Pound argues, "if an European were about to write of America." He attributes Williams's ability "to observe national phenomena" from without to Williams's multicultural "ancestral endocrines." Williams observes America from a "secure ingle" as "something interesting *but exterior.*" Such for Pound is Williams's version of modernist exile.[1]

Pound's major interest in his essay is Williams's prose (he finds Williams's attempts to enter the minds of his characters in *A Voyage to Pagany* [1928] not Williams at his best). But his perception that Williams views his world from within the space of a "secure ingle" sums up a central feature of the poetry, particularly when the poetry deals with the local community or a contemporary public event. While this characteristic is lessened in the post-1950s work, which often explores memory or emphasizes the poet's distance from the object world by foregrounding his physical handicaps, in the earlier poetry this "ingle"— sometimes spatial, sometimes temporal—can be carved out in the midst of a poem or sequence striving fully to engage the community and the pressure of a public moment. This split becomes itself a central theme in *Paterson*, and is one of the recurring meanings of the "divorce" motif that runs through the poem.

From the perspective of his temporal or spatial distance Williams assesses the unrealized significance of a public event within a context larger than its immediate moment or examines the community itself along with an implicit or explicit presentation of its unrealized potential. From the straightforward exhortations to "my townspeople" in *Al Que Quiere!* (1917) to the more complex strategies of later poems, Williams articulates a series of gestures toward the community from the distance of this demarcated space. In poems, many of which emphasize beginnings or locate an alternative space in the imagination expressed through art, Williams's distanced perspective finally looks to a space in the future to redeem the unfulfilled space of the present.

In *Paterson* (Book V of which was once to be titled "The River of Heaven") this future is as much his own as the future of the time and landscape the poem explores, although here and throughout his work the reach is also to a future for the poem itself as unfulfilled space. The strategy amounts to calling for a dialogue with the future from within the pressure of the moment, a call answered by a number of poets in the 1950s and later. The call in *Paterson* is explicitly answered by Allen Ginsberg and built into the narrative of the poem, but two other important later poets, Denise Levertov and Thom Gunn, have also acknowledged looking to Williams's work for strategies to articulate their own guarded responses to their particular communities.

Williams's divided response to Rutherford as a community, and as a representative community, emerges in his 1954 autobiographical essay "Seventy Years Deep," in which he asks, "What does my being a poet mean to the people of Rutherford?" The answer is guarded. "At first it was amusing to them; some were critical, others were unconcerned, and a very few were understanding." Then later in the essay he acknowledges that his "intimate contacts" with the individuals of the town have been the source of much of his writing.[2] In a late interview with Edith Heal, Mrs. Williams was more forthright about this division between intimacy and understanding: "There were no literary connections in Rutherford. I asked him not to read his poetry in Rutherford where he was misunderstood and parodied. I told him to cut it out. . . . 'They don't know what it's about . . . it's insulting to you and me.'"[3]

This division also characterizes the response of the community itself, including the city of Paterson, to Williams and his work, one well illustrated by the material collected over the past forty years by the

Rutherford Free Public Library.[4] While the library's collection of over
two thousand items (newspapers, magazines, books, photographs, au-
diovisual material, and general artifacts, largely donated by local
townspeople) is a remarkable tribute to the community's response to
the poet, the discussion of Williams in the local newspapers preserved
in the collection often reveals a somewhat bemused and often patroniz-
ing attitude. With what might be an accidental oversight, an early clip-
ping preserved from an unidentified local publication records that the
poet has just won the 1926 *Dial* award but identifies the recipient as
"William Corlas Williams." The *Bergen Evening Record* of 2 March 1932
records: "Williams, All But Unknown Here, Seeks to Restore Thought,
Life, with Word," while thirty-three years later, now titled the *Record*,
the paper headlines a nonevent on the second anniversary of Williams's
death with: "Paterson doesn't recall William Carlos Williams." Among
the obituaries published two years earlier, one notice in another un-
identified local publication records that the head of the Passaic County
Historical Society (located in the Lambert Castle of *Paterson* Book III),
D. Stanton Hammond, "Disliked Poet's 'Paterson.'" The historian com-
ments: "We had him come speak to the Manuscript Club of Paterson
and I told him then I didn't think much of his poem. . . . And Williams
told me that was my privilege." The notice continues, reporting the
historian's comments: "he didn't bother much with Paterson. 'He
flowed more in the New York direction. . . . He got too big for Pater-
son.'" Another newspaper item describes how a letter sent to Williams
with the address "Paterson, New Jersey" was briskly returned "ad-
dressee unknown."

Ginsberg, Levertov, and Gunn responded in their own ways to
these tensions in Williams's poetry, as they evolved their own particular
degrees of engagement with communities warily embraced and po-
tentially hostile. Levertov and Gunn, both working within a non-
native culture from early in their careers, and thus particularly sen-
sitive to tensions between the self and surroundings, have, in a number
of essays, discussed ideas of community in Williams's work. For Lever-
tov "there is virtually nothing that he wrote that does not—espe-
cially within the context of his work as a whole—have social im-
plications";[5] while Gunn, in early and recent essays on Williams,
has examined the poems in terms of the relationship they evince be-
tween the poet and the external world. This ranges from the "remark-
able . . . detachment" of "The Term" to the "new ease in his relationship

with the external world," suggested by the *Pictures from Brueghel* volume, "poems which twenty years before would merely have implied Williams as onlooker."[6] Ginsberg consistently sees Williams as both "the poet / of the streets" and a visionary. Ginsberg's "Death News," the poem on Williams's death in which the lines just cited appear, has an opening epigraph in which Williams contrasts two separate communities, the group within and the threatening community outside:

> *Visit to W. C. W. circa 1957, poets Kerouac Corso Orlovsky on sofa in living room inquired wise words, stricken Williams pointed thru window curtained on Main Street: "There's a lot of bastards out there!"*[7]

Poem III of *Spring and All* (later titled "The Farmer") is a central poem for both Levertov and Gunn to illustrate Williams's response to community. (The poem also begins Pound's selection of Williams's work in his 1933 *Active Anthology*.) For both Levertov and Gunn the key term in the poem is the artist/farmer's role as "composing / —antagonist." For Gunn the artist/farmer is "the antagonist to disorder," while Levertov develops the point further: "He is an *antagonist*—but to what? To the hostility of the environment, which, however, contains the elements that will nourish his crops." Both readings can be extended to emphasize that the artist/farmer, while actively "pacing," engaged in his immediate world of rain, fields, wind, water, weeds, and orchards, imagines (as do the opening pages of *Spring and All*) a possible "harvest" that could concretely embody what is now only his antagonistic "thought" and that would justify and qualify his current isolation. The space for thought is marked out within the physical world (with no compromise made in the engagement with that world's physicality): it "rolls coldly away / . . . leaving room for thought." The "room for thought" marked out in this poem by the farmer, and by the poet who invents and watches his activity, is the space Williams delineates for himself in poem after poem, the space from which to gain his distanced perspective upon community.[8]

Williams also marks out a potentially communal physical space at the center of the 1930s ten-poem group "Della Primavera Trasportata al Morale." Within the sequence's narrative of violence, rootedness, personal despair, and artistic triumph, the sixth poem, "The House," voices an unanswered invitation:

the whole house
is waiting—for you
to walk in it at your pleasure—
It is yours.

                                                          (CP1 341)

This sequence (its status *as* a sequence unclear in the 1951 *Collected Earlier Poems* from some confusion of titles in the headnote and intertitle pages) illustrates the way Williams can use the contextualizing potential of the sequence form to extend the themes of an individual poem. Surrounding "The House" and emphasizing, by contrast, the emptiness of its and the poet's space is "The Bird's Companion," while following "The House" is "The Sea Elephant," describing the physical dislocation of one important source of renewed language:

            —torn
from the sea.
(In

a practical voice) They
ought
to put it back where
it came from.

                                                          (CP1 342)

As the final poem of the sequence, "The Botticellian Trees," makes clear, the only space that can be filled imaginatively now is the space within Botticelli's frame and the poem that parallels it in the sequence, while the communal possibilities of the space in "The House" remain on the level of potential, the poet as displaced within his contemporary world as is the sea elephant; the poet, unlike the birds, is companionless (CP1 340–43).

A similar mapping out of unfulfilled space marking the distance from which the poet observes his community informs "The Attic Which Is Desire:" also of 1930. Looking out from

the unused tent
of

bare beams
beyond which

directly wait
the night

and day—

the poet watches, and incorporates visually into his poem, a space that
is filled with language—contrasting with the "unused" communal po-
tential of the attic itself:

```
*  *  *
*  S  *
*  O  *
*  D  *
*  A  *
*  *  *
```

(*CP*1 325)

In each of these three examples isolation is tempered by the prom-
ise that the space from which the poet watches the community might
become the space upon which that community could be met. This po-
tential is expressed in terms of imagination ("deep thought"), invita-
tion, and desire—terms also never far from the parallel sexual strat-
egies in Williams's engagement with his world. This marked-out space
within a hostile world (the "blank fields," the house, the attic) is con-
trasted in each case with an imaginative space (the harvest, "The Bot-
ticellian Trees," the soda sign) that is filled by the exercise of the imag-
ination as articulated through the poem. But the status of this imagined
space remains potential and serves to emphasize through its reach back
to the poet's own space the distance and isolation from which he en-
gages his community. The third book of *Paterson*, "The Library," func-
tions in much the same way. Here the poet / Dr. Paterson has retreated
to the wrong space from which to try to gauge communal potential and
recognizes this error through recalling his discovery—in another space,
"the basement"—of a physical embodiment of the "beautiful thing"
that throughout Book III is struggling to escape from the library.[9]
Some recent comments by Walter Benn Michaels on identity and
representation in Williams's work help further define this multiple
function of space in the poetry. Arguing that "the privileging of identity
and its transformation into a project" are defining characteristics of
American modernism, Michaels notes that in Williams's version "this

effort of identity takes the form of a critique of representation where representation seems essential (i.e., in language)",[10] for Williams a poem and a word must first and foremost represent itself, and this imperative is linked to a nativist poetics that must not "copy," that is, engage in representation that is merely copying "reality" (45, 39). Thus, the landscape in the first poem of *Spring and All* is primarily a place of language, with the repetitions of *spring* and *all* in its lines being its foremost "reality" (39). But Michaels points out that for Williams "the effort of imitation [through writing] is redeemed when it's mobilized on behalf of identity" (53). Thus, Poe is most "American" when he isolates himself from his community and clears the ground, "in order [Michaels quotes from Williams's *In the American Grain*] to let the real business of composition *show*" (45).

In Michaels's terms the full potential of the communal ground upon which poet and community could meet, and in turn realize their mutually reinforcing identities, can be illustrated through a "representation," by a "composing/antagonist," of the current fracturing of that potential, without giving up the claim that the poem is rooted in a space prior to meaning. The meaning that finally concerns Williams is one yet to be realized communally and that can only be represented by a space marked out by the imagination, in art, and/or in the future. Williams insists that this representation of what *could be* more clearly serves the community and delineates the artist of integrity's relationship to it than a representation of the local, which he would term merely "realistic."

The perspective upon the city of Paterson that this strategy produces in *Paterson*, as noted earlier, is one of the poem's central themes— the poet's "divorce" from his own culture and the people within it, an indictment charged in the poem's prose, for example, by "E.D." (68) and by "Cress" throughout Book II, and also illustrated in its central narrative. The poem records Dr. Paterson's confused and sometimes desperate search for ways to avoid a full confrontation with community, the prose in particular recording many deaths and various kinds of evasions. Book IV of *Paterson* ends with a somersault, another version of the multiple presence of potential action in space, and Book V with a dance—yet another. In what is apparently the latest manuscript we have of the barely started Book VI, beginning "Lucy had a womb," the fertility of space is illustrated through Lucy's thirteen children, the womb space always central to Williams both as doctor and as poet (240). The poem itself, despite the motions toward a form of closure at the end of Book IV, is one Williams could never finish, for, as previously noted, part of the space he looks to for an alternative includes his own future—for as long as he could imagine one.

This distanced perspective that Williams makes a central theme in *Paterson* has caused the poem to be criticized as not sufficiently engaged with the city that is its ostensible subject—and not only by the head of the Passaic County Historical Society. Charles Olson saw Williams's focus upon the "substance historical of one city" as making the poem time-bound and his treatment as essentially nostalgic, a "blueberry America," for "Bill, with all respect, don't know fr nothing abt what a city *is*." And this—in Williams's terms, narrow—assumption that the city in this poem is only its immediate urban presence (what for Williams, as noted earlier, would be mere "realism") is also behind Michael Bernstein's complaint in *The Tale of the Tribe* that "the political, historical, and economic reality of Paterson, its existence *as a city*, . . . is curiously missing, a virtual blank at the poem's core." For Bernstein these details of Paterson's urban reality only enter the poem with the inclusion of Allen Ginsberg's two letters in Book IV: "at the last moment, Williams does manage to retrieve his missing context. Fascinatingly, all of the suppressed details do enter the poem once, and in a form that reveals with uncanny precision just what *Paterson* had hitherto failed to confront."[11] But, when the poem is seen in the context of Williams's consistent treatment of community, this inability to confront the city itself is particularly emphasized—rather than the details being "retrieve[d]"—by the inclusion of Ginsberg's prose. The first edition's identification of Ginsberg's letter as from "A.P." (for "a poet," Williams told Ginsberg [*Paterson* 289]) further marks the voice as one with which Dr. Paterson might be able to fuse if the space separating voices, generations, and here too the prose and the poetry could be conflated, as they are in the world of the poem's space.

Ginsberg himself, in "Death News," presents his response to hearing of Williams's death while in Benares, India, as a conflation of spaces upon which the two poets can meet:

> If I pray to his soul in Bardo Thodol
> he may hear the unexpected vibration of foreign mercy.
> Quietly unknown for three weeks; now I saw Passaic
> and Ganges one, consenting his devotion . . .
>   . . . Riding on the old

rusty Holland submarine on the ground floor
Paterson Museum instead of a celestial crocodile.

His 1984 poem "Written in My Dream by W. C. Williams," from *White Shroud,* articulates another meeting on the common ground of imagination.

In an essential way community is the raw material of Williams's poems, and the imagined possibilities of communal space that come out of his distanced and critical response to that raw material are his invitation to the community to examine itself and its possibilities. The strategy is parallel to what Williams praised in Juan Gris's painting *The Open Window* in 1923: "the attempt is being made to separate things of the imagination from life, and obviously, by using the forms common to experience so as not to frighten the onlooker away but to invite him." The objects of everyday experience in this painting "are seen to be in some peculiar way—detached" (*CP1* 194, 197).

Apparently, Williams found such detachment difficult to build into his poems that respond specifically to public events or public figures. He often hesitated about publishing these poems and was uncertain about their quality, as if by setting a poem too closely alongside a public event his own distance might be dissolved by an implied degree of participation. These poems often remained unpublished for some years, as one way to gain at least temporal distance, while a number of poems responding to very specific local events remained, as far as Williams's wishes were concerned, unpublished or uncollected—too much, perhaps, still the raw material. Sometimes these poems were literally handed to local citizens. The record of some of these local gestures is in the material now part of the Rutherford Library collection.

The public event of Ford Madox Ford's death spurred the 1939 commemorative poem "To Ford Madox Ford in Heaven." Williams's uncertainties regarding the poem, its location of Ford within a particular locale and future, tell something of Williams's relation to his own community and of his doubts about this kind of poem. He wrote to his publisher, James Laughlin: "I like [the poem] but it's really the sort of occasional verse which I somewhat mistrust. The subject makes such demands on a man that he is likely for the moment to forget the poem in the occasion—somewhat topical."[12] Williams wavered in particular on the first stanza. He resisted Louis Zukofsky's suggestion to omit the entire poem from his 1944 collection *The Wedge,* although he apparently accepted every other suggestion of the younger poet. But he did leave out most of the first stanza, an omission that was restored almost twenty years later in the revised edition of *Collected Later Poems* (1963).

The omitted lines answer the question posed by the only line of the first stanza retained in the early version: "Is it any better in Heaven, my friend Ford, / than you found it in Provence?" The first stanza's omitted lines make clear that, for Williams, Ford had seen Provence in terms of the qualities of that "greater world where you now reside" (*CP2* 95–96). The remainder of the poem suggests that Ford's visionary sense of Provence had made him "homeless" in a physical and geographical sense while still, at the same time, very much a grunting and sweating "gross" part of the actual Provence he moved within and recorded in his writing. Ford is described here in terms resembling Williams's sense of his own distanced participation in his community and of the price paid in isolation for a perception of that community's larger potential.

Yet Williams's concern with the pressure of "the occasion," Ford's death, apparently led him to doubt the efficacy of describing the doubleness of Ford's communal commitment so explicitly in terms of "heaven"—despite the sanction, as David Frail has pointed out, offered by Ford's 1914 poem "On Heaven."[13] Although Williams retained the title, the omission of the lines in the first stanza blurred somewhat the double perspective. But, while the pressures of the occasion gave Williams pause, his strong wish to bring attention to Ford as a writer led him to try (unsuccessfully) to publish the poem where it would receive a wide circulation, in the *New Yorker* (*CP2* 466).

Of other poems concerning public events, "An Early Martyr," on the treatment of social activist John Coffey, waited ten years for revision and publication, and "Impromptu: The Suckers," on Sacco and Vanzetti, waited fourteen years. Both "An Elegy for D. H. Lawrence" and "The Death of See" (on Harry Crosby) first appeared five years after the deaths of the writers they commemorate and "To the Ghost of Marjorie Kinnan Rawlings" after seven years. Williams's tribute to Sibelius, written, like the Ford poem, in the year of the subject's death (1957), became—again as with the earlier work—a poem he continued to hesitate about; in this latter case he still apparently revised the poem after the publication of two previous versions (*CP2* 515–16).

A major exception, however, to this discomfort with poems on public figures and occasions is Williams's elegy to his friend Charles Demuth. Here Williams does not distance himself so much from the event and figure through time as from the event and figure as subject. Demuth is mentioned in the dedication but nowhere else in the poem, which subsumes the remembered painter within an organic presentation of one of his favorite subjects, flowers. Thom Gunn has perceptively articulated the doubleness at work in the poem, the physical and allegorical space of the language: "touch by touch, through qualifications and extensions of the literal, and through a constant attention to the double possibilities in words, an apt description of the physical becomes an apt rendering of the allegorical, and vice versa."[14]

The Rutherford Public Library collection has preserved a number of little-known Williams poems that directly address local events or persons. But Williams himself submitted only two of these poems for publication—"Peter Kipp to the High School" from 1921 and "Early Days of the Construction of Our Library";[15] he republished neither poem in any of his collections (and neither poem is recorded in Emily Wallace's *Bibliography*). Another poem, "The Post Office Clerk and His Daily Duty," was written for and given to local resident John Kirk in the late 1930s, according to the *Bergen Evening Record* of 5 December 1953 (the occasion of the 1953 article was Mr. Kirk turning up at a local library reception for the poet and telling the story). The poem, published in David Frail's book *The Early Politics and Poetics of William Carlos Williams* (but without the background story reported by the *Record*), concludes by ascribing to the postal clerk behind his counter the same dual role as community servant and community critic that Williams himself played:

By practice
grown familiar
I size you up
for what you are
But ask no questions
standing there
What I think
is my own affair.[16]

Of course, Williams's gesture of writing and donating the poem (after waiting in a line at the post office window, "Dr. Williams left and returned later with a poem," John Kirk reported) is a gesture of sharing "my own affair," but the poem remains an example of what I termed earlier the raw material of community, not a poem that points to future space but, rather, a gesture of the moment. "Plaint," however, another poem in the collection, unpublished to my knowledge, was written for—according to a note added by Professor John Dollar—and presented to two Rutherford parents "on the occasion of their naming their baby daughter Meredith." Often in Williams's work, a new baby represents the physical present and a future promise—and, if a patient of Doctor Williams's, his own delivery of that hope into its double presence.

Two further poems concerned with local matters preserved in the Rutherford Library archives appeared in local newspapers (the source of the clippings unrecorded in both cases). They have never been reprinted and, again, are not recorded in the *Bibliography*. Apparently, Williams was behind the publication of neither poem, each coming into the hands of a local newspaper columnist. Each poem, while clearly not fully developed, ends with its own version of a distinct backing away, a recognition of distance.

"The Old Steps of the Passaic General Hospital," apparently from the 1940s, equates the "bowed head" of the poet, as it runs into a new barrier where he expected to find entrance, with the figures—"heads often enough / bowed"—of another now "vanished" time, the experience a physical and temporal displacement:

"The Old Steps of the Passaic General Hospital"

With bowed head, walking toward the old steps
I ran into a wall. The old steps were gone.
The new start from another quarter more
convenient, safer, more protected from
the north wind and Summer sun, and the old
that led broadly to the carriage way from
the open porch above them are no more. There
chestnut branches leaned at one time and in
Autumn brown nuts would fall. Vanished now
with the men who mounted, heads often enough
bowed, to be led without twist, turn to
obstruction, discretely, straightaway upward

When the Rev. George Talbott published "The Old Steps of the Passaic General Hospital" in his local column, the context he placed the poem in was "the glorious tradition of William Wordsworth." While certainly one possible way of articulating Pound's view that Williams's perspective upon America is as an outsider, Rev. Talbott's gesture of association ("Wordsworth and Williams" is the title of his article) is one of inclusion, despite the poem's ambivalent attitude toward the change. Since Williams is, like Wordsworth, glorifying the "commonplace," Talbott's argument runs, he is a communal poet: "Dr. William Carlos Williams of Rutherford." But Williams is like Wordsworth in a more central way in this poem, setting the new "convenient" entrance against the old, in which heroic figures on missions of mercy battled against the nature whose beauty and force they would further battle inside.

The second poem, "My Nurses," is represented in the Rutherford collection by a clipping dated "August 1946." In May of that year Williams had an unsuccessful hernia operation at the Passaic General Hospital. "While there," the clipping records, "his nurses teased him into writing some verses commemorative of his immobilization in bed."

"My Nurses"

I can hear the rattle of their skirts
as I watch their minds
struggling to maintain the discipline
—of kindness—put to the test;
girls, that's all they are
softening their voices to
the adult necessity of their lives
tickling my toes but attentive
to the need but watching always—not
only the need but what I might be—
me, jagged stalagmite in this curious
cavern of a sick room for their wonder
Asking, asking and wanting to seem
not to ask; full of caresses—withheld

The double perspective of the last two lines, from the poet's and the nurses' view, encapsulates, as often in Williams's work, an unfulfilled sexual promise as part of its articulation of distance and potential.

This "commemorative" poem requested by the nurses found its way into print only through those it addressed. Meanwhile, Williams published "The Injury" (CP2 161–63) in the Nation, a poem that de-

scribes the same hospital stay but elaborates upon his feeling of isola-
tion entirely from his own point of view. Once again, though, he came to
be ambivalent about a poem centered upon a public event, albeit a
personal one. He decided that "The Injury" is a "weak" poem (*CP2* 476),
and he resisted, unsuccessfully, Randall Jarrell's inclusion of it in the
1949 *Selected Poems.*

Denise Levertov's interest in the "social implications" of Williams's
work comes from a poet who, like Ginsberg, is much more comfortable
in engaging with public events than is Williams. Levertov argues that
Williams's poem "In Chains" (1939) is "to me one of the most interest-
ing, and least known, of twentieth-century political poems," but her
analysis marks the crucial difference between the two poets' public
stances. Williams's poem lays out three ways of resisting "blackguards
and murderers" in positions of power ("to bend to their designs, / buck
them or be trampled"), all of which are finally rejected for a fourth
position: "to avoid / being as they are" and—with another image of
potential and of fertility—to

    learn . . .
           how love
  will rise out of its ashes if
  we water it, tie up the slender
  stem and keep the image of its
  lively flower chiseled upon our minds.

                           (*CP2* 65)

For Levertov, that Williams presents one of the three rejected options,
to "buck them," in negative terms is "a flaw of logic in the poem."
Williams's strategy of resistance, however, is one of patience and sym-
pathy ("love"), out of which could come growth, and not one of re-
sistance merely. Levertov's complaint that Williams fails to define the
nature of the resistance implied by "buck them" is answered by the
kind of resistance the poem finally posits. Something of the delicate
relationship Williams tries to articulate between the poet and "the
world" is further illustrated by his revisions to this poem. The poet's
degree of implication in a world that the "blackguards and murderers
. . . torture" shifts from 1944's distant "to torture it" to the final ver-
sion's "to torture us" with the revised *Collected Later Poems* of 1963,
while the early periodical publication's "we will water [love]" for the

final version's "we water" stresses more distinctly the status of the healing action as future potential.[17]

The essay of Levertov's from which these comments come was written in 1972, and it demands of Williams a political voice closer to the position of Levertov herself in the late 1960s and early 1970s than to the stance she had taken ten years earlier, when most influenced by Williams's work. A poem like Levertov's "A Map of the Western Part of the County of Essex in England" (from *The Jacob's Ladder* [1961]) is structured along the lines of Williams's position toward community and posits a duality of space in much the same way. The community here is the new world itself, the writer "less a / stranger here than anywhere else." The possibility of joining that community is explored through a memory of childhood places recorded within the space of a map and is seen as one of finding "ancient / rights of way" that could, through patience and imaginative expression, provide a guide to the problem of "picking up fragments of New World slowly, / not knowing how to put them together nor how to join / image with image." The degree of alienation from her adopted country and culture is heightened by the associations and names from a map representing the space of childhood, adolescence, and imaginative growth. But the map also shows the way, through an acknowledgment of the part of the self that remains tied to it, to connect to and articulate a response to the present: to discover, and write from, that "long stem of connection" Levertov sees as part of Williams's own poetics ("Williams: An Essay," from *Candles in Babylon* [1982]). By contrast, a Vietnam poem such as "Advent 1966" (*Relearning the Alphabet* [1970]), dating from the years of Levertov's comments on Williams's "In Chains," eschews any such alternative space from which to avoid fully engaging with the present culture and its actions. "Advent 1966" rejects any mediation that Southwell's poem on the burning Christ child might offer, or that the imagination might offer ("it is my own eyes do my seeing / . . . what I see is there), and—in an inversion of the strategy of "A Map of the Western Part of . . . Essex . . . ," and other early poems that are closer to Williams's poetics—to refuse to "look elsewhere" for any alternative to, or perspective upon, the present horror; "or if I look" to see only "whole flesh of the still unburned." Similarly, "Ways of Conquest" (from *The Freeing of the Dust* [1975]) is a poem that narrates the fusion of two spaces, rather than their, albeit connected, separation.[18]

With Thom Gunn, Pound's sense of Williams's "position" as that of a transatlantic observer comes full circle. In his comments upon Williams, Gunn has sought to bridge what he sees as a gulf between Williams's achievement and its appreciation in Britain. "He is somebody from whom it is time we started taking lessons" he told the readers of *Encounter* in 1965, and more recently Gunn has argued for the importance of Williams's *Collected Poems, Volume I.* As noted earlier, Gunn has commented upon the doubleness of space in Williams's poem "The Crimson Cyclamen," and in general his comments upon Williams's work might have pleased the Reverend Talbott as well as Pound. He sees Williams as occupying a place both of engagement with his American community and of reaching back for expression of that engagement to some central elements of the English tradition, whether "the seventeenth century" or "the Elizabethan conceit at its best."[19]

But Gunn's most direct attempt to use Williams is in a series of poems reflecting an ambivalent response to a community—his 1966 volume *Positives.* Gunn has said of this book, "I was consciously borrowing what I could from William Carlos Williams, trying as it were to anglicize him." But these poems on an England he had left ten years earlier produced a book all but dismissed in Gunn's *Collected Poems* (1994). "When I returned to San Francisco [after the year that produced *Positives*]," Gunn recalls, "it was with half thoughts of ultimately moving back to London"—although he didn't. Whatever Gunn's intentions in *Positives*, Williams's voice is an appropriate vehicle for the uncertain degree of commitment to the community that lies behind the book: a voice that comes out of a recent past and a potential future in another space, across the Atlantic.[20]

The character of the space from which Williams engages his community and speaks to its future—as well as to the future of poetry—receives different responses from Ginsberg, Levertov, and Gunn. But, whether that space is shaped by the European perspective Gunn describes, the visionary dimension emphasized by Ginsberg, or the connection to origins that concerns Levertov, each poet responds to some degree to Williams's call for a dialogue as part of dealing with his or her own contemporary questions of communal commitment. Williams's call for such a dialogue, along with his reach beyond the pressure of the moment, is what finally lifts his work out of what could have been the limitations of that moment and of his own particular brand of modernism. All three poets recognize that this most sexual of poets, so concerned with touch and contact, was at the same time the poet of "caresses—withheld."

NOTES

1. Ezra Pound, "Dr. Williams' Position," *Literary Essays of Ezra Pound* (New York: New Directions, 1968) 391–93.

2. "Seventy Years Deep," *Holiday* 16 (November 1954): 55, 78.

3. "Flossie," *William Carlos Williams Newsletter* 2 (Fall 1976): 10.

4. For a description of this collection, see *William Carlos Williams Review* 20 (Fall 1994): 52–57.

5. Denise Levertov, *The Poet in the World* (New York: New Directions, 1973) 259.

6. Thom Gunn, "Inventing the Completely New Poem," *Times Literary Supplement*, 19–25 February 1988, 180; "A New World: The Poetry of William Carlos Williams," *The Occasions of Poetry* (San Francisco: North Point, 1985) 33.

7. *Collected Poems: 1947–1980* (New York: Harper, 1984) 297.

8. Gunn, *Occasions*, 24; Levertov, "The Ideas in the Things," *New and Selected Essays* (New York: New Directions, 1992) 47; Williams, *The Collected Poems of William Carlos Williams, Volume I: 1909–1939*, ed. A. Walton Litz and Christopher MacGowan (New York: New Directions, 1986) 186. Hereafter cited in the text as *CP1*.

9. *Paterson*, ed. Christopher MacGowan (New York: New Directions, 1992) 125, 101. Further page references will be included in the text.

10. Walter Benn Michaels, "American Modernism and the Poetics of Identity," *Modernism/Modernity* 1 (1994): 53, 49. Further page references will be included in the text.

11. Charles Olson, "Mayan Letters," *Selected Writings*, ed. Robert Creeley (New York: New Directions, 1967) 82–84; Michael Bernstein, *The Tale of the Tribe* (Princeton: Princeton UP, 1980) 209, 212. Williams does not incorporate any notice of his subsequent tours of the city with Ginsberg into the poem; see Michael Schumacher, *Dharma Lion: A Critical Biography of Allen Ginsberg* (New York: St. Martin's, 1992) 143.

12. *The Collected Poems of William Carlos Williams, Volume II: 1939–1962*, ed. Christopher MacGowan (New York: New Directions, 1988) 466. Hereafter cited in the text as *CP2*.

13. David Frail, *The Early Poetics and Politics of William Carlos Williams* (Ann Arbor: UMI, 1987) 85.

14. Gunn, "Inventing the Completely New Poem," 179.

15. For the first poem, see *William Carlos Williams Review* 15 (Spring 1989): 2–3; and *CP1*, 566–67, from the third paper printing (1995). For the second poem, see *William Carlos Williams Review* 18 (Spring 1992): 50–51.

16. Frail, *Early Poetics*, 24.

17. Levertov, *Poet in the World,* 259. Also see Linda A. Kinnahan, *Poetics of the Feminine* (New York: Cambridge UP, 1994), for an argument that Levertov reads Williams in terms of her own move away from an object-oriented poetry to one that emphasizes female and maternal space.

18. *Poems, 1960–1967* (New York: New Directions, 1983) 21–22; *Candles in Babylon* (New York: New Directions, 1982) 59–60; *Poems, 1968–1972* (New York: New Directions, 1987) 124; *The Freeing of the Dust* (New York: New Directions, 1975) 19.

19. *Occasions,* 32–33; "Inventing the Completely New Poem," 179.

20. Gunn, *Occasions,* 191.

Modern Poetry after Modernism: The Example of Richard Wilbur

James Longenbach

Poem after poem is gracefully and competently done, there is good taste and intelligence throughout, there is variety of theme and an interesting, largely mythological, field of allusion. . . . But on the whole the poet's many evident talents only add to one's sense of frustration at the tameness and not-quiteness of his poetry; if this be the new decorum, I suggest we scoot back to modernism.[1]

Back to modernism: in the aftermath of the turmoil Pound and Eliot injected into the American literary scene, Richard Wilbur's poetry has sometimes seemed a little too calm, and this statement is similar to many responses his poetry received throughout the 1940s and 1950s. Randall Jarrell was sympathetic but skeptical: "who'd have thought that the era of the poet in the Grey Flannel Suit was coming?"[2] But poets such as Robert Bly weren't sympathetic at all. Writing in *kayak*, Bly quoted Wilbur's poem "Mind" and said, "as a fist, *kayak* is raised against stuff like this, crystallized flower formations from the jolly intellectual dandies."[3]

The battle lines of American poetry after modernism seem clear enough here (the bardic Bly and the fastidious Wilbur) and other poets have been quick to jump to Wilbur's defense. Anthony Hecht once praised Wilbur for standing apart from "this poetic era of arrogant solipsism and limp narcissism—when great, shaggy herds of poets write only about themselves."[4] That's one way to respond to Bly's fist: with another fist. Wilbur's response, "A Postcard for Bob Bly," took a different form: "Granted that it's a figurative fist," Wilbur admitted,

"That critics punch as harmlessly as kittens"; nevertheless, "when you incite to riot / Against your friend, he is not pleasured by it."[5] Refusing to raise a fist, Wilbur reminds Bly, whom he has known for years, that he retains a stockpile of ammunition. Bly and Wilbur were both at Harvard in the late 1940s, and Wilbur surely remembered (even if Bly didn't) the shaggy bard's earlier incarnation as New Critical aesthete. As the editor of the *Harvard Advocate*, Bly gave this slap on the wrist to Kenneth Rexroth:

> Perhaps it is unfortunate that Rexroth should have been let loose on the Romantics; there is, I think, a difference between the desire to express personal emotion by increased direct reference to the world of nature, and the desire to overthrow all external discipline of morals of government.[6]

The symmetries are perfect here. The early Bly offers an opinion of which the later Hecht might have approved. Wilbur stands in the middle of the fray, seemingly aware that an unnuanced extreme can too easily fold into its opposite.

Which is not to say that Wilbur is a poet without opinions. The quotation with which I began is in fact not a criticism of Wilbur (though it sounds like one) but Wilbur's own criticism of John Heath-Stubbs, offered in 1950. Even at this early point in his career Wilbur had little patience for the values that are usually ascribed to him (mere grace, taste, craft, or elegance), and, though it's tempting to say that Wilbur is criticizing himself in the mirror of Heath-Stubbs, I think that it's safer to say that Wilbur is that rare thing: a seriously misunderstood poet. Because the style of his poetry is so distinctive, so easily opposed to that of the later Bly, readers assume that Wilbur is deeply invested in distinctions. The poetry itself shows otherwise. Wilbur has gleefully gone "back to modernism" to learn from Moore, Stevens, Eliot, Frost, and Williams; at the same time, he has moved past it precisely because of his openness to modernism's variety of poetic practices.

Wilbur's respect for Williams offers one potent example of this openness. In the same review in which he found Heath-Stubbs's poetry tepid, Wilbur called the form of Williams's poetry "perfect" (though he confessed that he couldn't say exactly why it was so). A few years earlier Wilbur wrote a response to talks given by Williams and Louise Bogan at the now legendary Bard College poetry conference, organized by Theodore Weiss. Wilbur disagreed with Williams, who argued for the historical necessity of free verse, and agreed with Bogan, who maintained—brilliantly—that the last hundred years had witnessed not a steady opening up of poetic form but, instead, an "alternate and gradual loosening and tightening of form."[7] But Wilbur was adamant that "in criticizing Dr. Williams' criticism" he was "not out to attack free verse." Especially not Williams's free verse. Wilbur's prime contention was that "poets can't afford to forget that there is a reality of things which survives all orders great and small," and his examples of this "heartfelt subservience to the external" included Williams's "ashcans, wastepaper and red wheelbarrows," along with Marianne Moore's poems, Cézanne's paintings, and James Agee's *Let Us Now Praise Famous Men.*[8] Wilbur's own work, culminating in the poems of *Things of This World,* published in 1956, also displays a radical loyalty to the physical world, even though it doesn't sound at all like Williams.

In an essay on Wilbur's poetry of "being" Nathan Scott rehearses the great divide between New Critical and Black Mountain poets, suggesting that, "in the case of Wilbur at least, we may notice in one important particular this divide being surmounted, in the degree to which he appears to be seeking a kind of metaphysical ground not unlike that at which, say, a poet like Robert Duncan aims."[9] But, even while the metaphysics are similar, the verse sounds different. Like Elizabeth Bishop, from whom he first learned "the joy of putting a poem together,"[10] Wilbur never felt the need to overthrow or break through traditional poetic forms in order to bring his poetry closer to the physical world. No matter how fully engaged with the realities, natural and political, of his time, consequently, Wilbur's style made him seem "irresponsible." That is Wilbur's own word, but one could add (given the ways in which formal extravagance has been associated arbitrarily with certain values) *elitist, insincere,* and *reactionary.*

Wilbur is none of these things. The external world that elicits his loyalty includes laundry dazzled by sunlight, but it also includes the Vietnam War. And, though the laundry may seem more prominent, the political upheavals of the last fifty years have been the ballast of Wilbur's poetry. Writing "Little Gidding," T. S. Eliot worried that the poem required "some acute personal reminiscence (never to be explicated, of course, but to give power from well below the surface)."[11] In Wilbur's poetry the material that lies below the surface of the poem, giving it power, tends to be public and historical, rather than private and personal. On the surface Wilbur may not often seem like a political poet, but his inspiration has come consistently from the public events of his time.

Unlike Elizabeth Bishop, about whom this could also be said, Wilbur has written more than a few explicitly political poems ("Mined Country," "Speech for the Repeal of the McCarran Act," "A Miltonic Sonnet for Mr. Johnson," and "A Fable," to name only a few). Wilbur tends to engage the mainstream of American liberal politics in a way that Bishop (whose poems follow an equally powerful path) does not. But, like Bishop, Wilbur is uncomfortable with what he has called the "speechifying" of much political poetry, preferring to recognize the ways in which "any full poetry is bound to have an implicit political dimension."[12] The reason this dimension interests me is that, given the ways in which Wilbur's formal qualities have been apprehended, his poems have been misread as mere confections, pretty but irresponsible. In fact, Wilbur's poems have taken their extravagant shapes precisely because of his respect for the magnitude of the world, both lovely and horrific, outside the poet's mind.

The McCarran Internal Security Act, enacted by Congress in 1950, required members of the Communist Party to register with the attorney general; other organizations had to supply lists of their members. Wilbur's "Speech for the Repeal of the McCarran Act" was published only a few months later, and it grew from a long-standing opposition to government censorship and coercion. In 1938 the House of Representatives formed its special committee to investigate un-American activities. Wilbur's comment on its chairman, Martin Dies, appeared in the *Amherst Touchstone* in December 1938.

> He'd banish all the aliens
> If you gave him half a chance.
> The ample seat of Mr. Dies'
> Extremely ample pants
> Is filled with all the bitingest
> Of patriotic ants.[13]

This is one of the first poems Wilbur published, and, though it is clever, it is not an undergraduate's trifle. When one of Wilbur's classmates wrote to the *Amherst Student,* objecting to Wilbur's views in patriotic terms,

Wilbur's response was abrupt: "the primary threat to our democracy, as has been said often but not often enough, is that Red-baiters, Jew-baiters and professional patriots will impair our civil liberties in their haste to suppress those whom they believe threaten those liberties."[14]

Wilbur became the editor of the *Student*, and again and again his editorials defend the preservation of civil liberties. Characteristically undogmatic, Wilbur once remarked that "the question is not one concerning the merits of Communism."[15] And his satire on Martin Dies was published beside another on "Labor's William Green." But Wilbur also published his own interview (signed "Lenin") with Earl Browder, secretary of the American Communist Party, and it was with Browder that Wilbur's sympathies lay. Many years later Wilbur would remember his own brush with intolerance after he was drafted in 1942.

> Reporting for duty at Fort Dix, I was assigned to cryptographic training, and thereafter sent on to a secret cryptanalytic camp in the woods of Virginia, where (as I later discovered) my progress into cryptanalysis was cut short by adverse security reports from the CIC [Central Intelligence Corps] and FBI. It was quite true that I held leftist views and had radical friends, and that I had been so stupid as to keep a volume of Marx in my footlocker; but then as now I had an uncomplicated love of my country, and I was naively amazed to learn that my service record was stamped "Suspected of Disloyalty."[16]

Perhaps it was this experience that made Wilbur hold onto his reverence for civil liberties in the 1950s, when many members of his generation succumbed to a more urgent postwar sense of national security.

Wilbur had opposed the war, often writing in the *Student* about the dangers of dogmatic, unspecific patriotism. His position wasn't popular. "You're all afraid for your skins," shouted one professor to a group of anti-interventionist students; another told Wilbur that, "if we refuse to fight, we refuse to do our duty; there is, after all, a Christian way of fighting, a way of fighting with as much decency and good sportsmanship as possible."[17] But Wilbur took far more heat when he suggested that it was wrong even to expect the certainty of conviction from people of his generation: "What is taken for idealism in Youth is inexperience and verbosity, and our enthusiasm is the product of good health and bad judgment."[18] When the editor of the *Williams Record* wrote to protest this editorial, Wilbur responded by holding up the value of hesitancy and doubt in a time of easily adopted convictions:

> An education ought to disillusion, then reconstruct. Its disease and
> its glory is indecision. A man who is barely beginning his education,
> should be thoroughly maladjusted in the world of ideas. If
> hesitation and suspense of judgment strike him as "cowardly," it is
> evident that he is more interested in conditioning than free education.[19]

There's a touch of grandstanding here (the young Wilbur is enjoying his notoriety), but the position was neither jejune nor unique; more experienced journalists (like Kenneth Burke) were paying for it as Wilbur wrote. While the older Wilbur has understandably downplayed the interest of these early writings, his early impatience with dogmatism became the seedbed for his later nonoppositional thinking—the kind of thinking that allows him to learn from Williams even as he disagrees with him. Objecting to Wilbur's response to Williams and Bogan, James Breslin says that "Wilbur is so sensible, so balanced, has such 'complexity of attitude' on the question of form that he is left with no ground to stand on."[20] But the early political writings, in which Wilbur learned how to maintain such an attitude, show that doubt and hesitation offered him a solid foundation.

"The poetic position is seldom on the fence," lamented Wilbur in one of his few college editorials about poetry rather than politics: "Any grail will do. . . . The war is a natural, and the most stimulating side of the fence is the crusader's, of course." Just as Wilbur wondered about the ability of youth to cope with complicated political questions, he worried about the capacity of poetry too: "what are the natural limitations of emotional poetry?"[21] But when the United States entered the war Wilbur recognized sensibly that, while his poems could continue to sit on the fence, his actions could not: "now that we are fighting, what is needed is unanimity and determined action."[22] Even this level of conviction was not firm enough for Wilbur's critics, however; he quoted these sentences from the Pearl Harbor editorial of the *Williams Record* in order to justify his own eschewal of passionate conviction:

> We fight Nazis and Nipponese together, to crush a revolutionary
> nihilism that has sought to corrupt the world. We fight them with

our steel and our blood and our lives, until we build the nation of free peoples everywhere that alone can guarantee the life we cherish.[23]

Without ever adopting this sort of rhetoric, Wilbur served with the Thirty-sixth Infantry Division in Italy, southern France, and along the Siegfried Line in Germany. (The army overlooked his disloyalty, installing Wilbur as the division's cryptographer, when his predecessor suffered a mental breakdown.) Wilbur had considered a career in journalism, but it was during the war that he wrote his first serious poems: "My first poems were written in answer to the inner and outer disorders of the Second World War and they helped me, as poems should, to take ahold of raw events and convert them, provisionally, into experience."[24] His first professionally published poem, "Italy: Maine" (signed by Pvt. Richard P. Wilbur), appeared in the *Saturday Evening Post* for 23 September 1944. "Italy: Maine" remains uncollected, but from today's perspective the poem seems closer to Wilbur's mature voice than several of the poems that made it into *The Beautiful Changes*, his first book.

> Whose song is for swarm and surfeit, let him win
> This passive land, moist-green and sun-stunned.
>   I'll go after
> Spike grass, crab apple, gargoyle tamarack
> And the last crazy jack pine climbing Cadillac's back.

These final lines of "Italy: Maine" sound a note that will be richly harmonized throughout Wilbur's later poems: a devotion to the unmasterable and apparently insignificant details of the natural world, lovingly catalogued. But the lines are especially useful because they help to show how this aspect of Wilbur's sensibility was formed. In one of his Amherst columns Wilbur offered a list of trivial events (a hen laying a triple-yolk egg; the Song Writers' Protective Association voting 372–24 to censure "She Had to Go and Lose It at the Astor"; a member of the House of Representatives objecting so loudly to the Wages and Hours bill that his opponent's hearing was restored) that transpired along with the first battles of the world war:

> A daily reading of these items in this war year should be a tonic to us all, a reassurance that everything is not dramatic, world-shaking

and momentous, for these little stories are about the people whose lives are the true history of this year 1940 and of all years.²⁵

Visible here, as in "Italy: Maine," is the Wilbur who would more than a decade later complain that "there is at present no want of apocalyptic emotionalism or of connoisseurial detachment among us, but the poem of modest and genuine feeling does not seem to come readily."²⁶ Wilbur was trying to write those poems himself, and he would eventually offer a kind of credo for them in "A Wood," published in *Walking to Sleep:* "Some would distinguish nothing here but oaks, / Proud heads conversant with the power and glory," the poem begins. But Wilbur wants to notice the dogwood—"overshadowed, small / But not inclined to droop" (134).²⁷ And, given that the sun is, practically speaking, equally distant from dogwood and oak, he concludes that "no one style, I think, is recommended." Wilbur has always understood that his own style may cause him to be underestimated, no matter how timely his utterance. As James Dickey put it early on, "Wilbur's is not essentially a tragic mind, and the lack of this one quality will probably keep him, in the estimates of literary historians and other fossils, from being called a 'major poet': one having made large Miltonic or Poundian flights."²⁸

Once again the wartime context reveals the real power of Wilbur's position. After "Italy: Maine" Wilbur's next publication was a group of poems that appeared in *Foreground,* along with a harrowing prose account of wartime deprivation and displacement. "The Day after the War" culminates in this passage:

> When you have lost all identity, all relation, all significance of speech, all notion of belonging anywhere in the world, when you have experienced *nothing* as a real entity, touching, filling, numbing and abolishing you
>
> Then the passing of a truck will fill your whole head with the clatter of bouncing planking, and the sight of leaves silvered on the undersides by road-dust will please you to smiling, and the sight of a child suckling will make you want to fall to your knees, and the explosion of a thrush will make you laugh in your throat, and the rain falling on you and coursing down your face and plastering your shirt to your skin, running down your stomach and your legs and filling your shoes will make you grin like a fool.²⁹

As a student, Wilbur understood the value of little things; as a new private, just shipped off to Italy, he yearned for the particularity of Maine's landscape. More powerfully, Wilbur's full experience as a soldier taught him that the details of the most insignificant thing may, in a particular place and time, hold more power than the grandest Miltonic or Poundian flight.

Most of the poems published with "The Day after the War" were war poems ("Place Pigalle," "Potato," "Mined Country"), and among them "Potato" values what is "too common to cherish or steal" (345). But it was in "Cigales," published a few months later, that the power of particular things is explored most deeply. This poem, eventually chosen as the opening poem in *The Beautiful Changes*, contains lines that the deep imagist Bly might have written ("Even the leaves / have thick tongues") but builds on Marianne Moore's probing of the animal world's moral value. Wilbur's focus is the cicada and the way it resists any human effort to locate significance in its song: "Such a plain thing / morals could not surround."

> This thin uncomprehended song it is
> springs healing questions into binding air.
> Fabre, by firing all the municipal cannon
> under a piping tree, found out
> cicadas cannot hear.
>
> (337)

Wilbur had wondered, given most poetry's inability to sit on the fence, if it were possible to write an isolationist poem. "Cigales" is such a poem, for, despite Wilbur's rejection of any human meaning for this insect, its song functions as an emblem for poetry—especially poetry written in a time of war. Wilbur suggests that the poet sings as the cicada sings, deaf to the cannon's roar. And yet, like the self-made song of Stevens's poem "The Idea of Order at Key West," the cicada's song nevertheless becomes involved with the world it cannot sense. "Cigales" rejects the terms of most war poetry (terms implying, as Wilbur would later put it, that a poem is "'serious' and 'significant' because it mentions the atomic bomb") and turns from the momentous to the commonplace and the particular.[30] Yet Wilbur's position in *The Beautiful Changes* is not consistent enough to be dogmatic: while other poems in the volume (notably "Objects" and "A Dutch Courtyard") extend his

praise for minutiae, the poems immediately following "Cigales" in-
clude much grander images of war ("On the Eyes of an SS Officer"),
suggesting that it is difficult—an achievement rather than a retreat—to
keep the poem focused on little things.

Given the importance of Moore's example for Wilbur, it is interest-
ing to note that his way of responding to World War II was far closer to
Moore's than Bishop's. When Moore read Bishop's poem "Roosters"
she was shocked by what seemed to her the violence of its rhymes and
the coarseness of its images, going so far as to rewrite Bishop's text.
Moore might have approved of "Cigales," however, for, like Wilbur's,
her preoccupation with the commonplace was a response to the pres-
sure of wartime vulgarity. Moore's poem "Reinforcements," first pub-
lished in 1918 and ultimately excluded from her *Complete Poems,* begins
with these stanzas:

> The vestibule to experience is not to
>   be exalted into epic grandeur. These men are going
> to their work with this idea, advancing like a school of fish
>   through
>
> still water—waiting to change the course or dismiss
>   the idea of movement, till forced to. The words of the
>   Greeks
> ring in our ears, but they are vain in comparison with a sight
>   like this.[31]

Moore wants her title to invoke the idea of military reinforcements, but
the poem also addresses the ways in which the language of poetry—the
usual terms of war poetry—might become a "reinforcement" of war.
Faced with the vastness of war, the words of the Greeks ring in her ears,
but she is unwilling to exalt the experience with epic grandeur.

Moore's later response to the war was to write self-consciously
"little" poems rather than ambitious (and, for Moore, masculine) poems
that answer an epic challenge. Analyzing Moore's response to Bishop's
"Roosters," Betsy Erkkila shows that Moore's "moral, decorous, and
ladylike aesthetic posture" was, at least in the early years of Moore's
career, a finely honed weapon.[32] But by the time Bishop wrote
"Roosters" she was not interested in appearing ladylike, no matter
what powers might be derived from the posture. By extending Moore's
aesthetic, in contrast, Wilbur became a poet who was (like Jarrell) some-

times perceived as "ladylike," especially in a poetic climate that valued the transgression of all decorums.

Wilbur was undaunted by this perception, for the poems of his second volume extend Moore's method even as they cease to respond to warfare. *Ceremony* is clearly a postwar book, and its poems engage a different world. In "Driftwood" (321–22) Wilbur meditates on the particular qualities of a length of wood, considering how it once knew a "rapt, gradual growing" before it was "milled into / Oar and plank" and then released into "the great generality of waters." Human significance begins to accumulate: the living tree knew its "own nature only," and, even after it was subjected to the generalizing ocean, it did not "dissolve" but, rather, became "involved" with "the gnarled swerve and tangle of tides." At the end of the poem Wilbur (mindful of the lesson of "Cigales") addresses his own effort to understand driftwood as an emblem of integrity.

> In a time of continual dry abdications
> And of damp complicities,
> They are fit to be taken for signs, these emblems.

Although Wilbur might seem to offer driftwood as a timeless sign, these lines (first published in 1948) insist that driftwood is fit to be taken for a sign in a particular time—"a time of continual dry abdications / And of damp complicities." Wilbur is describing the initial years of the Cold War, as his note on "Driftwood" makes even clearer: "the poem began when a friend tried to argue me into a revolutionary political party on the grounds that there are at present two choices only, Communism or Fascism." Like Wallace Stevens, Wilbur distrusted political affiliations that were so single-minded that they could be easily adopted and just as easily dropped. His early drafts for the poem show that he began by describing generally this time of damp complicities before he focused on the emblematic qualities of driftwood: "On a day of an age when allegiance is always too heavy or light / I singular walk to myself on the glass banks of the sea."[33] As Wilbur recognized, he was assigning meaning to this landscape (and thinking perhaps too consciously of Whitman and Stevens), rather than deducing meaning, and he turned his eye to the particular qualities of driftwood as a better way of earning his convictions.

Wilbur may have been worried that in the process the political content of "Driftwood" was obscured: he first published the completed poem beside "We," which clearly locates the time of dry affiliations in the postwar years. Having once been an ally, Russia quickly replaced Germany as the enemy against which a fragile sense of American identity could be shaped.

> How good to have the Russians to abhor:
> It lets us dance the nation on our knee
> Who haven't been quite certain since the war
> Precisely what we meant by saying *we*.[34]

Wilbur never collected this poem. While it has some of the attractive verve of the political verse he wrote in college, it doesn't stand up against a mature poem like "Driftwood." I think Wilbur came to see that his particular strength did not lie in this kind of political poem—or in the kind of political poem that "Driftwood" appeared to be in its initial drafts. Ultimately, the final version of "Driftwood" didn't need "We" to bolster its examination of damp complicities: the struggles of the Cold War lay behind its metaphors in the way that Eliot wanted personal experience to stand beneath "Little Gidding."

Published along with "Driftwood" and "We" in 1948 was "To an American Poet Just Dead," a more clearly political poem that did make it into *Ceremony*. "It is out in the comfy suburbs I read you are dead," says Wilbur to the American poet Phelps Putnam, who won't be mourned by sprinklers, deep-freeze units, or Studebakers: "The suburbs deepen in their sleep of death" (329). Characteristically, Wilbur won't ignore the contradictions of his position; he admits that he himself lives in the suburbs. But over and over again throughout his poems of the 1950s Wilbur chastises the complacency embodied here in the word *suburbs* or (more surreptitiously) in the word *peace*. In "From the Lookout Rock" he surveys a world without any kind of vital contention, concluding that "for this was not the peace we prayed" (328). In "Grasse: The Olive Trees" he surveys a landscape in which "luxury's the common lot," but this condition is not pleasing to Wilbur, and he's relieved to notice that "the olive contradicts." These anxious, famished branches seem like "clouds of doubt against the earth's array," and Wilbur concludes that they teach "the South it is not paradise" (304–5). Neither of these poems refers openly to political complacencies, but, as in "Driftwood," Wilbur's metaphors stand on his awareness of the history of his time.

This distrust of suburbs, luxury, and paradise is especially interesting to me because Wilbur is often thought of as a poet who values these things above anything else: "The Poetry of Suburbia" was the title of Horace Gregory's review of *Things of This World*. This is one of the ways in which, as I began by saying, Wilbur is deeply misunderstood: the plain content of his poems is often overlooked because of associations readers bring to his formal dexterity. And even more suspicious than the use of meter and rhyme is the fact that Wilbur's style hasn't changed much over the years. In "Poetry and Happiness" Wilbur applauded Robert Lowell's transformation in *Life Studies*, saying that these poems represented a "withering into the truth" (Yeats's phrase) that at some point occurs "in the life of every poet," though not necessarily so dramatically.[35] But in the world after *Life Studies* free verse seemed essential to such a withering, and Wilbur's formalism seemed like the sign of complacency, luxury, suburbia—everything Wilbur abhors.

Wilbur's style hasn't changed much because it hasn't needed to. Unlike Lowell (but again like Bishop), Wilbur began writing with a purity of syntax and diction that never resulted in gnarled, encumbered poems. (And, in this regard, one might say that Lowell's early problem was not meter or rhyme but muscle-bound syntax: he had to throw out the former in order to achieve the clarity he admired in Bishop from the start.) But I think there is another reason for the relative stability of Wilbur's style. In the essay responding to Williams and Bogan, Wilbur was adamant that a "heartfelt subservience to the external" could be sustained only through a recognition (Wilbur compares the poet's formal ingenuity with a rain dancer's) of "the difficulty—the impossibility—of achieving a direct expressive relationship with the rain, or with any other real thing."[36] Wilbur never needed to buck the traditions of poetic form because he was comfortable with the idea that any human utterance is by nature indirect: wanting to cleave as closely to the external world as possible, he resists any mystical sense of the poet's ability to transcend the boundaries of language or thought. In an uncollected essay on landscape Wilbur said he was "not out to deny the distance" between himself and the natural world: "fusing [the landscape] with my thoughts and feelings and interpreting it through my human senses, it does not trouble me that my words do not essentialize it."[37]

Far from troubling him, the artificiality of language seems to Wilbur an unavoidable aspect of experience: in "An Event," published in *Things of This World*, he described the way in which a flock of birds disperses, resisting his metaphor ("drunken fingerprint") for its undulation: "It is by words and the defeat of words," he concludes, that "one may see / By what cross-purposes the world is dreamt" (274). Like Marianne Moore or the Williams of *Spring and All* before him, Wilbur feels that only an extravagantly artificial art may, by respecting the alterity of the genuine, approach it. ("What is more precise than precision?" asks Moore in "Armor's Undermining Modesty": "Illusion.") This healthy skepticism, not the formal artifice of his poetry, is what ultimately separates Wilbur from poets such as Duncan, whose allegiance to the physical world he otherwise shares.

That allegiance, apparent in earlier poems such as "Cigales" and "Driftwood," became the keynote of Wilbur's third book, published in 1956. *Things of This World* received both the Pulitzer Prize and the National Book Award, and the volume still stands, along with *Walking to Sleep*, as one of Wilbur's finest achievements. "Love Calls Us to the Things of This World" or "A Baroque Wall-Fountain in the Villa Sciarra" are as full of the joy of language as they are of the joy of the physical world: especially in the latter, language becomes a physical presence, the syntax so intricate, yet so plainly apprehensible, that it begs to be turned over in the mouth. The quieter "Love Calls Us to the Things of This World" (233–34) is, famously, a poem of immanence: angels exist because, for a moment, the mind imagines them in laundry hanging on the line. But this argument against a world-denouncing spirituality is only half of the poem's purpose. A more violent, urgent world is registered in Wilbur's diction: words like *rape* and *hunks* slip into his elegant vocabulary, and their prominence has sometimes troubled the poem's admirers. But Wilbur's point is that a devotion to laundry alone—to the world's sensual pleasures, physical and linguistic—may be as world-denying as the most ascetic spirituality. While the soul cries, "let there be nothing on earth but laundry," the language of the poem has suggested that this desire is unrealistic even before the poem's final lines (spoken by the soul as it descends into the awakening body) make Wilbur's position clear.

> "Bring them down from their ruddy gallows;
> Let there be clean linen for the backs of thieves;
> Let lovers go fresh and sweet to be undone,

And the heaviest nuns walk in a pure floating
Of dark habits,
                    keeping their difficult balance."

The balance here is not only between the physical and spiritual worlds
but also between the state of mind that dallies with physical pleasures
and the necessary awakening to a sterner, even more challenging
ground.

I wouldn't argue that "Love Calls Us to the Things of This World"
has much of (in Wilbur's phrase) "an implicit political dimension." But I
do think that the poem became possible because of Wilbur's earlier
meditations on wartime loss and postwar deprivation. Similarly, the
final poem in *Things of This World*, "For the New Railway Station in
Rome," grew from Wilbur's sense of the unreality of a Cold War doom
and gloom—the intellectual climate that prompted Wilbur's quip about
the poetry of the atomic bomb and encouraged one reviewer of *Things of
This World* to ask, "how can he be so damnably good-natured in an
abominable world?"[38] Like Randall Jarrell, Wilbur sided with Robert
Frost, who responded to postwar apocalypticism by pointing out that
every generation stakes its own claim for historical ultimacy: "I say they
claimed the honor for their ages. They claimed it rather for themselves.
It is immodest of a man to think of himself as going down before the
worst forces ever mobilized by God."[39]

"For the New Railway Station" (277–78) begins with a litany of the
doomsayers' favorite images (Rome, hurt pillars, rubble, dust, the
forum) before it upends a cliché: "there's something new / To see in
Rome."

> See, from the travertine
> Face of the office block, the roof of the booking-hall
>   Sails out into the air beside the ruined
>   Servian Wall,
>
>   Echoing in its light
> And cantilevered swoop of reinforced concrete
>   The broken profile of these stones, defeating
>   That defeat.

At this point the shards begin to speak as eloquently as Keats's urn. But
Wilbur's well-wrought stanzas (as masterful as those of "A Baroque
Wall-Fountain in the Villa Sciarra") do not trace the contours of an

ancient urn or fountain. Appearing after Wilbur's paean to Roman antiquity in *Things of This World*, "For the New Railway Station" assures by its very form that Wilbur is no antiquarian; the swoop of canti-levered concrete does as well as a "ragged, loose / Collapse of water" (271).

If all that Wilbur offered in "For the New Railway Station in Rome" were something new to offset the decline of civilization, he would tac-itly concede the doomsayers' point. (And, as the reviewer suggested, Wilbur would merely be good-natured.) Instead, the poem interrogates the means by which hurt pillars are taken as signs of decline—or con-crete swoops are taken as signs of progress. Wilbur's doomsayers "would not take the sun standing at noon / For a good sign." This line cuts two ways, for it suggests both that the doomsayers are insensitive to the daily particularity of their world and that they are incapable of taking anything for a good sign. Neither the Roman forum nor the railway station stands for our future, just as the song of the cicada doesn't naturally stand for anything: the human imagination invests these objects with meaning, producing signs whose arbitrariness the doomsayers have forgotten. Here, as in so many of his poems, Wilbur champions a deductive looking at particular shapes of things rather than an inductive attribution of qualities. But—again typically—he doesn't believe that things can speak to us outside the parameters of human thought or formal ingenuity. The speaking shards at the end of the poem are the product of a self-consciously flagrant act of human imagination, and their final words ("What does it say over the door of Heaven / But *homo fecit?*") could stand over all of Wilbur's paeans to particular things, beginning with "Italy: Maine."

"It is easy to prophesy against us," said Wilbur in "Poetry and Happiness,"[40] and the title poem of *Advice to the Prophet* builds on "For the New Railway Station," suggesting that prophecy will be believable only if it catalogues the simple, apparently insignificant things we could lose: "The dolphin's arc, the dove's return, / These things in which we have seen ourselves and spoken" (182–83). But *Advice to the Prophet* at large seems a little disappointing after *Things of This World*, in which one glorious poem seems to topple over the next. The disappointment is perhaps inevitable, given the midcareer achievement of *Things of This World*, but Wilbur himself has said that there are poems in *Advice to the Prophet* that he wishes he had never published. Any great writer's career has its lulls, but I think this moment in Wilbur's career is especially revealing of his strengths. A comment Wilbur once made about Day Lewis's later work may also describe the predicament of his own career: "He is left with his earnestness, his good-will, a poem manner appropriate to a matter [the political turmoil of the 1930s] which has deserted him."[41] The poems of *The Beautiful Changes* and *Ceremony* grew quite directly from Wilbur's engagement with wartime struggles, physical and ideological. In the poems of *Things of This World* those struggles are more distant, but they lurk beneath the surfaces of the poems (to continue with Eliot's metaphor) in identifiable ways. But by the time Wilbur wrote *Advice to the Prophet* that historical ballast was lost: a few poems retain a sense of urgency, but too many others finally seem like the extenuation of a *manner* after the *matter* that provoked it has dropped away.

Together with *Walking to Sleep*, published in 1969, *Advice to the Prophet* confirms my sense that Wilbur's best writing comes in connection with the events of his time: while the connection is too often missing in *Advice to the Prophet*, it is prominent throughout the poems of *Walking to Sleep*. Wilbur seems to have been reinvigorated by the historical challenge of the Vietnam War in particular and the 1960s in general. His manner faced a newly urgent matter, and the result was, with "In the Field" (the first section of *Walking to Sleep*), the finest group of poems that Wilbur has written.

Several pages away from this group stands "A Miltonic Sonnet for Mr. Johnson on His Refusal of Peter Hurd's Official Portrait." The octave's long subordinate clause compares Johnson's escalation of the Vietnam War with Jefferson's legacy of Enlightenment ideals; the sestet addresses Johnson directly:

> Rightly you say the picture is too large
> Which Peter Hurd by your appointment drew,
> And justly call that Capitol too bright
> Which signifies our people in your charge.

> > (144)

These lines are Miltonic in several ways, not least in the stern intrusion of the trochee (*Rightly*) at the sonnet's volta. But they are Wilburian too. After turning Johnson's criticism of the official portrait against him, Wilbur doesn't leave himself, one of the people, untainted by criticism. This turn was important to Wilbur for reasons he explained in an interview conducted a few months after the sonnet was written: "I recall that Allen Ginsberg recently asked an audience whether they would consent to the proposition that the United States government, in its foreign policy, is psychotic. Something like a third of the audience voted for that idea. They and Mr. Ginsberg are setting themselves up as supersane. . . . Though I can share all their objections to our Viet Nam policy, I'm all for institutions."[42] That last comment—as Wilbur well knew— could make him no friends in 1968. (And there might be a touch of grandstanding here too: in middle age, as in his youth, Wilbur sometimes enjoys the notoriety of standing apart.) But Wilbur's sonnet embodies the sentiment with greater power—both thematically, in its meditation on the office of the president, and formally, in its rejuvenation of Milton's trumpet for political poetry.

"A Miltonic Sonnet" is the only conventionally political poem in the volume, but, even if Wilbur had not included it, *Walking to Sleep* would still seem like a book provoked by wartime visions of carnage and wartime lapses of conscience. The book (and the group of poems called "In the Field") opens with "The Lilacs," which offers a simple story of the lilac's growth, cast in the Anglo-Saxon alliterative line. Recalling "When Lilacs Last in the Dooryard Bloom'd," Wilbur's metaphors tell a somewhat more complicated story: the stalks begin "Like walking wounded from the dead of winter"; their "bullet-shaped buds" grow out of "present pain and from past terror"; the blooms are "Healed in that hush, that hospital quiet." But the lilacs ultimately reveal nothing of "their mortal message"—unless we can measure the depth of hell by "the pure power of this perfume" (118–19). This concluding line of the parable offers Wilbur's characteristic moral about the hidden potency of earthly things. But the poem following "The Lilacs" gives historical weight to the parable's metaphors, forcing us to return to these lines with a more vivid sense of what the "present pain" may be: "some dirty war" (122) preoccupies Wilbur in "On the Marginal Way," transforming even casual fancies into images of violence.

Several of the poems of "In the Field" are themselves about this dialectic between metaphor and historical reality (or what Wilbur several times calls "fact"). But throughout "In a Churchyard" and "In the Field" itself (the poem that gives this section of *Walking to Sleep* its title) even the slightest reference to the "dirty war" drops away, leaving only the struggle of the dialectic itself. These poems seem to me even stronger than "A Miltonic Sonnet" or "On the Marginal Way": Wilbur works best when he feels the challenge of history but records the more surreptitious ways in which the challenge enters our lives and poems.

"In the Field" (131–33) begins with a recollection of a nighttime walk. Wilbur and his wife gaze at a sky that seems almost domestic in its familiarity: the field grass through which they wade is like "the cloudy dregs" of a teacup, and Andromeda, transformed into a constellation, is self-sufficient, requiring neither Perseus to protect her nor Euripedes to tell her tale. "But none of that was true": Wilbur is caught short, reminded that he's speaking of metaphors, of stories spun on filaments of light, and the sky suddenly seems emptied of human relevance. Initially, he doesn't let this emptiness include him:

> The heavens jumped away,
> Bursting the cincture of the zodiac,
>   Shot flares with nothing left to say
>   To us, not coming back
>
> Unless they should at last
> Like hard-flung dice that ramble out the throw,
>   Be gathered for another cast.
>   Whether that might be so
>
> We could not say, but trued
> Our talk awhile to words of the real sky,
>   Chatting of class or magnitude,
>   Star-clusters, nebulae.

Wilbur is an experienced fiction maker, knowing that to have abandoned one metaphor is only to have tried on another; dice replace the shapes that Greece or Babylon discerned. But he slips—perhaps knowingly, at first—when he imagines that he "trues" his thought with words of the real sky. This is the movement toward fact that "In the Field" shares with "On the Marginal Way" and "In a Churchyard," and throughout these poems the facts are anything but stable. In "On the Marginal Way" Wilbur fights off a vision of the Holocaust with geological facts, but the violence of volcanic eruption and glacial movement is no haven from imaginative vision. It is not simply the imagination's waywardness that leads him to find new horror in the facts; it is "the time's fright," his knowledge of "some dirty war" (121, 122). Wilbur is less specific about the "nip of fear" that approaches him in "In the

Field," but its effect is the same: metaphor takes the upper hand, and Wilbur is left with nothing—"All worlds dashed out without a trace, / The very light unmade."

This dialectic between imagination and fact is a messy one, for fact is conceived unusually as something comforting rather than something to escape; later, as imagination works on fact, the distinction between the two collapses, and there is nowhere to seek refuge but in the dialectic itself—the process of time and the mind's ability to conceive of it. Similarly, when fact interrupts the reverie of "In a Churchyard" (a pendant to Gray's "Elegy") in the form of a ringing bell, the real sound is "far more strange" than the imagined, "things that are" more mysterious than any vision. This is because the world of "things that are" includes mortality—"the darker dead"—the undeniable fact as well as the ultimate mystery (128).

The project of "In the Field" is to remain aware of this final reality but not be overwhelmed by it. In the second half of the poem Wilbur returns to the field during the day, his metaphor-making skills rejuvenated. Stars, invisible in daylight, are now "holes in heaven [that] have been sealed / Like rain-drills in a pond." The only starry sky now visible is on earth: "galaxies / Of flowers, dense and manifold." At night Wilbur only felt these flowers (he had mistaken them for field grass the night before) brushing against his legs. As in so many poems, he is saved by a close look at the particular character of the physical world: daisies, heal-all, and hawkweed, all of them committing "to air / The seeds of their return."

Behind that heal-all lurks the flower of Robert Frost's "Design," and Wilbur follows Frost in suggesting that no "design of darkness," independent of the mind's ability to imagine it, may "govern in a thing so small."

> We could no doubt mistake
> These flowers for some answer to that fright
>   We felt for all creation's sake
>   In our dark talk last night.

Just as Frost knows that birches aren't broken by boys, Wilbur knows that the field, imagined as an earthly heaven, is not really an answer to his fright. But, just as Frost knows that a spider is not brought to a heal-all by some force of evil, Wilbur now knows better that no design of darkness determines his place—or some dirty war's place—in the universe. Wilbur achieves no higher eloquence than the final lines of "In the Field": the poem is worthy to stand with "Directive," "The Idea of Order at Key West," or "At the Fishhouses."

This is company Wilbur wanted to keep from the beginning of his career. Discussing his first book, I concentrated on Moore's presence in the poems, but traces of Frost, Stevens, Eliot, and Williams are also apparent, sometimes overwhelmingly so. And, while it is a commonplace to notice Wilbur's early ventriloquism (he was sometimes chastised for it), I mention it again to suggest that the magnanimity of "In the Field" is the ultimate fruit of Wilbur's openness to his immediate predecessors. Reviewing Robert Graves in 1955, Wilbur quoted this statement about modernism: "the mainly negative work begun by the 'modernists' of the Twenties in exploring the limits of technical experiment is finished and done with." With Laura Riding, Graves had first voiced this opinion as early as 1928, in *A Survey of Modernist Poetry* (a book that must have influenced Randall Jarrell's similar statements, offered fifteen years later in "The End of the Line"). But Wilbur added a sentence to Graves's: "and indeed there are styles of the Thirties and Forties, *not* technically extreme, which would seem to have had their time of prevalence."[43] Unlike Graves, Wilbur is not battling modernism by suggesting that it has passed; casting his historical net a little wider, Wilbur sees that the first wave of postmodern reaction has also passed.

For reasons I've explored Wilbur is often understood as a reactionary poet, but he worked past that position early in his career, learning from a wide variety of poets even as his own poetry became utterly distinctive. Or perhaps I should say that his poetry became so utterly itself precisely because of his undogmatic openness. As Wilbur has explained in "On My Own Work," there is only one aspect of modern poetry that has not appealed to him.

> The revolution [in American poetry during the second decade of the century] was not a concerted one and there was little agreement on objectives; nor is there now any universal agreement as to what, in that revolution, was most constructive. But certainly it has been of lasting importance that Robinson and Frost chose to enliven traditional meters with the rhythms of colloquial speech; that Sandburg and others insisted on slang and on the brute facts of the urban and industrial scene; and that Pound and Eliot sophisticated

American verse by introducing techniques from other literatures, and by reviving and revising our sense of literary tradition.

Visible here is the same Wilbur who, as a young man, fostered an open political debate, even as his own convictions were clear. Visible, too, is Wilbur's lifelong caginess: he chooses his forebears carefully, knowing that few poets will champion Sandburg and Pound in the same breath. Wilbur's one disagreement with these modern poets is that he won't "exclude anything in the name of purity."[44] But I suspect that Wilbur knows, for example, that Pound's taste was rarely dogmatic; Pound promoted Sandburg, reviewed Frost glowingly when others rejected him, and even had a kind word for Robinson. This is why Wilbur is so careful to point out that the modernist movement was neither concerted nor single-minded—really not a movement at all. He knows that, at their best, the moderns were not manifesto writers but, rather, poets who worked to extend the possibilities of poetry. One of the joys of reading Wilbur is our knowledge that, with a long and productive career behind him, he is still continuing to extend those possibilities today.

NOTES

1. Richard Wilbur, "Seven Poets," *Sewanee Review* 88 (Winter 1950): 141.

2. Randall Jarrell, *Letters,* ed. Mary Jarrell (Boston: Houghton Mifflin, 1985) 413.

3. Robert Bly, "the first ten issues of kayak," *kayak* 12 (1967): 47.

4. In Wendy Salinger, ed., *Richard Wilbur's Creation* (Ann Arbor: U of Michigan P, 1983) 130.

5. Richard Wilbur, "A Postcard for Bob Bly," *kayak* 13 (1968): 15.

6. Cited in Ted Solotaroff, "Captain Bly," *Nation* 253 (9 September 1991): 270–71. On Wilbur's Harvard years, see Peter Davison, *The Fading Smile: Poets in Boston, from Robert Frost to Robert Lowell to Sylvia Plath, 1955–1960* (New York: Knopf, 1994).

7. Louise Bogan, "The Pleasures of Formal Poetry," *Quarterly Review of Literature* 7 (1953): 176. The conference itself took place in 1948.

8. Richard Wilbur, "The Bottles Become New, Too," *Quarterly Review of Literature* 7 (1953): 190, 187, 188. This essay is reprinted in Wilbur's *Responses* (New York: Harcourt, 1976) 215–23.

9. Nathan A. Scott Jr., *Visions of Presence in Modern American Poetry* (Baltimore: Johns Hopkins UP, 1993) 194.

10. See Bruce Michaelson, *Wilbur's Poetry: Music in a Scattering Time* (Amherst: U of Massachusetts P, 1991) 40.

11. See Helen Gardner, *The Composition of* Four Quartets (London: Faber, 1978) 67.

12. William Butts, ed. *Conversations with Richard Wilbur* (Jackson: U of Mississippi P, 1990) 43. For an analysis of Bishop's relationship to the idea of political poetry, see James Longenbach, "Elizabeth Bishop's Social Conscience," *ELH* 62 (Summer 1995): 467–86. In *American Poetry and Culture, 1945–1980* (Cambridge: Harvard UP, 1985) Robert von Hallberg points out that the notion of "protest" poetry limited the scope of political poetry during the 1960s (see 117ff.); see also his readings of Wilbur's "Speech for the Repeal of the McCarran Act" and "The Regatta" (122–26).

13. Along with two others, this poem appeared in *Touchstone* 4 (December 1938): 9. I am deeply grateful to John Lancaster, curator of Special Collections at the Amherst College Library, for helping me to locate Wilbur's early writings.

14. Richard Wilbur, "The Debate Continues," *Amherst Student* 72 (6 April 1939): 2.

15. Richard Wilbur, "Strange Setting for Intolerance," *Amherst Student* 73 (7 March 1940): 2.

16. Butts, *Conversations*, 117.

17. Richard Wilbur, "Fight, Fight, Fight," *Amherst Student* 73 (2 May 1940): 2; "Consequences of the War to Public Morals," *Amherst Student* 74 (16 December 1940): 2.

18. Richard Wilbur, "For the Record," *Amherst Student* 74 (22 May 1941): 2.

19. Richard Wilbur, "Reply to the Editor of the *Williams Record*," *Amherst Student* 75 (10 November 1941): 2.

20. James Breslin, *From Modern to Contemporary* (Chicago: U of Chicago P, 1984) 25.

21. Richard Wilbur, "Short Laments for Some Poets," *Amherst Student* 75 (25 September 1941): 2.

22. Richard Wilbur, "Now That We Are in It," *Amherst Student* 75 (8 December 1941): 1.

23. Richard Wilbur, "Decency, Honesty, Guts," *Amherst Student* 75 (15 December 1941): 2.

24. Wilbur, *Responses*, 118.

25. Richard Wilbur, "The Mock Turtle," *Amherst Student* 73 (13 May 1940): 2.

26. Richard Wilbur, "Robert Graves' New Volume," *Poetry* 87 (December 1955): 176–77.

27. Parenthetical references supply page numbers for Richard Wilbur's *New and Collected Poems* (New York: Harcourt, 1988).

28. James Dickey, *Babel to Byzantium: Poets and Poetry Now* (New York: Ecco Press, 1981) 172.

29. Richard Wilbur, "The Day After the War," *Foreground* 1 (Spring–Summer 1946): 112.

30. Richard Wilbur, "The Genie in the Bottle," in *Mid-Century American Poets*, ed. John Ciardi (New York: Twayne, 1950) 6.

31. Marianne Moore, *Poems* (London: Egoist Press, 1921) 13.

32. Betsy Erkkila, *The Wicked Sisters: Women Poets, Literary History, and Discord* (New York: Oxford UP, 1992) 125. See also David Bromwich, "'That Weapon, Self-Protectiveness,'" in *Marianne Moore: The Art of a Modernist*, ed. Joseph Parisi (Ann Arbor: UMI Research P, 1990) 67–80.

33. Wilbur made these comments about "Driftwood," including the earlier drafts, in *A Critical Supplement to Poetry*, ed. John Frederick Nims (December 1948): 2–7.

34. Richard Wilbur, "We," *Poetry* 73 (December 1948): 127–28.

35. Wilbur, *Responses*, 101.

36. Wilbur, *Responses*, 218, 220.

37. Richard Wilbur, "Poetry and the Landscape," in *The New Landscape in Art and Science*, ed. Gyorgy Kepes (Chicago: Paul Theobald, 1956) 89, 90.

38. See Salinger, *Richard Wilbur's Creation*, 68.

39. Robert Frost, *Selected Prose*, ed. Hyde Cox and E. C. Lathem (New York: Holt, Rinehart and Winston, 1959) 105.

40. Wilbur, *Responses*, 107.

41. Richard Wilbur, "Between Visits," *Poetry* 74 (May 1949): 116.

42. Butts, *Conversations*, 49.

43. Wilbur, "Robert Graves' New Volume," 175.

44. Wilbur, *Responses*, 122, 123.

The Once and Future Texts
of Modernist Poetry

George Bornstein

My title implies that the texts of modernist poetry might be divided into
those that are past, those that are passing, and those that are to come. Of
course, in view of its recent standing in some quarters of the academy,
one might wonder if modernist poetry *has* a future, textual or other-
wise. It certainly has a past, and its brief but glorious heyday often leads
modern detractors to forget for how much of that past poetic modern-
ism was, well, marginalized, abused, oppositional, and literally sup-
pressed, as with governmental banning of work by nearly every major
modernist writer. For example, the influential man of letters Arthur
Waugh (father of Evelyn) spoke for a good many of that minority who
had even heard of the modernists in 1915 when he compared them to
those at the very bottom of the social order rather than those at the top.
Reviewing Ezra Pound's *Catholic Anthology* of poetry (which included
work by T. S. Eliot, Pound, W. B. Yeats, Alice Corbin, Harriet Monroe,
and William Carlos Williams, among others) for the *Quarterly Review,*
Waugh worried about what he called "anarchy" and "red ruin": "It was
a classic custom in the family hall, when the feast was at its height, to
display a drunken slave among the sons of the household, to the end
that they, being ashamed at the ignominious folly of his gesticulations,
might determine never to be tempted into such a pitiable condition
themselves."[1] Waugh's charge that the modernists were left-wing and
hostile to established authority directly contradicts current notions that
the modernist poets as a group were conservative (or even fascist) and
upholders of established order, especially established capitalist order.
Yet Waugh's charges were more normative for their time than we now
often remember. In 1920, for example, a column in the *Morning Post*

abused modernist poetry under the title "Certain American Poets: The Bolshevist Touch." Improbably to our ears, the critic singled out T. S. Eliot of all people in this way:

> These scribbling Bolshies are not confined to the less cultured side of the Atlantic. We have so-called poets who will throw such similes as this at the head of poetical authority:
>> Let us go, then, you and I,
>> When the evening is spread out against the sky
>> Like a patient etherised upon a table.[2]

Such sentiments were far more widespread than we now sometimes remember, and they persisted much longer as well, to be revived with controversies after World War II such as the award of the Bollingen Prize to Pound for *The Pisan Cantos*. Nowadays, of course, the modernists are often abused as being politically right-wing rather than left-wing and, culturally, upholders of authority rather than its challengers.

Such wide swings in opinion suggest more the needs of their constructors than the merits (or demerits) of their objects. Certainly, the revolution has been nearly complete during the time of my own scholarly career. When I was a graduate student in the 1960s working on my first book, *Yeats and Shelley*, other students and my professors would say things to me such as "I can see that you'd be interested in Yeats, but why on earth would you want to work on *Shelley*?" Nowadays, the question might be reversed, with as little depth of knowledge. Instead of those who used to berate the romantics as overly emotional, adolescently exuberant, and careless in their craft, we now hear those who berate the modernists as overly intellectual, psychologically repressed, and overconcerned with formal technique. Once the darlings of the New Criticism, the modernists have become the roadkill of contemporary theory.

Modernist fortunes have sunk so low that perhaps they are bound to rise again. If so, future views of modernism will construct their subject far differently than the New Critics did, perhaps stressing fault lines rather than well-wrought urns, openness rather than closure, indeterminacy rather than fixity. Paradoxically, modernism may seem postmodern after all—not surprisingly, since the charges that postmodernism levels at modernism often replay those that modernism itself leveled at Victorianism. The political and social stances of modernism call for reassessment, too, particularly over notions of identity, gender, and ethnicity. The absence of women from most New Critical constructions of modernism now looks like a scandal, and so does the absence of many ethnic groups. Not only are well-known writers such as H.D. or Marianne Moore rightly assuming central roles, but so will myriads of women less often thought of in this way, such as George Yeats. Similarly, we need to pay more attention to the host of minority voices explicitly appropriating modernist strategies, whether of numerous Harlem Renaissance writers invoking Irish Renaissance examples as a model for self-assertion by previously oppressed groups or of writers such as Ralph Ellison declaring that his "entire conscious education in literature" came from reading *The Waste Land*, of all works. And our sense of the texts of such works themselves will change, both as copyrights lapse and as electronic media come to complement book displays of texts. Modernist texts are protean, existing in multiple and equally authorized forms, as we will increasingly see; to adapt the title of a recent incisive book on Emily Dickinson, "Choosing Not Choosing" was a hallmark modernist strategy. The conjunction of copyright protection and codex production have obscured that condition temporarily, reinforcing instead the tendency to think of such works as authoritative, hegemonic, closed products. With the demise of modernist copyrights and the rise of electronic media to complement or even challenge book distribution, the original protean nature of these contingent texts as ongoing processes will reemerge.

Just after publication of his elaborate edition of *Guido Cavalcanti Rime*, itself a fragment of a larger project, the modernist poet Ezra Pound exploded: "With plenty of printers, plenty of paper, plenty of ink, it is manifestly idiotic that we couldn't have the editions we want, but it is equally obvious that with more food than humanity can eat, more clothes than it can wear, it is quite idiotic for men to starve and go ragged."[3] Pound's comment exemplifies the concern for material creation and distribution of texts so pervasive among modernist writers, just as his concern for economic inequalities such as the distribution of food and clothing reminds us that actual modernist politics were more sympathetic to social distress than their occasional contemporary caricatures would suggest ("Parnell came down the road, he said to a cheering man; / 'Ireland shall get her freedom and you still break stone'" was Yeats's bitter couplet on the economic effects of the Irish revolution).[4] Modernist subversion of pieties extends to texts as well as to politics. Central to them is the notion of what editions we might want, and central to that is the notion of what editions have been chosen for us so far and why they are unsatisfactory. The major modernists worried continually about such problems, and their careers show extraordinary involvement in publishing institutions and textual design: think, for example, of Yeats's involvement in founding the Cuala (originally Dun Emer) Press run by his sisters and then with publishing his own successive volumes of verse there first, of Pound's supervision of the productions of the early versions of his epic *The Cantos,* of Marianne Moore's crucial role at the *Dial,* of H.D.'s preference for private editions produced by Darantière in France or by her companion Bryher's firm in England, or of Wallace Stevens's arrangements for small press first editions of his own mature volumes, like those from Alcestis or Cummington Press. Such arrangements bespeak both dissatisfaction with existing institutions and desire for alternate arrangements. And, if the modernists themselves were dissatisfied with any one form of editions of their work and instead explored alternatives, what should we say of our own editions of the modernist poets, the ones we studied at college or university and still assign to our students?

I would term even the best of those editions not "idiotic" but, rather, misleading. They are misleading because they present the modernist project as something fixed, stable, complete, and imposing. But, as Wallace Stevens remarked, "it must not be fixed."[5] Rather, the modernist project was restless, unstable, evolving—to use Sean O'Casey's phrase, always "in a state of chassis." Most modernist poems exist in multiple forms, more like a process than a product, with each form carrying its own authorization and validity. In that way the physical texts themselves resist hierarchy and hegemony, instead proclaiming a radical contingency of the versions that each of them constitutes and that together might be said to constitute "the" poem. To illustrate this I turn first to examples by Moore, Pound, and Yeats, then to economic and intellectual contingencies that have contributed to the erasure of variation by single-state forms of the text, and, finally, to recently emerging forces for recuperating the protean character of these elusive texts in the future.

Marianne Moore's poem aptly named "Poetry" provides a helpful place to start. A selective brief overview might run as follows: The poem first appeared in the July 1919 issue of the magazine *Others,* in a format of five eight-line syllabic stanzas rhymed *abcddeef* (because of line length, some readers take the stanzas as six lines with turnovers, rhymed *abbccd*). Here is the first stanza from that version:

> I too, dislike it: there are things that are important
> > beyond all this fiddle.
> > Reading it, however, with a perfect contempt for it,
> > one discovers that there is in
> it after all, a place for the genuine.
> > Hands that can grasp, eyes
> > that can dilate, hair that can rise
> > if it must, these things are important not because a[6]

Discovers is a keyword there, as the attentive reader gradually discovers both an order in the poem (the six stanzas, the calculatedly casual rhyme scheme, the strict syllabic pattern of the lines, the precise articulation of meaning through form) and a disorder struggling against it (the unconventionality of the stanzaic form, the demurely nonconformist typography, the enjambment preventing closure at the end of the stanzas).

Yet, despite the technical and thematic triumph of the poem, Moore reduced those forty carefully patterned lines to only thirteen lines of free verse for her own book *Observations* (1924). There only the first sentence remained from the first stanza, with the rest of the poem similarly condensed and the syllabic pattern broken. By her 1935 *Selected Poems* Moore reinstated the original stanzaic form, with some revisions and in a layout gesturing more toward six-line stanzas with turnovers than did the ambiguous layout of the first version. One of the two most available current texts, the 1951 *Collected Poems,* derives from the 1935 *Selected Poems,* again with revisions. But the other version, for the 1967 *Complete Poems,* was the most stunning change of all. There Moore reduced the entire poem to just three lines, set on a page by themselves and reading:

> I, too, dislike it.
> > Reading it, however, with a perfect contempt for it, one dis-
> > > covers in
> > it, after all, a place for the genuine.[7]

That combines half of the original first sentence of the poem with the second sentence, rearranged in a new display. The lines take their meaning partly from the absence of their original context; they act out their content by constituting and preserving the "genuine" that found a place in the original "poetry" (here brazenly dismissed). Yet, clearly, the final version gestures toward the deleted thirty-seven lines of the early versions and cannot be understood fully without them.

I hope that not even the most devoted admirer of Fredson Bowers and American eclectic editing would wish to banish all but the final three-line version in the name of final authorial intention. An adequate edition of the poem would have to include at least the original forty-line version (or a later variant of it), the thirteen-line free verse version, and the three-line final version. Several scholars have commented on the differences among these versions.[8] I wish to emphasize here, instead, the significance of the existence of such multiple versions: by displaying her poem in such radically different material forms, Moore creates not merely a series of variants but, more important, a physical enactment of the process of transmission of modernist poetry. The poem does not merely present a series of propositions about poetry, nor does it even add to those an enactment of its own semantic principles, but through its successive embodiments it *reenacts* important paradigms of poetic transmission, paradigms that remind us that poems exist in multiple, changing forms that constitute more an ongoing process than a final product. Poetry (as subject or quality) comes in multiple forms, and so does "Poetry" (as Moore's particular poem).

So far I have spoken of different "versions" of a poem as linguistic only. But those different linguistic versions are embedded in different material forms, which carry their own systems of meaning. In the chapter "What Is Critical Editing?" from his book *The Textual Condition* Jerome McGann proposes that we term the semantic aspects of a text's physical format—typography, page layout, book design, and the rest—the "bibliographic code," in distinction to the merely "linguistic code" of the words.[9] Our modern editions clearly scant the bibliographical code, focusing primarily or even exclusively on the linguistic code.

A glance at the publication history of Ezra Pound's early cantos will show us the importance of gesturing toward bibliographic codes in our current editions. The early magazine versions themselves contain important variations in the linguistic as well as bibliographic code, especially the three installments of "Three Cantos" published in *Poetry* for June, July, and August 1917, with their huge variations from the eventual linguistic code of that section of the poem. *The Cantos* appeared in book form first as *A Draft of XVI. Cantos* from William Bird's Three Mountains Press in Paris (1925), then in the uniform successor *A Draft of the Cantos 17–27* from John Rodker in London (1928), then in *A Draft of XXX Cantos* from Nancy Cunard's Hours Press in Paris (1930), and, finally, again as *A Draft of XXX Cantos* but in a different and barer format from Farrar in the United States and Faber in England (1933). Contemporary editions of *The Cantos* descend from the 1933 versions, which elide the elaborate bibliographical coding of the earlier versions and, thus, of the origins of Pound's poem.

Briefly, the 1925 and 1928 versions offered two-color (red and black) printing, illuminated capitals at the start of each canto, a modernized Caslon typeface, and oversized pages of expensive paper. The effect was to gesture at once backward and forward, to invoke the opposing bibliographical principles of Morris's Kelmscott Press and of Lane and Mathews's Bodley Head, of a medievalizing ideal and a modernizing aesthetic, of craft rather than industrial production, and through Morris of a set of socialist principles rarely identified with Pound. The 1930 *Draft of Thirty Cantos* functions as a halfway house between the gaudy originals and the quotidian current form of the text; it offers the same typeface but smaller pages and, in place of the elaborate, nearly Pre-Raphaelite early capitals, a set of more modern Vorticist ones designed by Pound's wife, Dorothy. By 1933 the format we still discover in the New Directions texts was set. In that product whole levels of meaning were lost, levels particularly pertinent to the project of a poem that begins with an entire canto on cultural transmission, including lines such as "In officina Wecheli, 1538, out of Homer." The erasure of those levels enables a misconstrual of the poem as fixed, authoritarian, and stable that a more adequate edition would prevent, even as it illuminated areas of complex cultural and political positioning that current editions remove.

The successive incarnations of Canto LXXIII ("Cavalcanti—Corrispondenza Repubblicana") illustrate the power of bibliographic codes to change the meaning of texts *even when the linguistic code remains the same.* One of the two "lost cantos" of the late fascist years, Canto LXXIII was published in February 1945 in *Marina Repubblicana,* a naval journal of Mussolini's fast-fading Salò Republic. There its story of a brave fascist girl deliberately leading a squad of Canadian soldiers into a minefield, where they all perish, clearly supports the failing fascist cause. The fact that it is written in Italian seems less an invocation of the language of Dante or even of the Cavalcanti alluded to in the title than of the fascist politicians and soldiers whom it both addresses and supports. Its closing apostrophe,

Ma che regazza!
        che regazze,
                che ragazzi,
                        portan il nero!
(But what a girl!
        what girls
                what boys
                        wear the black!)

alludes particularly to Mussolini's notorious Black Brigades.[10] The celebratory nature of the poem soon changed into shamefaced silence, signaled by the gap in printed collections of *The Cantos*, which moved abruptly from Canto LXXI to Canto LXXIV (the opening of the Pisan sequence). The silent gap signaled a suppressed secret, a part of the poem too embarrassing to print but which the gap in the numerical sequence kept calling attention to, a paradigmatic absent presence in which "Cavalcanti—Corrispondenza Repubblicana" had reversed its initial meaning of celebration to one of scandal.

But, partly as a result of discovery of a 1973 mimeographed "edition" distributed by the Pound estate to establish copyright, interest in the suppressed cantos continued to grow. The pair was included first in the 1985 Italian edition prepared by Pound's daughter Mary de Rachewiltz (in which their composition in Italian rather than English disappeared into the rest of the translation) and then at the back of the New Directions printing of 1986. The New Directions tactic reveals intricate bibliographic coding: by including the lost cantos at all, the text establishes them as part of the poem; but, by printing them out of sequence at the back, it seeks to exclude them from the main body of the text and consign them instead to an ancillary role, a sort of documentary afterthought. That changed again in still later printings of *The Cantos*, in which Canto LXXIII, like its companion LXXII, was silently inserted into its proper place in the sequence, for the first time acknowledging it as an integrated part of the poem and reproducing it accordingly. Each of these positions in different editions, or even spatially within successive printings of the same edition, shows the bibliographic codes changing the meaning of the linguistic code even though the linguistic code stays constant throughout. But its social and political meanings vary drastically. Ordinarily, bibliographic coding most strongly affects those aspects of texts.

Both Moore's revision of linguistic codes and Pound's of bibliographic ones find their analogues in Yeats, perhaps the greatest reviser of an age of revisers. No one text can pin down the political or poetic position of a writer who begins one of his characteristic presentations of Ireland as a woman, "Red Hanarahan's Song about Ireland," in this powerful way in the standard current edition:

> The old brown thorn-trees break in two high over Cummen
> Strand,
> Under a bitter black wind that blows from the left hand

but with this contrastingly tripping lilt in the original publication of 1894:

> Veering, fleeting, fickle, the winds of Knocknarea,
> When in ragged vapour they mutter night and day . . .[11]

Similarly, Yeats varied the bibliographic codes of his works, particularly with his increasing control from 1895 onward (and again with the establishment of Cuala Press after the turn of the century). The elaborately designed covers on which he often collaborated with the designer, the carefully meditated page layouts, and the thoughtful sequencing continually shift the meanings of poems more deliberately and no less strikingly than with Pound's Canto LXXIII, even when the linguistic code remains the same.

Yeats's best-known and best-selling book before the *Collected Poems* of 1933, his much reissued *Poems* volume of 1895, provides a ready example. Disappointed by the static design of angel, dragon, and rose-bushes produced by H. Glanville Fell for the original edition, Yeats arranged for the 1899 edition to feature a more vibrant cover design by Althea Gyles, with roses swirling outward from a central cross.[12] Gyles's design thus stressed both the Rosicrucian and dynamic aspects of the contents, rather than their static and more orthodox side. Similarly, her design for the spine of hands beseeching a female face on a rose tree called attention to the erotic elements of Yeats's Rose poems and other early lyrics.

"Dedication to a Book of Stories Selected from the Irish Novelists" provides an example of bibliographic context changing linguistic meaning even when the words remain the same. One of the few unrevised lines of the poem has the speaker announce, "I also bear a bell-branch full of ease" (*VP* 130). In the original context, in which the poem served as dedication to Yeats's own selection of *Representative Irish Tales*, the bell-branch clearly refers to the contents of the volume, the stories by the Irish fiction writers Maria Edgeworth, the Banim brothers, and William Carleton that immediately follow. But, when transferred to the context of Yeats's *Poems* or *Collected Poems*, the bell-branch instead refers to the other poems in the volume surrounding it.[13] The bibliographic code has changed the linguistic meaning.

But, having shown linguistic and bibliographical codes at work also in Moore and Pound in more detail, I emphasize here, instead, the radical instability of Yeats's entire canon. Briefly, this poet, who can contend for the modern world's record in articulating the shape of his work as a whole, left us varied and conflicting arrangements of it. That issue was at the heart of the quarrel over the order of Yeats's poems between Richard Finneran, who preferred the familiar arrangement deriving from *Collected Poems* of 1933, which put the lyrics first and the narrative and dramatic poems in a separate section at the end, and Warwick Gould and A. Norman Jeffares, who championed the more interleaved order of the never published Edition de Luxe. Yet even at the time Finneran pointedly noted that the idea of a definitive edition was a myth in this case and that such a thing would be neither possible nor desirable for Yeats.[14] That view has steadily gained dominance, with critics increasingly realizing that the point is that different arrangements are possible and even authorized by Yeats at different times and that such different arrangements carry claims of both social and authorial construction.

Such architectonics include whether a volume of collected poems should open with Yeats as an immediately Irish poet in *The Wanderings of Oisin* or as a derivative European one in "Song of the Happy Shepherd," coming to Irish themes only later. Correspondingly, Finneran's recovery of the close of the canon by reseparating *New Poems* (1938) from the posthumous *Last Poems* and then putting *Last Poems* in an order specified by Yeats made it clear that the final movement of Yeats's verse began, rather than ended, with "Under Ben Bulben." That is, it began with one of the harsh "inhuman" or "inhumane" poems and ended with the humanly moving "Circus Animals' Desertion" followed by the love envoi artfully entitled "Politics." We begin with a voice beyond the grave and an injunction to "Cast a cold eye / On life, on death" but end up back "In the foul rag and bone shop of the heart" (*P* 328, 348) with an exhortation toward human love.

That movement toward the human and the humane recurs throughout Yeats's mature arrangments of his poetry, in which the individual volumes regularly "refute" their opening lyrics, as *Michael Robartes and the Dancer* does by moving from its title poem to "To be carved on a Stone at Thoor, Ballylee," as *The Winding Stair* does by moving from "In Memory of Eva Gore-Booth and Con Markievicz" to "From the *Antigone*," or as *New Poems* does in moving from "The Gyres" to "The Municipal Gallery Revisited" and "Are You Content." *New Poems* is a particularly telling example. Its introductory piece "The Gyres" seems to dismiss the blotting out of existing beauty or worth with an insistent "what matter?" and to seek consolation in the concluding notion that a future time will see "all things run / On that unfashionable gyre again." In contrast, however much he may know intellectually that a future time will bring round a new gyre and new models of accomplishment, the more humanized speaker of the penultimate "Municipal Gallery Revisited" cries emotionally that "I am in despair that time may bring / Approved patterns of women or of men / But not that selfsame excellence again" (*P* 293, 320). Opening poems such as "The Gyres" are among those for which Yeats is most often attacked nowadays, but the volumes in which such works are embedded often critique them more harshly than do even the harshest of Yeats's critics. We might call such arrangements a "contextual code," to supplement the linguistic and bibliographical ones. Like the other two, its full deployment leads away from fixity, stability, and hierarchy and toward flux, instability, and something short of anarchy but still moving in the direction of radical textual egalitarianism. Yet none of the readily available texts of the modernist poets recaptures the process embodied in any of the codes. Why is that?

To begin materially: part of the problem has to do with the standardization provided by the institution of copyrights, whose current and ongoing expirations will again free the texts to resume their protean forms. Despite the early adroitness of Yeats, Pound, or even Eliot in manipulating editors and publishers (and they themselves were editors, of course), the modernists eventually settled into long-term copyright arrangements with their publishers: in the United States, if you wanted to read Yeats, you turned to Macmillan; if Moore, to Viking; if Pound or Williams, to New Directions; if Eliot, to Harcourt, Brace for the poetry and Farrar, Straus for the prose; and in England for Yeats again to Macmillan and for many of the other poets to Faber, where Eliot himself served as editor and director. The result was to "freeze" the principal texts in the form distributed by those publishers, to the loss of all earlier forms, and, if writers like Yeats continued their revisions, the latest ones were apt to shove aside all the others. Readers of Moore's "Poetry," Pound's *Cantos*, or Yeats's *Collected Poems*, for example, were simply furnished with the latest form of those poems, with little or no indication that earlier forms even existed, let alone what they were.

Thus, readers and critics interested in the early Yeats often use the "final" texts in his *Collected Poems* to discuss his poetic development, with no awareness that the versions of the early poems there often show heavy revision. To let a few examples stand for many, "Song of the Wandering Aengus" was originally entitled "A Mad Song," which undermines the claims of some critics to take it as a paradigm of male desire; lines that now refer bitterly to Ireland as "that country where a man can be so crossed; / Can be so battered, badgered and destroyed" originally called it wistfully "the willow of the many-sorrowed world"; and the section called *The Rose* never existed as a separate volume and was not printed in 1893 (*VP* 149, 130, and 64). In such ways projects that existed in ongoing states of evolution and change came to seem fixed and stable products rather than ongoing processes.

To understand the opportunity of undoing such distortion at the present time, it is helpful to glance back over the history of copyright. With the exception of a brief period in Roman antiquity, copyright seems to have arisen concomitantly with the invention of the printed book, or codex, and with the rise of capitalism. In Renaissance England the British Crown decided to grant copyrights not to protect authors but to enforce censorship and royal control over the newly emergent printing houses. Specifically, the Crown gave the guild of printers and booksellers known as the Stationers' Company exclusive rights to print and sell books, and the Stationers' Company bought the perpetual copyright of books from authors, ordinarily by a onetime payment. This system of control was enforced by the notorious Court of the Star

Chamber and lasted until the Cromwellian revolution, when a brief period of open publishing yielded to a new licensing act two years later.

Contemporary British and U.S. copyright law both depend on the Statute of Queen Anne passed in 1710, which for the first time explicitly acknowledged the exclusive rights of authors over printing their own works for a set period of years. U.S. copyright law took a separate course after the Revolution and did not develop protection for foreign writers and works until the end of the nineteenth century, starting with the Chace Act of 1891. Perhaps the most important discrepancy today is that British copyright recognizes the lifetime of the author plus fifty years (but is about to change again), whereas U.S. copyright now recognizes the same standard but grants an exemption to works that were still in copyright when the Copyright Law of 1976 was passed: they are entitled to protection for seventy-five years from first publication.[15] Such works include a large amount of major modernist poetry, which thus comes out of copyright in the United Kingdom fifty years after the death of the authors but in the United States seventy-five years from first publication.

Copyright law means that copyright protection for the modernist writers has already begun to expire and will continue to do so in the coming years. For example, Yeats's works came out of copyright in the United Kingdom in 1989 (fifty years after his death in 1939), but only those published by 1919 (seventy-five years ago) are out of copyright in the United States. In the United States all of Pound's poetry through *Mauberley* will have emerged from copyright restriction by the end of 1995, Eliot's *Waste Land* only two years after that, Wallace Stevens's *Harmonium* volume the year after that, and Marianne Moore's *Observations* in 1999, by which time H.D.'s *Sea Garden, Hymen,* and *Heliodora* will also all be available and Langston Hughes's *The Weary Blues* in the offing.

Obviously, not all of the results of this will be salutary, and we may have modern analogues to the unscrupulous early Victorian publisher Thomas Tegg who, when informed by his printer that he was running out of type for an edition of Milton's *Paradise Lost,* simply ordered the printer to put "Finis" at the end of book 10 and to sell the volume like that. The expiration of Yeats copyrights in the United Kingdom at the end of 1989 and of those of Joyce at the end of 1991 has led to a rash of editions there, some of varying scholarly merit but others of little value, whose sloppiness in text and apparatus does a disservice to their authors. And in the United States, with its different situation, we already have a book entitled *A Poet to His Beloved: The Early Love Poems of W. B. Yeats* (1985) that restricts itself to poems published before 1910 (and hence out of copyright by 1985; most of the later love poetry is still protected) yet unaccountably presents them in their "final" forms, in effect giving us "The Early Love Poems of W. B. Yeats as revised by the Later Yeats."[16] At least two further volumes, both entitled *Selected Poems,* have appeared since then, incorporating work from *Responsibilities* (1914), which itself emerged from copyright in the meantime. Neither edition explains either its choice of which textual version to use of the poems selected or the reasons for that choice. Yet, despite such disasters in the case of Yeats, not all copyright holders for other poets have been as cooperative or as scrupulous as the Yeats estate for works still under restriction, and the coming liberty will surely benefit the study of those poets even more. Freed of copyright restriction, the texts of modernist poetry can reassume their original protean forms.

Two factors concomitant with the expiration of copyright will help them do that. The first is the sea change in editorial theory over the past decade. Put briefly, the older theory of editing stressed the construction of ideal, eclectic texts thought to represent "the author's final intention" and thus aimed at establishing a single "definitive" form for the text. To our poststructuralist ears all three terms—*author, final,* and *intention*—raise problems. Instead of aiming at a single ideal form of the text, newer theories stress the legitimacy of various versions, the importance of social as well as authorial constructions of the text, and the historical contingency of both the linguistic and bibliographical codes.

These theories have so far found their fullest practical realization in Hans Gabler's edition of Joyce's *Ulysses* and of various work on Shakespeare's *King Lear,* and their best-known (though rarely definitive) early theoretical articulation in Jerome McGann's *Critique of Modern Textual Criticism.* The older editorial theories carried an implicit congruence with New Criticism in their emphasis on an ideal, unitary state of a dehistoricized artwork. Correspondingly, the newer theories fit better with poststructuralism in their emphasis on multiple, often contradictory states of historically contingent texts and in their bent for a resistant heterogeneity rather than a totalizing hegemony. Just as the older editorial theory supported the New Critical distortion of modernism, so will the newer theories join with the expiration of copyright to re-enable alternate constructions.

In their different ways several advanced modernist editions produced under the old dispensation gesture toward the new, among them the facsimile edition of Eliot's *Waste Land*, the documentary Cornell Yeats, and the archival *Ezra Pound's Poetry and Prose*. Publication of the facsimile *Waste Land* in 1971[17] revealed for the first time the contingent nature of that poem, assembled from various possibilities with heavy editorial input from Ezra Pound. Unexpectedly, the most prototypical and imposing work of poetic modernism appeared to be one of a series of possible incarnations that could have been assembled in different ways; indeed, the very existence of the facsimile edition itself, with its inclusion of a wide range of eventually discarded materials, gesture toward another such way. Further, the centrality of Pound's role in construction and revision of the poem pointed to a collaborative rather than solitary model of authorship.

The ongoing Cornell Yeats project, which aims to publish the manuscript and draft materials for all of Yeats's poetry,[18] in addition to many plays and selected ancillary material, similarly took the documentary record back before the published variants recorded in the *Variorum Edition* and revealed the original scenes of composition and alternate forms of published works, including some that Yeats "published" only in manuscript albums. Its diplomatic transcriptions and generous use of facsimiles gesture toward usually neglected bibliographical codes as an integral part of the editorial project, indicating that the level of physical inscription of manuscript gatherings such as "The Rosy Cross: Lyrics" or "The Flame of the Spirit" carries important aspects of the meaning.

And, third, the recently published eleven-volume *Ezra Pound's Poetry and Prose* both brings together a dizzying mass of material beyond the more familiar works by Pound and also reproduces it in photofacsimile.[19] In so doing, the edition points toward the original bibliographic coding of the materials, revealing them as contingent historical and social products often in a state of flux rather than as transhistorical objects beyond the material world. All three projects, in effect, extend existing technology to its limits, producing advanced works of codex construction that call the limits of the medium itself into question.

Such editions suggest the final factor I want to identify in this essay: new technologies. Ordinary print media pose definite limitations on the display of alternate versions and bibliographical codes. Codex display can easily handle two versions of a poem, whether on facing pages (as is now frequent in editions of Wordsworth's *Prelude*) or in different type sizes, as in Timothy Webb's interesting display of early and later versions of Yeats's selected poems. But print becomes increasingly unable to deal with larger numbers of versions, usually consigning them to a system of collation at the bottom of the page or back of the book that almost nobody understands or can decipher. Thus, the paradoxical effect of editions such as *The Variorum Edition of the Poems of W. B. Yeats* is to enshrine whatever version the edition uses as its base text (usually, the latest) and cause the reader to skip over the very apparatus that would allow reconstruction of alternate versions. And the apparatus itself suffers from the dilemma of having to opt either for a display that makes it easy to see all the variants of a single line but hard to reconstruct globally entire alternate versions or for a seriatim printing of versions that makes the tracing of local variation difficult.

In contrast, electronic media can with proper tagging handle multiple versions and display them in alternate ways—whether locally in different versions of a line or globally in different versions of an entire poem or arrangements of a book of poems—at the touch of a toggle switch. Similarly, digitized scanning makes possible the tracking of multiple bibliographic codes of cover design, page layout, typeface, and the like; some advanced scanners can produce both ASCII and digitized files at the same time, which can be linked to become machine searchable. The different versions of Moore's "Poetry," the different bibliographic codes of Pound's early cantos, and the contextual codes of Yeats's poetic arrangements could all be captured in an electronic edition, which, equally important, could allow for multiple constructions of the texts and their arrangement.

Planning the electronic editions of the future needs to move forward to exploit the possibilities of the new media itself. Just as the first printed books tended to resemble manuscripts in appearance, so has much thought and effort so far tended to think of an electronic edition as a sort of superbook, using the medium principally to overcome limits of codex display and storage. As future editions begin to explore the possibilities created by electronic media themselves, they may alter our entire conception of what an edition is. One major component will likely be hypermedia, combining words, images, and sound in linked formats. A second might be new conceptions of display that will either revise or altogether obviate current notions of the need for a base, or copytext; a hypermedia edition might offer an archive rather than a critical text as understood in much twentieth-century editing. One advantage helping to propel the rise of SGML (Standard General Markup Language) is its alleged openness to freeing future work from the limits of particular platforms and applications, allowing room for the unforeseen; already, for example, it is clear that the tertiary tag set developed by the TEI (Text Encoding Initiative) to allow for information on bibliographic codes needs elaboration. (A disadvantage of SGML is that it is so labor-intensive as to require extensive initial funding; commercial publishers may prefer to work within the limits of existing hardware and software, and to recode at some future point.)

As a member of the team now planning a hypermedia edition of W. B. Yeats, I find electronic prospects exciting. Yet it is important to remember that an electronic edition does not merely incorporate previous editions and versions: it changes them in the act of incorporation and itself constitutes a new version, albeit one in some ways the sum of previous versions. In his last completed canto Ezra Pound spoke of his poem as

> the record
>   the palimpsest—
> a little light
>   in great darkness—

and then wondered "who will copy this palimpsest?"[20] All modernist poetry is a palimpsest, an ongoing record of processes whose protean development has been artificially limited and distorted by a particular conjunction of copyright protection, critical and editorial theory, and codex display. All three now are yielding to alternative formations, enabling recovery of the heterogeneous achievements of modernist poetry. It is we who must copy—or, better yet, construct—the next stage of that palimpsest.

NOTES

1. Arthur Waugh, "The New Poetry," *Quarterly Review* 226 (October 1916): 386.

2. E. B. Osborn, "Certain American Poets: The Bolshevist Touch," *Morning Post,* 28 May 1920.

3. "Rime MSS," Beinecke Library, Yale University, as quoted in David Anderson, *Pound's Cavalcanti: An Edition of the Translations, Notes, and Essays* (Princeton: Princeton UP, 1983), xxvii.

4. W. B. Yeats, *The Poems*, ed. Richard J. Finneran, rev. ed. (New York: Macmillan, 1989), 312. Hereafter cited as *P* followed by page number.

5. Wallace Stevens, *The Necessary Angel* (New York: Vintage, 1965), 34.

6. *Others* 5 (July 1919): 5.

7. Marianne Moore, *Complete Poems* (New York: Macmillan/Viking, 1967), 36.

8. The best overall discussion of Moore's revisions is Andrew J. Kappel's "Complete with Omissions: The Text of Marianne Moore's *Complete Poems*," in *Representing Modernist Texts: Editing as Interpretation*, ed. George Bornstein (Ann Arbor: U of Michigan P, 1991), 125–56.

9. Jerome J. McGann, *The Textual Condition* (Princeton: Princeton UP, 1991), 48–68. The following discussion of the early printings of Pound's *Cantos* is indebted to McGann's book.

10. Ezra Pound, "Cavalcanti—Corrispondenza Repubblicana," *La Marina Repubblicana* 2.3 (1 February 1945): 7. For a facsimile reprint see *Ezra Pound's Poetry and Prose*, cited below.

11. *The Variorum Edition of the Poems of W. B. Yeats*, ed. Peter Allt and Russell K. Alspach, corrected 3rd printing (New York: Macmillan, 1966). Hereafter cited as *VP* followed by page number.

12. For reproduction of the designs and a brief discussion, see appendix 3 of my edition *W. B. Yeats: The Early Poetry, Volume II—Manuscript Materials* (Ithaca: Cornell UP, 1994).

13. For a fuller discussion of this example and the theoretical point implied, see my essay "What Is the Text of a Poem by Yeats?" in *Palimpsest: Editorial Theory in the Humanities*, ed. George Bornstein and Ralph G. Williams (Ann Arbor: U of Michigan P, 1993), 167–93, esp. 173–79.

14. See "Prolegomena: The Myth of the *Definitive Edition*," in *Editing Yeats's Poems*, ed. Richard J. Finneran (New York: St. Martin's, 1983), 1–4. Some key documents of the subequent controversy include: Warwick Gould's appendix "The Definitive Edition: A History of the Final Arrangements of Yeats's Work," in *Yeats's Poems*, ed. A. Norman Jeffares (London: Macmillan, 1989), 706–49; Finneran's revised version of *Editing Yeats's Poems: A Reconsideration* (London: Macmillan, 1990); and his essay "Text and Interpretation in the Poems of W. B. Yeats," in *Representing Modernist Texts*, 17–47. It is time for Yeats studies to move beyond the controversy.

15. As a result of the United Kingdom joining the Common Market, British copyright law is about to change again. Many observers expect that the copyright terms will be lengthened once more, thus bringing back under copyright protection some works (like those of Yeats) that have recently emerged from it.

16. *A Poet to His Beloved: The Early Love Poetry of W. B. Yeats* (New York: St. Martin's, 1985).

17. T. S. Eliot, *The Waste Land: A Facsimile and Transcript of the Original*

Drafts, Including the Annotations of Ezra Pound, ed. Valerie Eliot (New York: Harcourt Brace Jovanovich, 1971).

18. At the present time six of the poetry volumes have so far appeared in print from Cornell UP, with others in various stages of production: my own editions of *The Early Poetry,* vol. 1 (1987) and vol. 2 (1994); Carolyn Holdsworth's edition of *The Wind among the Reeds* (1993); Thomas Parkinson and Anne Brannen's edition of *Michael Robartes and the Dancer* (1994); Stephen Parrish's edition of *The Wild Swans at Coole* (1994); and David Clark's edition of *The Winding Stair 1929* (1995).

19. *Ezra Pound's Poetry and Prose: Contributions to Periodicals,* prefaced and arranged by Lea Baechler, A. Walton Litz, and James Longenbach (New York: Garland, 1991).

20. Ezra Pound, *The Cantos* (New York: New Directions, 1986), 797.

Wandering in the *Avant-texte:* Joyce's "Cyclops" Copybook Revisited

Michael Groden

"Facts are simple and facts are straight," remarks David Byrne (with his Ulyssean name) in "Crosseyed and Painless," a Talking Heads song. Facts about James Joyce's writing of *Ulysses* abounded in my 1977 genetic study, *"Ulysses" in Progress,* and they have held up fairly well over the years as facts. Yet, Byrne continues: "Facts all come with points of view / Facts don't do what I want them to." I researched and wrote *"Ulysses" in Progress* in ignorance of anything that might be called "theory," and its facts were gathered and presented as part of an argument that took for granted the unity of the published *Ulysses* and the secondary position of the prepublication documents in relation to the finished book. At the time I didn't pay much attention to the interpretation, the point of view, that I was putting on the facts. For several years now I have been curious to see how the facts offered in the book and the evidence mounted to present the argument might look in light of the recent theorizing about texts, writing, and authorship and especially in light of the theoretical essays and the specific studies of Joyce and other writers produced under the auspices of the Institut des Textes et Manuscrits Modernes (ITEM) of the Centre National de la Recherche Scientifique in Paris. The method of *critique génétique* that has come to be associated with ITEM studies, paying attention to the *avant-texte* (sometimes translated as "pre-text" or "foretext") as a vital object of study and aware of contemporary theory, would seem to offer an ideal new "point of view" for the facts. Since the first version of *"Ulysses" in Progress* was a Ph.D. dissertation written under the supervision of A. Walton Litz, I have taken this collection of essays honoring Litz as an opportunity to follow through on this curiosity, and so what follows are some speculative ruminations about one major part of *"Ulysses" in Progress,* the *avant-texte* of the "Cyclops" episode.

"Ulysses" in Progress is representative of a genetic-teleological model of Joyce's writing of *Ulysses.* It argued that Joyce wrote *Ulysses* in three stages—which it labeled as early, middle, and late—with the early stage focused mainly on the novelistic story of Leopold Bloom, Molly Bloom, and Stephen Dedalus; the middle stage a transitional one in which Joyce turned to parody styles; and the late stage more concerned with stylistic elaboration, symbolistic details, and Homeric parallels. I assumed that "once [Joyce] finished the book . . . the tasks of interpreting and assessing the complete book necessarily take precedence over any questions about the methods of composition" (200–201). I also argued, though, that "Joyce's book was composed in ways so idiosyncratic as to be interesting in themselves" (202) and that "the processes by which he wrote the book cannot be separated from other aspects of its meaning" (203). I took for granted that a literary work was characterized, even defined, by unity—even if *Ulysses* itself caused a lot of problems for this assumption. Because of the assumption, I glossed over the difficulties in bringing these three statements together into one argument. Instead, I argued that the radical dichotomies within *Ulysses* could be reclaimed for a unified concept of the book within such formulations as "a 'both/and' approach which seems to me the most fruitful critical one to *Ulysses*" (51) and "the most valuable [responses to one-sided readings of *Ulysses*] have been attempts to incorporate both the human drama and the symbolic structure into a unified theory of the book" (21). And I assumed that a history of Joyce's composition of the book would reveal the ultimate unity coming into being, even if unity meant "a multiple or ambiguous combination" of opposed tendencies (4). The suggestion of a middle stage of composition between the early and late ones was designed to show a gradual, evolutionary procedure rather than an abrupt, radical break, but my metaphors of palimpsest (4, 23) and superimposition (32) were offered in the service of a view of the book as a unity, even if a complex one.

Needless to say, conceptions of a literary work have changed drastically since *"Ulysses" in Progress* was written. Roland Barthes, for one, has traced a path "from work to text": "the work is a fragment of substance, it occupies a portion of the spaces of books (for example, in a library). The Text is a methodological field. . . . [T]he work is held in the hand, the text is held in language. . . . *[T]he Text is experienced only in an activity, in a production"* (57–58). Conceptions such as Barthes's emphasize openness, splits, and fissures, anything but closure and unity. The text's methodological field, or "network," includes other texts, whether these are preexisting texts—"influences" or "sources" in other contexts but now called "intertexts"[1]—or, specifically for the purposes of *critique génétique*, the *avant-texte*, the text's own past. The old terms *prepublication documents* and *finished work* are usefully superseded by *avant-texte* and *text*, and the sense of a teleological movement from early stages to finished product can be replaced at least provisionally by one of a textual field that extends backward and forward between *avant-texte* and text. Thus, for Hans Walter Gabler *critique génétique* is "concerned with the *différence* of all writing as it materializes in variants and in the advancing and receding of textual states" ("Textual" 713). Seen in this way, the process need not be interpreted as heading towards "one great goal," as Garrett Deasy in the "Nestor" episode claims all history tends to do (*U* 2:381), and the published text can be reconceived as a provisional central point, a "caesura" in the line of writing (Cerquiglini 118).[2]

The *Ulysses avant-texte*, and especially that of "Cyclops," offers a gold mine of material for these purposes. The *avant-texte*—notes (British Museum notesheets, Buffalo notebook V.A.2), lists (Buffalo MS V.A.7, Cornell item 55), drafts (Buffalo MSS V.A.8 and V.A.6, plus short passages in Buffalo notebook V.A.2, MS V.A.7, and MS V.A.9), manuscript (Rosenbach MS), typescripts (Buffalo TSS V.B.10.a and 10.b), *Little Review* serialized version, and proofs (Harvard, Buffalo V.C.1, Texas, Princeton)[3]—can show *Ulysses* coming into being, as *"Ulysses" in Progress* attempted to do, but it can also tell other stories. (In "Does 'Text' Exist?" one of the central statements of *critique génétique*, Louis Hay notes that, "in defining the pre-text as a constructed object, one must accept the existence of a variety of possible constructions" [70].) For one thing the *avant-texte* shows that the text of *Ulysses* can indeed be seen as a caesura within the full "Cyclops" archive, since there is what Hay calls an *après-texte* (71) of "Cyclops" in the various notebooks and other documents for *Finnegans Wake*. The *avant-texte* can also tell other stories involving the form and structure of *Ulysses*, concepts of characterization, and the role of the author in the text.

As almost everyone has noted who has looked at Buffalo MS V.A.8, the earliest extant draft of "Cyclops" (it can be dated around June 1919), this copybook is rare among the documents for *Ulysses* in containing a draft that was written before Joyce's sense of the episode's structure had solidified.[4] The copybook contains eight scenes, all quite sketchy. The first four, drafted in ink, move from the beginning of the episode ("In ^ green Erin of the west Inisfail the fair^ there lies a land, the land of holy Michan.") to the end ("And they beheld Him ^ in His Glory ascend to Him Who in Heaven in the direction of a beeline over Hogan's in Little Green Street. amid Clouds of Glory angels ascend to the Glory of the Brightness at an angle of fortyfive degrees over Hogan's Donohoe's in Little Green Street like a shot off a shovel.^").[5] Scenes 5–8, written in pencil, add some sections for the middle of the episode. The copybook ends in the middle of scene 8, and a note on page 23r of the twenty-four-page book referring to page 28, plus the continuation of scene 8 in Buffalo MS V.A.6, which contains the next draft of scenes 5–8, indicates that there was at least a second document that continued on from MS V.A.8 but that hasn't survived. When he was working on *Finnegans Wake,* Joyce told Frank Budgen: "I am boring through a mountain from two sides. The question is, how to meet in the middle" (qtd. in *UP* 124), and the copybook serves as an earlier instance of Joyce trying to meet in the middle. But it can also show his willingness not to push too hard to meet. For someone as obsessed with form and structure as Joyce was, the copybook is surprisingly unconcerned with form. Barthes describes "the classical sign" (or the "work") as "a sealed unit, whose closure arrests meaning, prevents it from trembling or becoming double, or wandering" ("Theory" 33), and the draft is a wonderful example of wandering—authorial, textual, or Odyssean— without too great a concern for the destination. As a document, it can enjoyably be read in a spirit of wandering.

The third scene of the copybook consists of talk about the Keogh-Bennett fight and about Irish sports. It contains dialogue, a rudimentary narrative voice, and two passages of "gigantism" (Joyce's term for his technique in the episode in his 1921 schema): the accounts of the fight and of the "most interesting discussion" of "the revival of ancient Gaelic sports." In *"Ulysses" in Progress* I discussed part of the scene in terms of Joyce's "problem of developing an alternative" to the interior monologue technique that he was dropping from *Ulysses,* and I offered an example in which I claimed that "several of his initial problems are evident" (126):

—I wouldn't like to see that, —— said. And those butting matches they have in California, going for each heads down like a bull at a gate.

—And bullfighting, Mr B ——, and cockfighting all those sports are terribly inhuman and hare hunting

—Well, yes, of course . . .

—What about bughunting, —— asked with a grin.

—*Cimex lectularius*, L—— put in.

—Isn't it what you call brain versus brawn

—They are simply disgusting, Bloom said. Brutal.

He walked to . . .

—Did you twig the one I gave him? —— said, about the buggy jews?

—Still and all, —— said, he's a humane chap.

—He is that, —— said sourly. He'd shove a soft hand under a hen. But I'd like to see him in the nine acres in a hurley scrap.

^Gara klooklooklook. Black Liz is our hen. She lays eggs for us. When she lays her egg she is so glad. Gara klooklooklook. Then comes good uncle Leo. She puts his hand under Black Liz and takes her fresh egg. Gara klooklooklook.^

He sang the Pæan of the Games of the Gael: he sang the Deeds of his Prowess. Youthful he drove the Wolf and the Boar: in the Chace he led the Knights of Uladh. From his godlike Shoulder sped the Stone: terrible, swift as the Glance of Balor.

—Ay, that's a fact, —— bore out. ^He was.^ How many feet could you put it?

—And that's what ^⟨you⟩ we^ want in Ireland today. Fine open air games. Irish games. Irish strength and skill. Hurley, Gaelic ^⟨slogger,⟩ soccer.^ Racy of the soil. That's what'll build up men Ireland a nation once again.[6]

Brief conversations come and go here, jokes are uttered and ignored, questions get asked but not answered. "Ay, that's a fact" serves as a transition from the speaker who would like to see Bloom "in the nine acres in a hurley scrap" to the question, "How many feet could you put it?" but it seems to be responding to something reported only in the gigantism style: "He sang the Pæan of the Games of the Gael." The conversations themselves are aimless, and they come from speakers whose names, and whose individual identities, don't seem to matter. Like several other parts of the copybook, the passage uses ——'s and *X*'s in place of characters' names. (As the copybook moves along in its eight scenes, names become more prominent. Even in scene 2, though, Alf Bergan, Ned Lambert, Bob Doran, and John Wyse Nolan are named.) Only "B ——" and "L ——" emerge here from the indistinguishable dashes; "B ——" expands once to "Bloom," and the reader probably fills in "L ——" to "Lenehan" on the basis of scene 5 in the copybook and later documents from the *avant-texte* and the text.

In *"Ulysses" in Progress* I discussed these details as evidence of Joyce's struggle with the details of characterization (139), but the situation can also be read in terms of the words in the conversations, as they are reported in this written text, taking precedence over the identity of the particular speakers who utter them. The language predominates over any identifiable center of attribution. If in "The Dead" Gabriel Conroy's "identity was fading out into a grey impalpable world" (Joyce, *Dubliners* 223), here voices predominate over identity, words are spoken in a convincing way from sources who can't be identified or who could be identified in one of several ways. The effect is like overhearing a conversation whose speakers can't be specified (as happens later at different points in "Circe" and especially in the last pages of "Oxen of the Sun"), but because of the ——'s and *X*'s it isn't quite this. Rather, speech comes from figures whose identity has not yet emerged from the "grey impalpable world," from speakers whose identity perhaps cannot emerge in this way. It is tempting to supply the speakers' identities from the text of "Cyclops" and to read these fragmentary conversations with that awareness (thus supplying not only Bloom and Lenehan but also Bergan, Joe Hynes, and the citizen), but if, as Gabler and others have argued, there is a "circularity" in the relationship between text and *avant-texte* ("Joyce's Text" 229), then the text can just as validly be read with an awareness of the *avant-texte* in mind. Read this way, the "characters" of "Cyclops" oscillate with the identity-less speakers of the copybook, and it then seems as if little more than the presence of the characters' names (as John Eglinton asks and Stephen Dedalus repeats twice in "Scylla and Charybdis," "What's in a name?" [*U* 9:901, 927, 986]) turns the copybook speakers into the recognizable characters of the text.

The text's wandering involves not only the conversation and the characters, who in the copybook as well as in the text drift in and out of the barroom, but also the imagery. Animals of all kinds—bulls, cocks, hares, a hen, a wolf, a boar—move in and out of the dialogue with surprising speed. Mr B ——/Bloom sets himself up to be the butt of a joke when he takes literally one speaker's simile involving a bull; in a context in which "that's a fact" is only a figure of speech, it's dangerous to treat any language as anything but figurative. In a quip that pleases its speaker Bloom is called a bug (expanded by another speaker to bedbug, *Cimex lectularius*), and then he is considered "humane" because of his concern about animals. When the conversation turns to sports (are the "men" of "Ireland a nation once again" the last items on the list of animals?), the contrast between the "soft" Bloom ("He'd shove a soft hand under a hen") and the "hard" Irish athletes ("From his godlike Shoulder sped the Stone") is far more obvious in this document than in the text of "Cyclops." By rearranging these details, the text presents the contrast less explicitly and less directly throughout the episode.

In *"Ulysses" in Progress,* looking for unity, I claimed that "only the combination of first-person narration and parodic exaggeration provides the double, two-eyed vision that is lacking in all the characters except Bloom" (129). Missing in this claim for "two-eyed vision" is the way in which the copybook scenes and the text itself work in terms of the relationship between the separate visions (or voices) rather than the ways in which the voices can be brought together. The passage in question, and much of the "Cyclops" copybook, illustrates very well M. M. Bakhtin's claim that novelistic language "is a *system* of languages that mutually and ideologically interanimate each other" (47). The bits of dialogue come from at least two recognizable positions, those of B —— /Bloom and of the other Dubliners in the pub, and they contrast with the position represented by the passages of gigantism, identifiable in general terms within their own intertextual networks (the Butcher-and-Lang *Odyssey,* newspaper sports reporting, etc.) but not more specifically. Within these networks the words that are used in the gigantism passages (like everything in "Oxen of the Sun") support Bakhtin's claim that words in a novel "have 'conditions attached to them,'" that each language system represents "a working hypothesis for comprehending and expressing reality" (65, 61). Thus, whereas it is possible to see the copybook as revealing the different parts of "Cyclops" developing in the order in which Joyce refined them (*"Ulysses" in Progress* argued that the gigantism passages came first, then the dialogue, and finally the "I" narrator [124]), it is also possible to see it as a Bakhtinian site in which the systems of language are privileged. Only after these systems develop do names get attached to them and delimit them in terms of specific speakers and styles. Reading the *avant-texte* into the text allows the Bakhtinian nature of the dialogue, and the dialogism, of "Cyclops" to stand out from the details (names, etc.) that gained prominence in the episode after the copybook.

The copybook with its fragmentary dialogue and unattributed speakers is Bakhtinian in yet another way. For Bakhtin "there is no unitary language or style in the novel. But at the same time there does exist a center of language (a verbal-ideological center) for the novel. The author (as creator of the novelistic whole) cannot be found at any one of the novel's language levels: he is to be found at the center of organization where all levels intersect" (48–49). Bakhtin's formulation is opposed to John Eglinton's statement in the "Scylla and Charybdis" episode that Shakespeare "is all in all" (*U* 9:1018–19); the author for Bakhtin is not incarnated in all or any of the characters. Nor should the author be configured, New Critical style, as either Wayne Booth's "implied author" (71 and elsewhere), posited between the historical writer and the fictional narrator, or as David Hayman's "arranger" (84 and elsewhere), located between the implied author and the narrator. Bakhtin collapses the author-implied author and author-arranger distinctions, but at the same time he avoids the assumptions of a unified authorial consciousness that underpin Booth's and Hayman's formulations. Bakhtin's author-as-organizational-center is a meetingplace, a network hub ("Hello There, Central!" [*U* 7:1042]), anything but a unified whole. The voices without names and the gigantism passages without specific identifiable sources, and eventually the "Cyclops" episode's "I" narrator, come together in Bakhtin's terms only at the level of the author defined in this way.

The "Cyclops" copybook seems to accept, even to welcome, this formulation of the author and of authorial presence. For example, in the example there is at first a direct transition from the dialogue to the "He sang the Pæan" passage of gigantism. Except for B ——/Bloom's words, all the dialogue is implicated in the demeaning barroom deflation of everything it mentions, whereas the "He sang" passage can do nothing but heroically inflate its subject. The neat, and obvious, dichotomy between these two dialogic systems is disrupted by the addition of a third one, the voice of the "Gara klooklooklook" passage. Also a voice of inflation, but less easily attributable than other gigantism passages to a generic source, the insert upsets the easy dualism that the passage had developed until now. Furthermore, as it exists on the page of the copybook, it visually disrupts any smooth movement. Joyce signaled the insert with a superscript *F* at the end of the "hurley scrap" sentence on page 12r of the copybook, and this refers the reader (including Joyce himself) to the verso of page 11 for the passage (*Archive* 13:106–7). The *F* signaling the "Gara klooklooklook" insertion, as has often been noted, is a very common feature of the documents of the Joycean *avant-texte*, and it helps to create another impression of textual instability, this time a visual one. In the Rosenbach MS of "Cyclops" (more so in the middle thirty folios than in the first or last fifteen) and the typescript, and throughout the placards and page proofs, the document usually assumes the form of basic text plus extensive augmentation, with Joyce's ubiquitous *F*s and his other letters (*H, M, S, T,* etc.) indicating an addition somewhere on the same page or a nearby one.

During the work in progress Joyce thought of his texts as fluid and in motion; as he wrote to Frank Budgen when he sent him a manuscript version of the "Penelope" episode, "This is only the *draft* a great deal will be added or changed on 3 proofs" (*Letters* 1:171). *Finnegans Wake*, in a section describing ALP's letter, notes "all those red raddled obeli cayennepeppercast over the text . . . flinging phrases here, there, or returns inhibited, with some half-halted suggestion, Ł, dragging its shoestring" (120.14–15, 121.6–8). Startling in their own right, these flung phrases can be seen not as insertions to be incorporated into the next transcription (typescript, proof, or published book) but, rather, as part of a multidirectional text moving out along innumerable lines from a physically centered but sometimes verbally dwarfed text. (There are proof pages on which the handwritten revisions overwhelm the printed text.) While he was writing the "Ithaca" and "Penelope" episodes, at the same time as he was correcting and adding to the proofs for earlier parts of *Ulysses*, Joyce compared himself to "the man who used to play several instruments with different parts of his body" (*Letters* 1:179), and the *avant-texte* documents have the appearance of a textual body with appendages jutting out in many different directions. In a way only an electronic medium such as hypertext can begin to match Joyce's presentation; traditional print media, with the possible exception of Gabler's synoptic text, can offer only pale, dull substitutes.[7]

A second passage that can be looked at anew is the copybook draft's opening scene. As *"Ulysses" in Progress* observed, the draft begins not with the "I" narrator, dialogue, or interior monologue but, instead, with a gigantism passage (124, 130–31). I assessed the opening there as revealing "an easy mock-heroic attitude toward the events to follow" (130) and noted the technical advance that Joyce accomplished after he developed the "I" narrator. The copybook opening can, however, be analyzed in other ways. The opening is in two parts:

> In ^⟨green Erin of the west⟩ Inisfail the fair^ there lies a land, the land of holy Michan. There rises a watchtower beheld from afar. There sleep the dead as they ^⟨slept in life⟩ in life slept^, warriors and princes of high renown. There wave the lofty trees of sycamore; the eucalyptus, giver of good shade, is not absent: and in their shadow sit the maidens of that land, the daughters of princes. They ^sing and^ sport with silvery fishes, caught in silken nets; their fair white fingers toss the gems of the ^fishful^ sea, ruby and purple of Tyre. And men come from afar, heroes, the sons of kings, to woo them for they are beautiful and all of noble stem.
>
> ⟩⟨O'Bloom went ^⟨by⟩ on^⟩ Who comes⟨ through Inn's quay ward, the parish of saint Michan. ⟩^⟨He moved⟩^ [^the son of Rudolph^] It is O'Bloom, the son of Rudolph ⟨the son of Leopold Peter, son of Peter Rudolph⟩ he of the ⟨⟨intrepid heart⟩ heart impervious to all fear⟩ ^moving,^⟨ a noble hero, eastward towards Pill Lane, among the squatted ^stench of^ fishgills, and by the gutboards where lay heaps of red and purple fishguts ^of gurnard, pollock, plaice and halibut^ He went by the city market, [O'Bloom ^a man^ of the intrepid heart.] ⟩Gurnard & plaice those are. Speckled backs. One after another hook in their gills. Can't be hunger drives them. Probably curiosity. Curiosity killed the fish⟨
>
> There rises a shining palace with crystal glittering roof, beheld from afar by mariners who traverse the sea in barks: and thither come the herds, the firstfruits and the offerings of that land for O'Connell Fitzsimon takes toll of them there, a chieftain descended from chieftains. Thither the wains bring foison of fruits and vegetables in their seasons, golden potatoes and seagreen kale and onions, pearls of the earth, and lustrous apples and strawberries fit for princes and raspberries from their canes. And thither wend ^herds innumerable^ ^⟨the heavyuddered⟩ ⟩heavytreading⟩^

heavyhooved⟨ kine, from pastures of Lusk and ^from Carrick-mines^ ⟩streamy vales⟨ Ossory and Coosbaragh, their udders swollen with abundance of milk and butter and rich cheese and eggs, ^various in size,^ the agate ^⟨and⟩ with^ the dun.⁸

And on the dexter hand in solemn array are set forth the accoutrements of noble heroes: there hangs the breastplate of Brian, by whose might the Vikings were brought to nought: there, the helm of Oscar, son of Finn: there the bardic cloak of Ossian, the sightless seer, wanderer to many shores.

Bloom went by Mary's Lane and saw the sordid row of old clothes' shops, the old hucksterwomen seated by [the] baskets of battered hats, amid the dangling legs of ^⟨?⟩ legless^ trousers, ^⟨culprits limp⟩ limp^ coats [hung by the neck.] [manless]

Like culprits. Be taken to the prison from whence you came and there be hanged by the neck till you are ^⟨bought⟩ sold^ and may the Lord. ^Emmet. Martyrs they want to be. My life for Ireland. Romance. Girl in a window watching. Wipe away a tear. ?Hung up for scarecrows. Quite the ?contrary effect. Of course— where was it battle of Fontenoy they charged. Remember Limerick.^ Hard times those were in Holles street when Molly tried that game. Nothing in it: blind ?rut. Chiefly women, of course. Devils to please. Come back tomorrow Ta, ta.⁹

Three different voices coexist in Bakhtinian dialogue here: the narrator of the gigantism passages, the narrator accompanying Bloom's interior-monologue passages ("Bloom went by Mary's Lane and saw the sordid row of old clothes' shops"), and Bloom's interior-monologue voice. In *"Ulysses" in Progress* I talked about this section of the "Cyclops" copybook, with its few examples of Bloom's monologue that soon disappeared, as "the precise chronological point at which [Joyce] stopped writing one kind of book, basically concerned with Stephen and Bloom, and began to write another, in which a succession of parody styles, and eventually a group of schematic correspondences, began to take over" (126). I emphasized the relative obviousness and awkwardness of the gigantism passages as a sign of Joyce's uncertainty as he made the transition, but the passages can be seen in other ways as well. The copybook's second scene introduces the "I" narrator—"Little Alf Bergan popped in and hid behind Barney's snug, squeezed up laughing. ^I didn't know what was up.^"[10]—and the characters' dialogue, so the first three copybook pages contain at least five systems of dialogic voices, without distinguishing among the different speakers in the pub or the different gigantism narrators. This group of voices represents as complex a situation as Joyce had created up to this point in *Ulysses,* and even though most readers would probably not want to sacrifice the increased subtlety of the three systems that he retained—"I" narrator, gigantism narrators, spoken dialogue—the subtlety does come at the expense of the elaborate network that Joyce briefly worked with in the first pages of the "Cyclops" copybook.

If the athletics passage is dominated by animal imagery, here there is slaughter of various kinds, from the fish and meat in the market to the old clothes that, hung as they are in windows, remind Bloom of hanged men. The sequence of paragraphs in the second passage—gigantism-narrator's description of the heroes' objects; Bloom-narrator's description of presumably the same objects, now "brought to nought" like the Vikings; Bloom's thoughts inspired by the clothes—offers three takes on the same scene. Like much of the copybook, this passage presents the gigantism version first as the "ground," then offers a "translation" (here into the Bloom-narrator) before presenting the more obviously subjective account in Bloom's mind. Later, after Joyce developed the "I" narrator, that narrator's version tends to appear first, so that the gigantism passages appear as "translations" of the narrator's account. *Translations* needs to be kept in quotation marks; these passages are excellent examples of Bakhtin's argument that a novel is "a dialogue between points of view, each with its own concrete language that cannot be translated into the other" (76). The opening copybook paragraphs contain no realistic ground against which other elements might be measured, and in this way they resemble the kind of radical disruption introduced by the opening fragments of the "Sirens" episode and later in the *avant-texte* by the first newspaper head in the "Aeolus" episode. (Joyce added the newspaper heads to "Aeolus" on the first proofs for that episode two years after the "Cyclops" copybook.)

Many of the details from the first paragraphs of the "Cyclops" copybook remain in the text, but they appear in altered, sometimes greatly altered, contexts. The gigantism passages of the first and third paragraphs remain relatively intact (*U* 12:68–117), but they are delayed to follow the introduction of the "I" narrator and Joe Hynes and then the Moses Herzog contract (which, rather than one of the "heroic" translations of mundane action, becomes the first passage of gigantism). The two paragraphs are split into three (fish, fruits and vegetables, meat and dairy products), and all are expanded. The first paragraph, with its "fishful streams," "lofty trees," and "lovely maidens," acquires some of the details about fish from the abandoned paragraph describing Bloom's walk through the market, and it also, in subsequent revisions, gains adjectives ("wafty sycamore," "eugenic eucalyptus"), items for lists ("the gibbed haddock, the grilse, the dab, the brill," "creels of fingerlings"), and long, encyclopedic passages, as the "heroes" eventually come "from Eblana to Slievemargy, the peerless princes of unfettered Munster and of Connacht the just and of smooth sleek Leinster and of Cruachan's land and of Armagh the splendid and of the noble district of Boyle." Also, by the time of the Rosenbach Manuscript the paragraph has acquired its tendency to self-destruct, as the "maidens" who are now "lovely," sit by "lovely trees," sing "lovely songs," and play with "lovely objects," all of which are introduced in a list that begins "as for example." The fruits and vegetables passage, smoothly written out in the "Cyclops" copybook, remains remarkably intact throughout the *avant-texte* and into the text, with the predictable exception of additions to the lists of examples at all stages of the manuscript, typescript, and proofs. Third, the paragraph of meat and dairy products, separated from the description of fruits and divided from it by the cry of Moses Herzog—"*I dare him*, says he, *and I doubledare him*"—gains many new details in its lists of examples.

The Bloom passages, with their inchoate interior monologues, differ the most from later documents in the *avant-texte* and from the text. Bloom's walk toward Pill Lane, partially retained in the text in a gigantism passage, is first mentioned by the "I" narrator, who says that "I saw him . . . sloping around by Pill lane and Greek street with his cod's eye counting up all the guts of the fish" (*U* 12:213–17; "and Greek street" is an addition). The walk by the clothes shops disappears as a separate unit, but the "noble heroes" Oscar, Finn, and Ossian are all part of the list of "the twelve tribes of Iar" enumerated in a gigantism passage (*U* 12:1127–29). The references to Fontenoy and Limerick become part of a patriotic remark uttered by John Wyse Nolan, while Bloom tries unsuccessfully to join the conversation (*U* 12:1380–82). Bloom's monologue thoughts about Robert Emmet and martyrs, here inspired by the appearance of the clothes, relate to and seem to be a continuation of his sight of Emmet's last words in a window at the end of "Sirens," the previous episode, and his thought, "Martyrs they want to be," is similar to his reactions to the Ormond bar scene during Ben Dollard's singing of "The Croppy Boy."

Has part of the text of "Sirens" wandered into the opening pages of the "Cyclops" copybook? Gabler talks about Joyce's use of "pre-text from within the *oeuvre*," by which he means that the intertextual network connects to a bit of text not from another author but, rather, from Joyce himself, even from *Ulysses* itself; Gabler thus talks of "the *oeuvre*'s intratextuality" ("Joyce's Text" 219). This process is most evident in "Circe," in which the text regularly seems to be quoting itself. In *"Ulysses" in Progress* I said that *"Ulysses* itself becomes one great 'character': like strands of thought in Bloom's and Stephen's minds, any themes or correspondences in *Ulysses* become usable sources of new juxtapositions or cross-references" (55), but it isn't necessary to anthropomorphize the text in this way. For Gabler, for instance, the text of *Ulysses* becomes "increasingly capable of oscillating between text and pre-text functions" ("Joyce's Text" 228). The "Emmet" passage shows this beginning to happen. If it somehow wandered from "Sirens" into "Cyclops," it eventually found its way back to "Sirens," since various parts of the "Emmet" sentence here became a typescript addition to that episode: "To wipe away a tear for martyrs that want to, dying to, die" (*U* 11:1101–2).[11] The most elaborate reuse of material involves the sentence "Hard times those were in Holles street when Molly tried that game." Molly's attempt to sell old clothes in Holles street after the "hard times" when Bloom lost his job at Wisdom Helys was already mentioned in "Sirens," when Ben Dollard talked about borrowing clothes and Simon Dedalus quipped that "Mrs Marion Bloom has left off clothes of all descriptions" (*U* 11:496–97), and *Ulysses* goes on to include in the Holles Street scene not only the selling of old clothes but also the selling of Molly's hair combings, Bloom's suggestion that she pose for nude photographs, and his washing and (in a "Circe" passage) wearing of Molly's underwear (*U* 15:2986–88; see also *U* 13:840–41; *U* 16:716–17; *U* 18:560–62). Given the extensive connections regarding both the martyrs and the clothes to other parts of *Ulysses*, it is possible that, like the Emmet passage, this one may not be part of "Cyclops" at all; it may be just visiting or have wandered in. Once it joins the copybook context, though, it takes on the atmosphere of male nastiness, bigotry, and violence that pervades so much else of the copybook and of "Cyclops."

Does it matter whether this passage was ever intended for "Cyclops?" For certain genetic histories of *Ulysses,* surely it does; it is important to document and understand the genesis of the book to the extent that documentation and understanding are possible. But Louis Hay cautions that "even the most detailed and well-conserved documentation reveals but a fraction of the complicated mental processes to which it bears witness. The ink on the page is not the writing itself" (68–69). If this is always the case, Joyce is a particularly acute reminder of it. Much of his creative efforts were not written down; he seems to have turned to paper only when the "writing" had advanced to a certain stage. Regarding "Sirens," he told Harriet Shaw Weaver that "the elements needed will only fuse after a prolonged existence together" (*Letters* 1:128), and this fusion presumably happened in his head. Gabler notes "the importance which the pre-writing processes had for Joyce's writing" and calls the written documents Joyce's "secondary *loci* of writing" ("Joyce's Text" 224).

It is tempting to see this process as a further way that Joyce found to confound his critics and guarantee immortality ("I've put in so many enigmas and puzzles that it will keep the professors busy for centuries arguing over what I meant, and that's the only way of insuring one's immortality" [qtd. in Ellmann 521]), but it also ensures that the origin of the text—whether it be the original idea for *Ulysses* as a whole or for "Cyclops" or the author's interpretation of the relationship between the *Odyssey* and *Ulysses*—remains private, inaccessible to the most scrupulous and diligent genetic critic. This inevitable gap—Hay discusses "the moment of the writing itself" as "stretched out between the author's life and the sheet of paper like a drumskin on which the pen beats its message" (73)—can throw us back to conceptions of the author as the genius at the heart of the mystery, but it can also lead to a willingness to live with and enjoy wandering through the evidence that does survive, looking not at Joyce the genius but at Joyce the author, who functions at the Bakhtinian center of various systems of discourse in dialogue with one another, the author as "the man who used to play several instruments with different parts of his body."

The drafts can, finally, open up at least one other kind of possibility. Gabler refers to "the interdependence of text and pre-text" and to "the ultimate circularity of their relationship" ("Joyce's Text" 229). If it is possible to read the *avant-texte* into the text of *Ulysses* as well as reading the text back into the *avant-texte,* then another "text" is created that is neither *Ulysses* itself nor any of its earlier documents. Hay suggests that "perhaps we should consider the text as *a necessary possibility,* as one manifestation of a process which is always virtually present in the background, a kind of third dimension of the written work" (75).[12] With its nascent Bloomian monologue, its gigantism opening, and its inter-changeable characters, "Cyclops" is an ideal test case of this claim for a "third dimension" that an awareness of the *avant-texte* can provide. Most startlingly, the presence in two of the copybook's scenes of Ste-phen Dedalus and other characters from "Aeolus" (Prof. MacHugh and O'Madden Burke; plus Lenehan, J. J. O'Molloy, and Ned Lambert, who remain in the text of "Cyclops"), not to mention the attribution to Ste-phen of the words "when he is quite sure which country it is" in answer to the question of why a Jew can't love his country,[13] opens up the possibility of the reader oscillating between recalling Stephen in the deep background of the episode and accepting his absence from the text of *Ulysses* between the "Wandering Rocks" and "Oxen of the Sun" episodes. Instead of revealing "false starts and uncertainties" or "un-clear" plans (*UP* 135, 137), the copybook and the other documents from the *avant-texte* can reveal alternate states, ones that became superseded but ones that, once encountered, are never entirely canceled. The text's network thus extends not only out in many directions in space but also back in time to encompass the rich alternatives offered in the *avant-texte* (and occasionally, but particularly in Joyce's case, in the *après-texte*).

So, I find that the facts of *"Ulysses" in Progress* can tell more than one story. The Talking Heads song goes on to say, "Facts are written all over your face / Facts continue to change their shape." Further shape changes will surely come; as David Byrne sings in the last line of "Crosseyed and Painless," "I'm still waiting. . . ."

NOTES

1. The concept of intertextuality, developed by Julia Kristeva in her read-ing of Bakhtin, is summarized concisely by Roland Barthes in "Theory of the Text" (39). I wish to thank Daniel Ferrer of the Institut des Textes et Manuscrits Modernes of the Centre National de la Recherche Scientifique for his valuable advice and suggestions regarding this essay.

2. Scholars working on and editing manuscripts of other authors have also argued that the relationship between early drafts and published work need not be one of preliminary to final state of a work. See, for example, Brenda Silver's essay "Textual Criticism as Feminist Practice" (esp. 204ff.).

3. *UP* (120–21) provides a tabular account of the "Cyclops" documents. See also Robert Scholes, *The Cornell Joyce Collection*; Peter Spielberg, *James Joyce's Manuscripts and Letters at the University of Buffalo*; Phillip F. Herring, ed., *Joyce's "Ulysses" Notesheets in the British Museum* and *Joyce's Notes and Early Drafts for "Ulysses": Selections from the Buffalo Collection*; *Ulysses: A Facsimile of the Manuscript* (the Rosenbach MS); the drafts, typescripts, and proofs for the episode in the *James Joyce Archive*; and the early "Cyclops" versions in the *Little Review*.

4. *UP* 115–65, esp. 139, 151–52; Herring, *Joyce's Notes* 124–49, esp. 128, 149; Gabler, "Joyce's Text" 230.

5. Buffalo MS V.A.8, 1r, 20r; *Archive* 13:85, 121; Herring, *Joyce's Notes* 152, 166. To indicate Joyce's revisions I have retained some of the symbols that Hans Walter Gabler used for the synoptic text in *Ulysses: A Critical and Synoptic Edition*. A pair of carets (^/^) indicates the first revisions to a passage. Second and third layers of revision are indicated by rotated carets (second = ⟩/⟨; third = ⟨/⟩). Text that Joyce deleted and replaced with other text is indicated by pointed brackets (⟨/⟩); text that Joyce deleted without a replacement is indicated by square brackets ([/]).

6. Buffalo MS V.A.8, 11r, 11v, 12r; *Archive* 13:105–7; *UP* 126–28; Herring, *Joyce's Notes* 161–62.

7. The synoptic text in Gabler's *Ulysses: A Critical and Synoptic Edition* can up to a point provide a schematic account of the genesis of the text and hence of the *avant-texte*. But the synoptic text is primarily a display indicating how Gabler constructed his edition's copytext, the continuous manuscript text; it is not a presentation of the genesis of *Ulysses* (although it overlaps with the genesis in many ways). See also Michael Groden, "Afterword" to *Ulysses*.

8. Buffalo MS V.A.8, 1r, 2r; *Archive* 13:85, 87; *UP* 125, 130–31; Herring, *Joyce's Notes* 152–53.

9. Buffalo MS V.A.8, 1v, 2r; *Archive* 13:86–87; *UP* 125; Herring, *Joyce's Notes* 153–54.

10. Buffalo MS V.A.8, 2r; *Archive* 13:87; Herring, *Joyce's Notes* 154.

11. See *Ulysses: A Critical and Synoptic Edition*, 1:616.

12. In discussing three different versions of Marianne Moore's "Poetry," Jerome McGann notes that we probably still "read" the longer thirty-line version when we see in front of us the three-line version that she published in *Complete Poems*, and he calls this process a "close encounter of a third kind" (87).

13. Buffalo MS V.A.8, 22r; Buffalo MS V.A.6, fol. 2r; *Archive* 13:125, 134c; *UP* 133–34, 135–37; Herring, *Joyce's Notes* 170, 181.

WORKS CITED

Bakhtin, M. M. "From the Prehistory of Novelistic Discourse." Ca. 1940. Trans. Caryl Emerson and Michael Holquist. In *The Dialogic Imagination: Four Essays*. Ed. Michael Holquist. Austin and London: U of Texas P, 1981.

Barthes, Roland. "From Work to Text." 1971. Trans. Richard Howard. *The Rustle of Language*. New York: Hill and Wang, 1986.

————. "Theory of the Text." 1973. Trans. Ian McLeod. In *Untying the Text: A Post-Structuralist Reader.* Ed. Robert Young. Boston, London, and Henley: Routledge and Kegan Paul, 1981.

Booth, Wayne C. *The Rhetoric of Fiction.* 1961. 2nd ed. Chicago: U of Chicago P, 1983.

Cerquiglini, Bernard. "Variantes d'auteur et variance de copiste." In *La Naissance du texte.* Ed. Louis Hay. Paris: José Corti, 1989.

Ellmann, Richard. *James Joyce.* New York: Oxford UP, 1959. Rev. ed., 1982.

Gabler, Hans Walter. "Joyce's Text in Progress." In *The Cambridge Companion to James Joyce.* Ed. Derek Attridge. Cambridge: Cambridge UP, 1990.

————. "Textual Criticism." In *The Johns Hopkins Guide to Literary Theory and Criticism.* Ed. Michael Groden and Martin Kreiswirth. Baltimore: Johns Hopkins UP, 1994.

Groden, Michael. "Afterword" to *Ulysses.* Ed. Hans Walter Gabler with Wolfhard Steppe and Claus Melchior. 1984, 1986. Reprint London: The Bodley Head, 1993.

————. *"Ulysses" in Progress (UP).* Princeton: Princeton UP, 1977.

————, ed. *The James Joyce Archive (Archive).* 63 vols. New York: Garland, 1977–79. Esp. vols. 12, 13, 19, and 25.

Hay, Louis. "Does 'Text' Exist?" 1985. Trans. Matthew Jocelyn, with Hans Walter Gabler. *Studies in Bibliography* 41 (1988):64–76.

Hayman, David. *"Ulysses": The Mechanics of Meaning.* 1970. 2nd ed. Madison: U of Wisconsin P, 1982.

Herring, Phillip F., ed. *Joyce's Notes and Early Drafts for "Ulysses": Selections from the Buffalo Collection.* Charlottesville: UP of Virginia, 1977.

————, ed. *Joyce's "Ulysses" Notesheets in the British Museum.* Charlottesville: UP of Virginia, 1972.

Joyce, James. *Dubliners.* 1916. Ed. Robert Scholes. New York: Viking, 1968, reprinted with corrections, 1969.

————. *Finnegans Wake.* New York: Viking, 1939, reprinted with corrections, 1958.

————. *Letters.* 3 vols. Vol. 1. Ed. Stuart Gilbert. New York: Viking, 1957, reprinted with corrections, 1966.

————. *A Portrait of the Artist as a Young Man.* 1916. Ed. Chester G. Anderson. New York: Viking, 1964.

————. *Ulysses: A Critical and Synoptic Edition (U).* 1922. Ed. Hans Walter Gabler, with Wolfhard Steppe and Claus Melchior. 3 vols. New York and London: Garland, 1984. 2nd impression, 1986.

————. *Ulysses: A Facsimile of the Manuscript.* Ed. Clive Driver. 3 vols. New York: Octagon; and Philadelphia: Philip H. and A. S. W. Rosenbach Foundation, 1975.

Little Review 6:7–10 (November 1919–March 1920).

McGann, Jerome J. *The Beauty of Inflections: Literary Investigations in Historical Method and Theory.* Oxford: Clarendon, 1988.

Scholes, Robert E., comp. *The Cornell Joyce Collection: A Catalogue.* Ithaca: Cornell UP, 1961.

Silver, Brenda R. "Textual Criticism as Feminist Practice: Or, Who's Afraid of Virginia Woolf, Part II." In *Representing Modernist Texts: Editing as Interpretation.* Ed. George Bornstein. Ann Arbor: U of Michigan P, 1991.

Spielberg, Peter, comp. *James Joyce's Manuscripts and Letters at the University of Buffalo: A Catalogue.* Buffalo: U of Buffalo, 1962.

Talking Heads. "Crosseyed and Painless." Lyrics by David Byrne and Brian Eno. *Remain in Light.* Sire Records Co., 1980. Sound recording.

H.D. Prosed: The Future of an Imagist Poet

Robert Spoo

As a scholarly field, modernism is still in its emergent phase, however dominant it may seem to its champions or residual to its detractors. Critical and pedagogical reshapings of the canon together with the release of unpublished and out-of-print materials continue to challenge any consensus about modernism even as these activities guarantee that modernism will return in ever new and diverse forms. It is impossible to predict the future of a literary period that has yet to step forth fully from the archives. Of the known letters of James Joyce, for example, approximately fourteen hundred, or just under half, remain unpublished, and that number will grow in the years to come. Editions of the correspondence of W. B. Yeats, T. S. Eliot, Marianne Moore, Samuel Beckett, and other writers are in preparation. Despite the steady stream of collections of Ezra Pound's letters in the last two decades, a truly representative sampling of his vast epistolary output will be as challenging a project as a complete edition seems an unlikely one.[1] The research of Ronald Bush and Richard Taylor promises to reveal much about the genesis of Pound's *Cantos*, but as of this writing they have yet to conclude their formidable projects.[2]

Of all the modernists-in-progress none has been more dramatically altered by archival revelations than H.D. At the time of her death, in 1961, she was just beginning to emerge from the obscurity that had enveloped her and her work from the 1930s on. Between 1956 and 1961, with the help of her friend and literary advisor Norman Holmes Pearson, she published her memoir *Tribute to Freud*, her autobiographical novel *Bid Me To Live*, the long poem *Helen in Egypt*, and her *Selected Poems*. Since that time many of her earlier works have been reissued by publishers such as New Directions and Black Swan Books. Even more striking is the list of her works published for the first time between the early 1970s and the present: the poems in *Hermetic Definition;* a memoir of Ezra Pound, *End to Torment;* an account of her childhood, *The Gift;* the autobiographical novels composed in the 1920s, *Paint It Today, HERmione* (or *HER*), and *Asphodel;* the essays *Notes on Thought and Vision* and *H.D. by Delia Alton;* the unpublished and uncollected poems printed in *Collected Poems, 1912–1944.*[3] This list could easily be extended, and editions of other unpublished writings are in preparation.

H.D.'s posthumous career is nothing short of astonishing, rivaling in quantity and quality the works she published during her lifetime. If the publication of her long poems *Helen in Egypt* and *Trilogy* forced a late revision of "H.D. Imagiste"—the poet of brief lyrics of Hellenic clarity—then the recent spate of memoirs and autobiographical novels has given us a wholly different H.D., a writer of prose works that are, in Susan Stanford Friedman's description, "gendered more directly than her lyric poetry, linguistically more experimental in its excesses . . . a difference that necessarily makes a difference in our reading practices."[4] In this essay I explore the implications of this new H.D. and give some sense of the range and quality of her prose. So rapidly have these works appeared, so avidly have they been assimilated to the polemical concerns of academic criticism—notably, revisionary feminism—that we stand in need of calm, cool assessment of our new riches. As the editor of one of H.D.'s recently released novels, *Asphodel,* I am alarmed by the lack of rigor with which some of these texts have been prepared for publication. H.D.'s particularly subtle *écriture féminine* can only benefit from careful philological work, and the future of H.D. and of her place in literary modernism may depend on the credibility of these and forthcoming editions.

The H.D. Papers at Yale University's Beinecke Library were acquired by Norman Holmes Pearson over the course of a long friendship with H.D., during which he encouraged her to send him manuscripts, including those he had urged her to write or revise, for safekeeping at Yale. At the time of her death this archive contained a veritable treasure of unpublished materials. A rough tally of the prose writings alone yields the following: nine novels, a double handful of short stories, and close to a dozen memoirs, journals, and extended essays (genres that tend to blur together in the case of H.D.). It is no exaggeration to say that until recently only a fraction of H.D.'s literary output has been known to the general reading public, and as of this writing six novels, to say nothing of the other genres, remain unpublished ("Pilate's Wife," "Majic Ring," "The Sword Went Out to Sea," "White Rose and the Red," "The Mystery," and "Magic Mirror"). Some of these manuscripts may never find a publisher, and perhaps they should not, at least not until her published fiction has established itself more firmly and generated a stable context for the reception of new work.[5] H.D.'s careful preservation of unpublished materials puts one in mind of Emily Dickinson's meticulously packeted hymnody of the attic, her unmailed letters to the world.

An unusual feature of recent H.D. criticism has been its willingness to treat her published and unpublished writings as if they enjoyed the same sociohistorical status. At least as early as Friedman's *Psyche Reborn: The Emergence of H.D.* (1981), works known to only a few archive-going scholars, such as *HER, Asphodel,* and *Paint It Today,* were receiving sustained exegesis as integral parts of H.D.'s oeuvre.[6] Frequently critics would forgo the quotation marks customarily placed around an unpublished work's title to indicate its merely potential status and use italics, as if the text were available in libraries and bookstores. Quite apart from questions of sociohistorical text production that these critics left largely unaddressed, what came into being was a set of phantom texts whose virtual reality was inseparable from the critical discourse they inhabited, for there was no way, short of visiting the Beinecke Library, to measure the accuracy of a critic's claims or to assess the true nature of the work under discussion. We were and are indebted, of course, to those who have provided snapshots of H.D.'s unpublished writings in the form of exegesis and summary, but these glimpses make it all the more imperative that we have the texts themselves, both for their intrinsic value and for the role they must play in testing and modifying the reader response they have evoked. Once published, these works take on an unprecedentedly metacritical function, for they are in a position to explicate the explicators as well as to explain themselves. But until that point we have no choice but to say, without any paradox of ontology or epistemology, that there is no text in this class; there is only an interpretive community.

The anomaly of these two faces of H.D.—the living author who participated in the shaping of her canon and the posthumous figure whose oeuvre has grown under the aegis of the academy—has led Lawrence S. Rainey to challenge this new H.D., whom he regards as little more than a species of author function "created largely in the 1980s

. . . constructed through different legal, textual, and ideological conventions, fashioned through a canon of works unlike any that prevailed in the lifetime of the earlier H.D., and forged with the assistance of an apparatus of support literature issued by biographers and scholars offering new evaluations of her work."[7] In his provocative essay "Canon, Gender, and Text: The Case of H.D." Rainey finds a contradiction between the historical H.D., who led a privileged life with her wealthy companion, Bryher (Annie Winifred Ellerman), and enjoyed the benefits of "coterie publishing," and the H.D. of the academy, who has become "the canonical figure for a poetics of political correctness," a rallying point for feminist engagements with marginality and subversiveness (116). Rainey never explains why an author who lived in material comfort should be unable to question the status quo (especially in matters of gender, sexuality, and personal identity) any more than he tackles the case of an author like Ezra Pound, whose modest means did little to temper an authoritarian politics.

Yet Rainey is right to point out that scholars have largely ignored the "specific sociohistorical matrix" in which H.D. wrote and published and, likewise, have taken for granted the new, posthumous context in which her works are produced, disseminated, and studied—though H.D. scholars are surely not the sole offenders, in this regard, among modernist critics. From these premises Rainey draws two conclusions that pervade his essay: first, that H.D.'s reluctance to submit certain of her works, notably her experimental prose writings, to the rigors of the ordinary literary marketplace stemmed from her affluent circumstances and the narcotic satisfactions conferred by an admiring coterie; and, second, that an ideologically driven academy has celebrated what it takes to be H.D.'s message—an antipatriarchal politics encoded within an avant-garde poetics—and, as a result of such content-based preoccupations, has blinded itself to formal aesthetic criteria, the real, transhistorical stuff of literary art.

Rainey's undisguised distaste for much of H.D.'s poetry and prose, for her "limited perceptions and impoverished resources of diction" (118), is conveyed with elegant authoritativeness, yet it should be evident that he deals in well-turned non sequiturs, that the aesthetic poverty he alleges does not necessarily follow from either of the sociohistorical matrices he cites: the coterie mode of production during H.D.'s lifetime or the more recent academic mode of production. He offers little in the way of proof when he does come down to cases, confining his discussion mainly to H.D.'s poem "Leda," a work little known until recent years that he proceeds to break on the rack by comparing it line by line with Yeats's "Leda and the Swan." Also, by selectively quoting from her long poetic sequence *Trilogy*, he gives the impression that H.D.'s major effort of World War II reduces to a self-indulgent blend of astrology and pop occultism, an orgy of naive asseverations and pretty bromides. Disappointingly, Rainey does not offer comparably detailed analyses of her prose fictions and memoirs—conspicuous products of the recent H.D. boom and presumably the chief culprits in his view— and leaves us with a sense that what was to be demonstrated has been quietly evaded.

Rainey's general point about recent interpretations of H.D.'s "Leda"—that critics have ignored the history of representations of Leda's rape and consequently overstate the subversive potential of H.D.'s poem—is well taken and should be borne in mind whenever we feel tempted to make sweeping claims about an author's revisionary art. But the problem with Rainey's reading is one that typifies his entire essay: he elevates a single poem in H.D.'s corpus to representative status and offers this partial truth about the author as the whole truth about her. He also commits the fallacy of reading a reductive version of feminist criticism back into H.D.'s art and then hastens to define the latter in terms of the former, as if the two inhabited the same ontological order and historical moment. In this he reenacts the occasionally malign strategy of critics of modernism who substitute a simplified notion of New Critical formalism for the irreducibly complex poetics of writers like Yeats, Pound, and Eliot, a strategy with which Rainey probably has little patience.

I have spent so much time with Rainey's essay because it raises timely, sobering questions about the academic construction and reception of H.D. and, by implication, about the future of H.D. studies. Perhaps his most challenging suggestion is that the posthumous publication of works that H.D. herself did not try to publish is an illegitimate venture underwritten by an ideological climate and an academic agenda conveniently unaware of the historical perversion thus perpetrated. The result, according to Rainey, is a "wholesale transformation in the context for the study of her work and career" (102–3). Yet he ignores the profound continuity between the two sociohistorical matrices he himself has isolated, for the last fifteen years of H.D.'s life were marked by her gradual incorporation within the very academy that

Rainey characterizes as an opportunistic latecomer to her cause. In fact, it was his predecessor at Yale, Norman Holmes Pearson, professor of English and American Studies, who cultivated H.D.'s friendship, encouraged her to write and revise, wrote criticism of and forewords to her texts, exposed his students to her work, purchased her literary copyrights, received power of attorney, acted as her literary executor and as an intermediary with publishers, and, most important for her future reputation, collected her manuscripts and worked tirelessly to establish her papers as part of Yale's Collection of American Literature. Pearson was the personal embodiment, if anyone could be, of modernism's transition from one mode of production to another, its passage from coterie publishing, limited deluxe editions, and small readerships to the great Chautauqua of the postwar American university.

As their unpublished letters abundantly attest, H.D. depended heavily on Pearson for encouragement and advice, confessing to him in 1949, "Your spiritual help and understanding of the MSS has meant everything to me."[8] Their detailed exchanges at every stage of the composition of *Helen in Egypt* reveal an intellectual and spiritual entente of signal richness, and Pearson motivated her to complete other writings, including a number of still unpublished personal essays. His practical exertions on her behalf were no less vital to her career. Among other tasks he saw to the publication of *Bid Me To Live* by Grove Press in 1960 and arranged for the publication a year later of *Helen in Egypt*, a copy of which was placed in H.D.'s hands the day before she died. And Pearson's labors did not end with her death. As literary executor and holder of her copyrights, he saw into print *Hermetic Definition* (1972), *Trilogy* (1973), and an expanded version of *Tribute to Freud* (1974), and penned the forewords to these volumes. Writing of H.D.'s memoir *End to Torment*, Michael King notes that Pearson "encouraged H.D. to complete the memoir, gave it a title, and was preparing it for publication when he died in 1975."[9]

Works by H.D. published after Pearson's death, such as *HERmione* (1981) and *The Gift* (1982), also bear traces of his influence, and it could be argued that texts such as *Asphodel* and *Paint It Today*, both published by university presses in 1992, extend the spirit of the H.D.-Pearson collaboration into the present decade. It is undeniable that the modes of modernism's production have changed since H.D. wrote and published, but they have changed in comparable ways for all the modern-

ists, and superficial differences should not obscure the deep con-
tinuities uniting the past and the present, in particular the socio-
economic base provided by a dense nexus of university and commercial
presses, undergraduate and graduate programs, changing canons and
revised syllabi, publishing scholars and paying students. Modernism's
history began in the flats and garrets of London and Paris, but its real
success came when it entered the academy through a complex process
of institutionalization that may also have been its salvation. Far from
being an anomaly, the case of H.D. is a representative chapter of that
history.

Despite H.D.'s failure or reluctance to publish certain works dur-
ing her lifetime—whether out of fear of personal exposure, uncertainty
about the quality of the writing, preference for different versions, or
self-censorship in reaction to a hostile patriarchy[10]—it is equally true
that from the late 1940s on she worked at revising her unpublished
materials and preserving them for the "shelf" Pearson had established
for her at Yale. Even when she directed that a text be "destroyed," as in
the case of *Asphodel*, she usually managed to tuck a copy away for
safekeeping.[11] Her letters attest to a quiet resolve, shared by Bryher and
Pearson, to tidy up and preserve manuscripts for possible future pub-
lication. As late as 1959, two years before her death, H.D. was sorting
through typescripts of her autobiographical novels and writing Bryher,
"I don't want to discard *destructively*—so must pick sections for pos-
sible re-writing." In her reply Bryher urged her to "keep one copy at
least of old manuscripts. Who knows, after Madrigal [*Bid Me To Live*,
published the next year], they will probably want others."[12]

Far from flouting or distorting her intentions, then, recent editors
and publishers might be said to be collaborating with H.D. in this new
phase of her publishing career; the fact that in her final years she
worked with Pearson to bring out several important volumes of prose
and poetry, volumes she might not have published without his help,
suggests that the current scholarly establishment has in a sense as-
sumed the role that Pearson played and continues to honor, as he did,
her implied last will and testament regarding her manuscripts. Again,
the socioeconomic matrices linking the various H.D.s—the coterie au-
thor of private editions, the more extrovert and mainstream author of
Helen in Egypt and *Bid Me To Live*, and the academically sponsored
author of recent decades—are less discontinuous than they might seem

at first glance. All of these H.D.s have their legitimate place in the institution of modernism, and the future of that institution will no doubt see more and different H.D.s.

As of this writing, several editions of her unpublished works are in preparation. Jane Augustine has completed a new edition of *The Gift*, H.D.'s memoir of her Moravian upbringing in Bethlehem, Pennsylvania. H.D. composed this work, with Pearson's encouragement, in London during World War II. German bombs fell on the city as she wrote, and the text interweaves, subtly and movingly, her past with her present, memories of her childhood in a peace-loving religious community with the fiery nightmare of embattled London. In 1982 New Directions published an abridged—some would say mutilated—version of *The Gift*, omitting substantial portions of every chapter as well as the whole of the crucial chapter 2 ("Fortune Teller"). Augustine has restored the text to its uncut form and included H.D.'s hitherto unpublished research notes on the Moravian church. Augustine is also completing an annotated edition of "The Mystery," a densely symbolic novel set in eighteenth-century Prague at an important moment in the history of the Moravian church. Completed in 1951, this work is a curious blend of modernist historiography and occultism. Its oblique narrative is ruptured by sudden shifts of character and incident that capture something of the strangeness and opacity of history itself, the apparent lack of coherence as events are unfolding counterpointed by transcendent meanings that emerge from the chaotic quotidian.[13]

Equally important are the editions-in-preparation of H.D.'s letters. Until recently only a few samples of her large correspondence have been available, mostly in scholarly journals. But recently Robert J. Bertholf has published the surviving correspondence—thirty-five letters—between H.D. and Robert Duncan. Caroline Zilboorg's *Richard Aldington and H.D.: The Early Years in Letters*, with its informative introduction and notes, is valuable even though it contains no letters by H.D. (Aldington apparently destroyed most of her early letters to him.) Zilboorg has now published a second volume covering the later years of this correspondence, in which H.D. is substantially represented.[14] Also in preparation are the letters between H.D. and Bryher during H.D.'s two analyses with Sigmund Freud in the 1930s; edited by Susan Stanford Friedman and to be published by New Directions, this volume will add to our knowledge about these sessions and the importance Freud's theories held for H.D. and her circle. Equally significant is the edition Donna Hollenberg is preparing of the selected letters of H.D. and Norman Holmes Pearson, which will document their friendship and literary collaboration in great detail. A representative sampling of the massive H.D.-Bryher correspondence (apart from the period covered in the Friedman collection) is also badly needed, as is a more probing account of their life together than can be found in existing biographies.

The release of these volumes will strengthen the biographical and philological base of H.D. studies. It will also underscore a transformation that is already at work in the ongoing career of H.D., for in the last decade or so she has emerged as a prose writer of originality and versatility. It is no longer accurate to classify her as a poet who occasionally indulged an aberrant penchant for fiction writing and memoirs, as it was possible to do even as late as 1980. With the publication, in 1992, of *Asphodel* and *Paint It Today* the core of H.D.'s autobiographical novels, which also includes *HER* and *Bid Me To Live*, is at last readily available to scholars and students. These novels tell and retell, with different emphases and large, shifting casts of characters *à clef*, the story of H.D.'s life in Pennsylvania after meeting Ezra Pound, her subsequent romances and friendships in America and Europe (with Frances Gregg, Richard Aldington, Bryher, and others), her experiences in London during World War I, and the birth of her daughter in 1919.

The decade extending roughly from 1908 to 1918 remained for H.D., throughout her life, a haunting, traumatic period of initiation, a time of growing into history and into knowledge of expatriation, creativity, procreativity, and a complex, restless sexuality. H.D. herself referred to these novels as her "Madrigal" cycle and thought of them as a single "novel" or "story" told in different moods and modes that slowly, collectively evolved toward a satisfactory account of her life and loves in those years. She felt that this process came to fruition with her revisions of *Bid Me To Live* (which she wanted to call "Madrigal") in 1949–50: "We began on that vineyard in 1921. . . . But the grapes were sour. We went on. It was a pity to let that field (1914–1918) lie utterly fallow. We returned to it, from time to time. At last, winter 1949, we taste the 1939 gathering. Impossible but true. The War I novel has been fermenting away during War II."[15]

H.D.'s teleological language downplays the variety of forms taken by the earlier "versions" of this novel as well as the fact that each one is a discrete, unified work of art. Friedman has provided the most comprehensive and influential reading of the Madrigal cycle to date, arguing that *Paint It Today, Asphodel,* and *Bid Me To Live* are "distinct layers in a composite 'text' that is structured like a psyche, interpretable through the lens of psychoanalytic concepts such as the censor, the dream-work, transference, and working through."[16] Further, she sees each of the novels as shaped by a different sexual thematics: lesbian love, lesbianism grading into pregnancy and childbirth, and heterosexual love, respectively. Though at one time she considered *HER* to be part of the Madrigal cycle, Friedman now prefers to read it as a related but independent work. Her powerful analysis of these interlocking texts has much to recommend it, but it would be a shame if her boldly schematic theory were taken as definitive rather than as one suggestive way of approaching this cluster of novels.

To read these works, as Friedman does, as a series of "rescriptions" of a painful ur-story is to perceive only one trajectory of their compositional history, and her approach runs the further risk of substituting an abstract Freudian model of H.D.'s text production for local knowledge that can be obtained from more traditional philological research. Although regarded by critics prior to its publication as an early "version" of *Bid Me To Live* (a view shared by H.D. at certain points in her life), *Asphodel* is in fact a carefully wrought and snugly fitting sequel to *HER*. H.D. probably revised and polished *Asphodel* at around the time that she completed *HER*, and in later years she referred to it as "a continuation of HER."[17] Restoring the novels to their original relationship as a sequence not only provides important information about H.D.'s writing and revising practices in the 1920s, but alerts us as well to aesthetic and thematic consistencies we might otherwise miss. *Asphodel* completes the Ezra Pound and Frances Gregg stories begun in *HER* and makes use of the same fictional names for real figures that appear in that novel (George Lowndes for Ezra Pound, Fayne Rabb for Frances Gregg, and so on). Moreover, *Asphodel* richly resumes and consummates *HER*'s undulating, madrigal-like pattern of relationships, its interwoven variations on the beloved.

For all of the critical commentary that has been devoted to H.D., there have been few sustained efforts to describe the aesthetic qualities of her prose texts. The *HER-Asphodel* sequence in particular lends itself to formal analysis. Each novel is divided into two parts that contain smaller narrative divisions resembling ordinary chapters; each chapter is in turn made up of long paragraphs that first fix an image or emotion in the manner of H.D.'s early poems, then proceed to stretch and develop it in a discourse that is private, sometimes cryptic, digressive and recursive, full of wanderings and returns. The emotional or narrative datum that initiates a rippling of consciousness may seem insignificant, like a pebble dropped in a pond, but, as in Henry James and other authors of the interior, the circles emanating concentrically and eccentrically from the event take on an independent value.

Asphodel, with its two parts consisting of fifteen chapters each, is an unusually clear example of H.D.'s love of structural patterns and parallels, of lapidary symmetries that complicate even as they assist the linear thrust of the narrative. H.D. typically and strategically has it both ways: her "borderline" temperament (a favorite concept of hers) was in one sense deeply conservative, for she desired to give up neither the static intensities of her Imagist days nor the kinetic exhilarations of her newfound narrative art. In her novels a passionate architectonics is matched by language that resists boundary and definition; ornately framed motifs (typically having to do with love, death, birth, war, and art) try to contain a feverish narrative voice that exceeds all devices for framing.

This narrative voice, which is almost always a *voice* and not an authorial presence carefully refined out of existence, is itself woven of tensions and contradictions. Often it is garrulous and informal, full of conversational tics and plucky inexactitudes that express the uneven development of the heroine, Hermione Gart (the H.D. figure), and the strain of her arduous *Bildung*: "The thing that Darrington said was not exactly the right thing to say on the verge of George Lowndes' engagement. But that was the nice thing about Darrington. He said the wrong thing in the right voice."[18] At other times a more exalted, ecstatic style and diction take over: "Is Christianity then that? Is Christ the soft mist, the blue smoke of altar incense hiding the beauty of the thing itself? Is Christianity then that, at its best, a curtain, woven of most delicate stuffs to hide reality, the white flame that is Delphi, that is Athens?" (20). Here H.D.'s Symbolist-decadent inheritance and her passion for Greece lend a hieratic breathlessness to the loose American orality of the narrative.

H.D.'s handling of dialogue is unusually skillful in *HER* and *Asphodel*, in which she uses crisp individuation and alert mimicry to exploit a wholly different aesthetic from the labile subjectivity of the narrative passages. Here is George Lowndes (Ezra Pound) trying to explain to Hermione why he tried to seduce her when he was already secretly engaged:

> George had pulled her down beside him where he curled half hidden by the very grand baby-grand. "Listen Dryad darling—" "O George you might—you might have told me—" "Dryad developing a Puritan conscience—" "No. That isn't the argument. It doesn't—seem—right—" "Well, Dryad as I never see my—ah—fiancée save when surrounded by layers of its mother, by its family portraits, by its own inhibitions, by the especial curve of the spiral of the social scale it belongs to, I think you might be affable." (*Asphodel* 96)

Pound's bumptious-bohemian prolixity is nicely caught here, and H.D. is similarly successful with characters such as Jerrold Darrington (Richard Aldington), whose banter in the course of the novel registers his decline from the jaunty sensitivity of a prewar poet to the coarse jingoism of an officer on leave.

Perhaps the least discussed aspect of H.D.'s narrative language is its strange, varied rhythms and its spectral glidings from third-person-limited discourse to first-person memoir to intimate, visceral stream of consciousness. Yet it is here, if anywhere, that H.D.'s claim to a unique feminine language must be staked. In *Asphodel*, for example, when Hermione wanders the cliffs of Cornwall alone in the intervals of time spent with her new lover, Cyril Vane, a tender, contemplative interior monologue reflects her abstracted melancholy: "I am lonely in this paradise. Look at me bird, you hate me. I found you, I got you. I don't care how your parents screech and wheel above me, you are old enough to leave your nest and you fill a hollow of my arms. There is some hollow of my arms you fill. You fill it completely" (151). The pulsing, run-on clauses with their sprinkle of commas suggest a sad, displaced maternal instinct lavished on the young bird she has found, and the language hints, just barely, at her troubled awareness that she is pregnant by Vane ("I found you, I got you").

Hermione has the baby, and when her husband, Jerrold Darrington, returns from the war and in a rage breaks his promise to register the child, Phoebe, as his own, the prose records Hermione's incredulous panic: "Trampled flowers smell sweet. But there is a murderous ox foot, a cloven devil foot. Was it the war simply, that walked forward that would crush with devil horns and great brute devil forehead the tenderest of growths—Phoebe. Phoebe" (198). Here an idiosyncratic, though for H.D. characteristic, use of commas—a needless inclusion here, an omission there—conveys a sense of alarm, a staggering and stumbling, a juggernaut male presence pushing past a mother to clutch at her infant. H.D.'s commas frequently have this kind of emotive-mimetic function, but just as often they pursue their own willful course. Comma phrases are often irregular, inconsistent, begun but not concluded—a series of broken pledges and torn contracts. Yet they rarely fail, however random they may seem, to discriminate some new inflection or deflection in the heroine's consciousness.

H.D.'s commas might be thought of as indicating a voice pause or a mental "breathing," an emotional hiatus rather than a division of syntax. In this they are not unlike Emily Dickinson's dashes—those rhythmic stitches taken in the text's fabric—and H.D. is no less liberal with her dashes and hyphens:

> "Will you look—after—it?" "Look after it? I only want the war to be over, us to get some way on firm ground—I only want your wishes in the matter." This is not what lizard-Hermione wanted. This is not what eel-Hermione, what alligator-Hermione, what seagull Hermione was after. (*Asphodel* 158)

It is at this busy microlevel of her prose—the level of unconsummated commas, disruptive hyphens and dashes, spellings that switch back and forth between American and British styles—that H.D.'s much-discussed female difference is so richly and materially evoked. Late in life she went through some of her earlier published prose writings, meticulously adding (less often deleting) hyphens and commas, and in this, too, she was encouraged by Pearson.[19]

Her molten, mutating accidentals are crucial to her creative project and self-expression, for they choreograph a revisionary dance with syntax, odd rhythms, and pulsations that complement the volatile narrative voice. These phenomena are entirely consistent, moreover, with theories of a maternal semiotic, or presymbolic language, which Julia Kristeva has defined as "enigmatic and feminine, this space underlying the written . . . rhythmic, unfettered, irreducible to its intelligible verbal translation . . . musical, anterior to judgement, but restrained by a sin-

gle guarantee: syntax."[20] H.D.'s playfully errant punctuation drama-
tizes in microcosm themes that the narrative develops on the level of
plot and character: the hyphenated maternal self, both animal and hu-
man (as in the passage quoted above); the Januslike indecisiveness of
the expatriate conscience; the passion play of unintegrated bisexuality.
H.D.'s gender politics of the borderline proceeds from and in turn
generates an aesthetics of oscillant indeterminacy. Ideology in these
texts is ultimately inseparable from the letter's subtle mode of pro-
duction.

Yet recent editions of her prose writings are anything but faithful to
the experimental letter of her texts. Although critics have deplored the
aggressive pruning of *The Gift* by in-house editors at New Directions,
no one has raised questions about the same publisher's less con-
spicuous but still troublesome alterations to *HER* (retitled *HERmione*).
Here an irregular and unstated editorial policy saw fit to correct mis-
spellings (such as *theorum*) in some places but not in others and to
convert British spelling to American in a hit-or-miss fashion. The
swarm of hyphens in H.D.'s original typescript is thinned to an occa-
sional buzzing: curious and striking constructions such as *still-born,
grave-yard, Queen-Anne's lace, wood-path, over-grown,* and *de-flowered dog-
wood* are silently standardized. H.D.'s substantive intentions are also
ignored, as when her archly transparent coinages, "Vanmaur" and
"Point Distant," are converted by an editor's literalizing pen back to
"Bryn Mawr" and "Point Pleasant." Other interventions include dele-
tions of phrases and sentences and several ad lib decisions to begin a
new chapter where H.D. indicated only a line break. These changes do
not drastically affect the spirit of her work, but they point to a certain
disregard for the aesthetic specifications of her text.

New Directions retains, laudably, the enthusiasm of the avant-
garde concern that James Laughlin founded in 1936 to publish works by
Pound, Williams, and other living writers. To some extent their asser-
tive editing of H.D.'s texts reflects the spirit of active collaboration with
authors that prevailed in earlier decades, and New Directions has never
pretended to be a scholarly publisher, despite the fact that classroom
and academic sales now constitute one of its chief markets. University
presses, targeting new audiences generated by women's studies pro-
grams, have also begun to add H.D.'s writings to their lists, but it is not
certain at this point that a higher standard of editing will result. Femi-
nist scholars, who might reasonably be looked to as custodians of

H.D.'s intricate *écriture féminine*, have not uniformly taken pains to develop coherent policies of editing but, instead, have devoted their energies to providing biographical and critical orientations, sometimes to the neglect of the less spectacular rigors of responsible textual editing.

A case in point is the edition of H.D.'s *Paint It Today* published in 1992 by New York University Press in its series "The Cutting Edge: Lesbian Life and Literature." The editor, Cassandra Laity, devotes more than twenty pages of useful introduction to the thesis that this novella, written in 1921, is one of H.D.'s "most overtly homoerotic novels" and pursues this claim with the somewhat contradictory argument that the work's lesbian discourse is "extremely coded," a lyrical transposing of Romantic conventions for the purpose of recording "transgressive desire."[21] In contrast to this sustained exposition, she spends exactly two sentences discussing the challenges of editing H.D.: "The novel is published here exactly as H.D. wrote it. With the exception of typographical and grammatical corrections, and the transformation of British spelling and usage to its American counterpart, the text is presented in its original form" (xxxviii). Tantalizingly vague phrases—"exactly as H.D. wrote it," "in its original form"—jar with confessions of editorial intervention and tell us nothing about the archival status of the text: how many versions exist, whether it is in manuscript or typescript or both, what related documents (such as the portion of *Paint It Today* published some years ago or other published or unpublished texts by H.D.) were enlisted to identify and adjudicate textual error.

Laity's edition does not present *Paint It Today* "exactly as H.D. wrote it." In the space of a single chapter consisting of eight pages in her edition (chap. 6, "Sister of Charmides") she has altered (added or deleted) nearly forty commas, over twenty-five hyphens, and has made changes to capitalization, italics, and other features of H.D.'s typescript. As promised in her brief note on the text, she consistently alters British spelling to American style and regularizes usage (*dreamt* becomes *dreamed* [63])—operations that erase H.D.'s characteristic wavering between British and American forms and thus expunge one textual manifestation of her expatriate sensibility. Substantive changes seem even more meddlesome: H.D.'s archaic *drear* becomes *dreary* (59); the expressive inversion "interdependent one on another" becomes the flat "interdependent on one another" (61). Inattention or eye skip is perhaps responsible for the change from "startled at its beauty" to "startled by its beauty" and "our old selves" to "our selves" (65). Misreading turns "His head" into "His hand" (62) and "full leafed spring trees" into paradoxically "fall-leafed spring trees" (64). Despite the assurance in her textual note that misspellings will be attended to, Laity allows *Mycene* to stand (62) and substitutes her own "Luxumbourg gardens" (59) for H.D.'s "Luxumburg gardens."[22]

Errors of execution aside, Laity is free, of course, to pursue any editorial policy she chooses, but some record of her procedures should be made available to scholars. As long as H.D.'s texts are so blithely changed to conform to prevailing (academic) standards of spelling and usage, at the expense of the teeming textual details on the pages of her typescripts, it will be hard to believe that critics are truly committed to the contradictory play of her feminine discourse, to the "difference" her texts evince at the level of words, variant spellings, commas, and hyphens. In this respect, as in others, H.D. studies lag behind work on other modernist figures, such as Joyce, Pound, Williams, and Woolf. Criticism and theory, however ambitious and illuminating, will not be enough to sustain H.D. through the changing critical fashions of the years to come. We need access to more of her unpublished correspondence and personal essays. Regularly updated bibliographies, sound biographies and source studies, detailed annotations of her densely allusive texts, have yet to be produced, though such apparatus have long existed for other modernists.[23] Lacking a stable philological foundation—which must include informed textual editing—a superstructure consisting entirely of critical and theoretical writing bears too heavy a burden, and the chief casualty will be H.D. herself, whose bid for canonization will be lost in the collapse.[24]

Criticism and theory are important, but they should remain flexible and responsible. The strategy of "decoding" H.D.'s writings, from her early lyrics in *Sea Garden* (1916) to recently published works such as *Paint It Today*, seeks to go beneath aesthetic conventions to locate personal and social realities that concerned H.D. and her friends: lesbian and heterosexual desire, the constraints of gender, the circumstances of the female artist.[25] We should take care, however, that our decoding does not yield the same message over and over again, that these "codes"—which are, after all, the aesthetic forms H.D. chose for her craft—do not become mere husks that we remove and discard in our quest for thematic kernels. Decoding H.D. without cherishing the code itself opens the way for a critical opportunism that might end by depriving her of her painstaking achievement.

Impatient as she sometimes was of "H.D. Imagiste," Hilda Doolittle remained proud of her early career, just as surely as she did not fear to venture beyond the security of a limited fame in pursuit of nonpoetic genres. Recognizing differences among the various interwoven H.D.s that literary history shows us is as important as perceiving difference within her texts. H.D.'s autobiographical novels remind us that things we often take to be fixed or given—love, sexuality, gender, the boundary between poetry and prose—are caught up in creative, often painful negotiations, tautly braided opposites that cannot be disentwined by any ingenious decoding, whether the critic's or the artist's. The nervously oscillating consciousness of *HER* and *Asphodel* strains to inhabit past forms and selves without becoming mired in them, a both/and passion that informs everything from H.D.'s representations of bisexuality to her asides on the predicament of the expatriate artist: "We are here. We are *there*. We will go mad being here and there unless we give up simply, stay here and are lost, stay there and are dead. To be here and there at the same time, that is the triumph" (*Asphodel* 46). Living life on the borderline, expatriated from her native land no less than from any doctrine of the old stable ego, Hermione Gart knows that madness may be the price of refusing fixity. Claire Buck aptly cautions H.D. critics against the "use of the 'I' of the texts as a confirmation and defense of an essential female subject."[26]

We have the good fortune to be able to observe a career in Phoenix-like rebirth, a neglected modernist entering a bright new phase at a rather terrific speed. H.D. the poet is becoming, with equal power and dignity, H.D. the prose writer. This is one meaning of my title. But H.D. is in danger of being "prosed" in another sense. Critics and editors are too ready to thematize her newly published writings in accordance with reigning theoretical categories and ideological tastes and are less prepared to do the work of responsible editing, patient explication, and self-effacing annotation, which, if less glamorous, may be a surer means in the long run of promoting her work and showcasing its beauties. In particular, the *écriture féminine* of her prose memoirs and fictions must be allowed, within the limits of editorial responsibility and publishers' constraints, to be heard in all its otherness—from the largest motifs to the smallest accidentals—and not be made a mere instantiation of our current preoccupations. No longer reduced to quoted snippets held captive within our critical discourse, H.D.'s prose difference must be emancipated from our eager patronage in other ways as well.

NOTES

1. A. Walton Litz is currently addressing himself to this challenge: a new selected letters of Ezra Pound (to be published by New Directions Publishing Corp.), a badly needed update of *The Selected Letters of Ezra Pound: 1907–1941,* ed. D. D. Paige (1950; rpt. New York: New Directions, 1971).

2. Bush, *The Genesis of Ezra Pound's "Cantos"* (Princeton, NJ: Princeton UP, 1976), and Taylor, *Variorum Edition of "Three Cantos" by Ezra Pound: A Prototype* (Bayreuth: Boomerang, 1991), are important contributions to our understanding of Pound's compositional process. Bush is currently studying archival materials relating to the growth of the Pisan Cantos, and Taylor is at work on a complete, computer-generated variorum of published versions of the *Cantos.*

3. A list of H.D.'s works mentioned in this essay, together with relevant dates of composition, is appended at the conclusion.

4. Susan Stanford Friedman, *Penelope's Web: Gender, Modernity, H.D.'s Fiction* (Cambridge: Cambridge UP, 1990) 32.

5. Some of these unpublished novels strike even a sympathetic reader as very long, forbiddingly private, at times diffuse and repetitious. H.D. tried and failed to place two or three of these works with publishers.

6. Susan Stanford Friedman, *Psyche Reborn: The Emergence of H.D.* (Bloomington: Indiana UP, 1981). Other studies that include sustained discussion of unpublished works are Rachel Blau DuPlessis, *H.D.: The Career of That Struggle* (Bloomington: Indiana UP, 1986); and *Signets: Reading H.D.,* ed. Friedman and DuPlessis (Madison: U of Wisconsin P, 1990).

7. Lawrence S. Rainey, "Canon, Gender, and Text: The Case of H.D.," in *Representing Modernist Texts: Editing as Interpretation,* ed. George Bornstein (Ann Arbor: U of Michigan P, 1991) 102. Hereafter cited parenthetically in the text.

8. Letter from H.D. to Norman Holmes Pearson, 8 August 1949; quoted in Friedman, *Penelope's Web,* 371 n. 35.

9. H.D., *End to Torment: A Memoir of Ezra Pound,* ed. Norman Holmes Pearson and Michael King (New York: New Directions, 1979) xi.

10. I give here the chief reasons offered by critics, feminist and nonfeminist, for H.D.'s accumulation of unpublished manuscripts. Each of these factors played a role at some point, and all are attested by H.D.'s correspondence and by other sources.

11. Rainey notes that H.D. scrawled "Destroy" on the sole surviving typescript of *Asphodel,* adding that "it says much about her own opinion of her work, which may have been prompted by shrewd self-assessment" (104). Here he mischievously credits H.D. with an aesthetic taste he denies her elsewhere. It is true that she came to feel that *Asphodel* was a less effective version of *Bid Me To*

Live, but this was due mainly to her delight at completing the latter novel, a work quite different from the earlier *Asphodel*. Rainey also fails to mention that the surviving typescript of *Asphodel* is a carbon copy and that in the last decade of her life, as her correspondence at the Beinecke Library indicates, she tried to round up and destroy extra copies of her manuscripts. Rainey faults H.D. scholars for disregarding philological matters, but an inspection of the archival record housed at his own institution would have enlightened him on this matter. See also Spoo, "H.D.'s Dating of *Asphodel*: A Reassessment," *H.D. Newsletter* 4 (1991): 31–40.

12. From unpublished letters by H.D. to Bryher, 12 October 1959, and by Bryher to H.D., 14 October 1959, in the H.D. Papers at the Beinecke Rare Book and Manuscript Library, Yale University.

13. Portions of "The Mystery" were published in a limited edition prepared by Eric W. White, *Images of H.D. and from "The Mystery"* (London: Enitharmon, 1976). The manuscript materials for "The Mystery" as well as for "The Gift" are at the Beinecke Library, Yale.

14. *A Great Admiration: H.D. / Robert Duncan Correspondence, 1950–1961*, ed. Robert J. Bertholf (Venice, CA: Lapis, 1992); *Richard Aldington and H.D.: The Early Years in Letters*, ed. Caroline Zilboorg (Bloomington: Indiana UP, 1991); *Richard Aldington and H.D.: The Later Years in Letters*, ed. Zilboorg (Manchester: Manchester UP, 1995).

15. H.D., *H.D. by Delia Alton* (*Notes on Recent Writing*), ed. Adalaide Morris, *Iowa Review* 16 (1986): 212.

16. Friedman, *Penelope's Web*, xi.

17. Letter of H.D. to Bryher, 18 April 1949; quoted in H.D., *Asphodel*, ed. Robert Spoo (Durham, NC: Duke University Press, 1992) xiii.

18. *Asphodel*, 100. Hereafter cited parenthetically in the text.

19. A case in point is H.D.'s *Kora and Ka* (Dijon: Darantiere, 1934), two "long-short stories" ("Kora and Ka" and "Mira-Mare") published together in a small volume of just under one hundred pages of text. In the 1950s she carefully marked corrections in two personal copies of the work. By my rough count she added 145 hyphens, deleting none, and inserted 55 commas, removing only 9. On receiving corrected copies of *Kora and Ka* and other works from H.D., Norman Holmes Pearson wrote to her: "The whole matter of corrected copies is a good thing. . . . I am not really thinking of typographical errors, but a feeling for commas, hyphens, the occasional word" (unpublished letter, 19 April 1959). The Pearson letter and the corrected copies of *Kora and Ka* are at the Beinecke Library, Yale. New Directions has reissued *Kora and Ka* in its Bibelot series, with an introduction and note on the text by Robert Spoo. The text is a photo-reproduction of the limited Darantiere edition of 1934. The note on the text lists the substantive changes that H.D. wished to see incorporated.

20. Julia Kristeva, "Revolution in Poetic Language," in *The Kristeva Reader*, ed. Toril Moi (New York: Columbia UP, 1986) 97.

21. H.D., *Paint It Today*, ed. Cassandra Laity (New York: New York UP, 1992) xvii, xxi. Hereafter cited parenthetically in the text.

22. I do not mean to imply that the editorial policy I adopted for *Asphodel*,

detailed in my edition (xvi–xix), is unassailable but merely that such a policy should be accessible. See Robert Spoo, "Editing H.D.'s *Asphodel*: Selected Emendations and Notes," *Sagetrieb* 14 (Spring and Fall 1995): 13–26.

23. An important recent contribution to H.D. studies is Michael Boughn's *H.D.: A Bibliography, 1905–1990* (Charlottesville: UP of Virginia, 1993), which covers both primary and secondary materials. H.D. scholarship is moving so rapidly, however, that bibliographic updates are already needed.

24. A disturbing sign was the recent demise of the *H.D. Newsletter*, founded by Eileen Gregory in 1987 for the purpose of disseminating biographical, bibliographical, and other research-oriented information about H.D. Essays of a strictly critical nature were not ordinarily accepted. Gregory, who edited the journal, told me that a large factor in her decision to discontinue it was the paucity of appropriate submissions.

25. For analyses of H.D.'s "encoded" poetry and fiction, see Friedman, *Penelope's Web*, 51–62; Laity, "H.D.'s Romantic Landscapes: The Sexual Politics of the Garden," in *Signets: Reading H.D.*, 110–28; and Laity's introduction to *Paint It Today*.

26. Claire Buck, "Freud and H.D.—bisexuality and a feminine discourse," *m/f* 8 (1983): 59.

WORKS BY H.D.

The following is a list of H.D.'s works cited in my essay. Where relevant, I have included dates of composition.

Asphodel. Ed. Robert Spoo. Durham, NC: Duke UP, 1992. Written 1921–22, 1926–27.

Bid Me To Live: A Madrigal. 1960. Redding Ridge, CT: Black Swan, 1983. Written 1939, 1947–50.

Collected Poems, 1912–1944. Ed. Louis L. Martz. New York: New Directions, 1983.

End to Torment: A Memoir of Ezra Pound. Ed. Norman Holmes Pearson and Michael King. New York: New Directions, 1979. Written 1958.

The Gift. New York: New Directions, 1982. Written 1941–44.

H.D. by Delia Alton (Notes on Recent Writing). Ed. Adalaide Morris. *Iowa Review* 16 (1986): 174–221. Written 1949–50.

Helen in Egypt. New York: Grove, 1961. Written 1952–55.

Hermetic Definition. New York: New Directions, 1972. Written 1957–61.

HERmione. New York: New Directions, 1981. Written 1926–27, 1930.

Kora and Ka. Dijon: Imprimerie Darantiere, 1934. Written 1930. Reissued, with an introduction and note on the text by Robert Spoo. New York: New Directions, 1996.

Notes on Thought and Vision. San Francisco: City Lights, 1982. Written 1919.

Paint It To-Day (first four chaps. only). Ed. Susan Stanford Friedman and Rachel Blau DuPlessis. *Contemporary Literature* 27 (1986): 441–74. Written 1920–21.

Paint It Today (complete). Ed. Cassandra Laity. New York: New York UP, 1992.

Selected Poems. New York: Grove, 1957.

Tribute to Freud. 1945–46, 1956. New York: New Directions, 1974. Written 1944, 1948.

Trilogy. New York: New Directions, 1973. Written 1942, 1944.

The Electronic Future of Modernist Studies

Mary FitzGerald

Like the Tasmanians who are said to have lost the art of making fire, generations of book readers have grown accustomed to doing without what they lost long ago, when mechanically printed texts replaced the idiosyncratic dazzle of manuscript illumination and superseded the real-world variety of lettered texts and marginalia inscribed by human hands. Print technology regimented individual artistry and supplanted it with rigorous linear regularity in a fixed codex format. Although the efficiency of the printing press made its results seem beneficial—who could deny that mass distribution of information was an improvement?—the mechanical replication of words cost us dearly. The technology of the printed page imposed limits on our imaginative expression in ways we are just beginning to notice, now that the new Prometheus, electronic technology, is firing imagination once more.

As we accustom ourselves to computers, we notice that the print technology we have long taken for granted has not been an unmixed blessing. As Richard Lanham notes in *The Electronic Word: Democracy, Technology, and the Arts* (1993):

> We have come to regard print as so inevitable that we have ceased to notice its extraordinary stylization. Print . . . [is] not a historical inevitability. Print represents a decision of severe abstraction and subtraction. All non-linear signals are filtered out; color is banned for serious texts; typographical constants are rigorously enforced; sound is proscribed; even the tactility of visual elaboration is outlawed. Print is an act of perceptual self-denial, and electronic text makes us aware of that self-denial at every point and in all the ways which print is at pains to conceal. (73–74)

It is heartening, then, to realize that the technology of light that is replacing the Procrustean bed of print is a profoundly human way of recording and transmitting thought. Electronic text promises to restore to us the freedom we sacrificed to Gutenberg and to bestow on us a greater power of information mastery than anything humankind has ever known. Different though it may at first seem, electronic text is no less natural than print, and it may in fact be *more* natural. It is far less cumbersome, after all, to store thoughts as the electric impulses they are than to encode them as marks on stone or paper. That we have been chiseling and inscribing them for millenia will no doubt ensure that deep patterns of inscription will continue to dominate our encoding processes for some time, shaping whatever thoughts come along. With the new tools in our hands, however, we will eventually be able not only to extend the metaphoric structure of thinking beyond jot-by-jot linearity but also to expand it into a rapidly connecting network of mental links, whose speed and intensity of processing will feel like fire at our fingertips.

Aristotle defined *technē* as knowing by virtue of the hands. Our own generation has already accustomed itself to the transition in hands-on knowledge from the "digital" technique of laboriously inscribing research notes to the digitized technology of photocopying them. In short order, we have welcomed the first flickerings of the technology of light and adjusted ourselves simultaneously to the ways in which our manner of knowing was altered by our first encounters with the *technē* of rapid electronic duplication. Electronic photocopying not only relieved our cramping fingers and shortened our research time, but it also produced a copy that closely resembled the original. Because of that, we learned to value precisely rendered appearance and to pay greater attention to visual context. If we were now able to give our students copies of an early version of a Yeats poem that looked exactly like the poem in its first printing, that was somehow better and more complete than giving them the words as reconstructed from a variorum. When the students themselves copied research material for term papers, they copied more copiously and more comprehensively, because the god in the machine was Phoebus Apollo, driving his chariot across the page, converting light energy into knowledge at their command—and occasionally blinding them at the edges of books copied too copiously or too fast. Their notes contained fewer errors than before, because photographic duplication eliminated scribal lapses and obviated the need to decode their own hand. It hardly seemed possible that so great an improvement in the convenience factor of scholarly work should itself be superseded by an even faster, better, easier and vastly more capable method of locating, copying, storing, retrieving and writing. But we have it now, and it is constantly improving.

We already know that the twenty-first century in higher education will be like nothing we have experienced before. Modernist scholars and faculty in all fields are availing themselves of the electronic technology that enables them to locate a strange attractor in chaos, map the mind in action, decode the human genome, walk in virtual reality through the Parthenon, access remote archives, address distant audiences, and network across time and space. Global access will make our universities more universal, and humanists as well as scientists have reasons to welcome that. Classicists were among the first humanists to take advantage of electronic research technology, and the compilers of the *Oxford English Dictionary* were not far behind. Any novice can now ask the CD-ROM *OED* for every English word first found in Shakespeare and receive the list instantaneously. And, as Peter Shillingsburg notes in an essay in *Palimpsest* (1994), "*The English Poetry Full-Text Database,* providing the works of 1,350 poets from A.D. 600 to 1900 on CD-ROM and magnetic tape, is the harbinger of comprehensive text data bases for a world that begins to see libraries as information centers, mere accesspoints to texts, rather than as collections of books and periodicals" (29). Museum archives have been similarly affected: research libraries and archives are available at a keystroke. In the very near future our students will come to class, whether in person or in virtual reality, armed with a level of preparation that should lift even ordinary discussion of a text well beyond business as usual. Interactive multimedia software will greatly improve the university, and it will also make possible a greater depth of independent study and a greater breadth of independent scholarship. People with an interest in Pound will be able not only to attend Pound conferences but also to hold discussions in electronic chat rooms in the virtual community. Our students can join them or listen in, trying their ideas with greater freedom against a broader range of contrasting viewpoints than they would customarily expect to encounter in a classroom headed by one of us. And, the more they know, the sharper and more computer friendly we will have to be.

Those who have not had the delightful experience of playing with interactive software may find it hard to imagine its potential for enhancing teaching and learning. To get some idea, one might watch an elementary school student ask a CD-ROM disc for the location of Togo, for example. Not only does the map of Africa appear on the screen, with Togo duly highlighted in red, together with a side order of hypertextual links to tempt further inquiry, but simultaneously in the foreground the Togo flag ascends a flagpole, accompanied by a rousing rendition of the Togo national anthem. If we translate that technology—already years old—into a university-level multimedia edition of James Joyce's "Araby" or "The Dead," we can easily imagine the proliferation of possibilities. The children who are playing with such toys will be our university students in the new century, and they will be accustomed to what Richard Lanham rightly calls a "new Eden":

> Imagine growing up as an electronic reader, used to . . . broad interactive enfranchisements. . . . How would you feel about *Paradise Lost* as presented to you in a codex book? Probably you'd prefer to access it from the CD-ROM disk which, in a few years, will contain all the texts you were asked to read —or ever could read—in your undergraduate career. Wouldn't you begin to play games with it? A weapon in your hands after 2,500 years of pompous pedantry about the Great Books, and you not to use it? Hey, man, how about some music with this stuff? Let's voice this rascal and see what happens. Add some graphics and graffiti! (7)

It is pleasant to share Lanham's futuristic vision of students who are tempted to lose themselves in Milton with an energy and enthusiasm with which they now master the arcana of unbelievably intricate video games, and Lanham's projections into the future are very likely to come true. (Yeats scholars take note: the Fomorians and Balor of the Evil Eye are in the game stores.) Because hands-on learning is engaging and interactive, it is a very enticing learning tool, and different levels of hypertextual links challenge users to move to more sophisticated levels of inquiry. We ought to prepare ourselves for this kind of work. It goes without saying that such hypertextual texts will require scholarly editors who will see to it that the best possible materials are made available. Clearly, university scholars will have plenty of opportunities in the years ahead to create the software that makes such learning tools possible or to lend expertise to those corporations that will be taking advantage of the market, whether the universities recognize the oppor-tunity or not.

As Nicholas Negroponte notes in *Being Digital* (1995):

> The population of the Internet itself is now increasing at 10 per cent per month . . . [and] . . . the real cultural divide is going to be generational. When I meet an adult who tells me that he has discovered CD-ROM, I can guess that he has a child between five and ten years old. When I meet someone who tells me she has discovered America Online, there is probably a teenager in her house. . . . Both are being taken for granted by children. (7)

The day when Chaucer's Clerk of Oxenford climbed onto his scrawny horse and lugged his precious books across half a country so that he could sit at the feet of the best scholars and read in their library is vanishing into the mists. While that thought may fill us with nostalgia, there's not much point in traveling back to that world. Indeed, scholars won't especially have to travel anywhere in the twenty-first century, at least not to get most kinds of useful information. The information will travel to us. We will only have to summon it to our screens—or to whatever has replaced screens in our futuristic offices. Art historian Oleg Grabar described the electronic office of a scholar in his field "a generation from now" in an essay on "The Intellectual Implications of Electronic Information," presented at a conference on Technology, Scholarship, and the Humanities: The Implications of Electronic Infor-mation, 30 September–2 October 1992, at the Arnold and Mabel Beck-man Center of the National Academies of Sciences and Engineering in Irvine, California:

> His or her desk would go around the room and will have equip-ment that could offer simultaneously all of the following (all my examples are based on programs I know to exist or to be fairly along in planning, especially in my own, underdeveloped, field of the history of Islamic art): a personal word processor containing bibliographies, draft or completed studies, and dozens of special lists adjusted to one's scholarly and personal concerns; dictionaries of a dozen languages; immediate access to a complete index of all monuments of Islamic (or other) art or relevant texts in one's field; a thesaurus of texts in Arabic characters (let's say) indexed like the

Thesaurus Linguae Graecae; an access to the catalogue not only of
the nearest scholarly library but of hundreds of other research
libraries; access to hundreds of bibliographical databases through
commercial sources such as DIALOG; a computer-assisted design
(CAD) program for architectural and urban investigations; some
printers; one screen available for whatever visitors bring; a ma-
chine to reconcile disks from different sources; a modem-equipped
telephone; and a fax machine.

With a few modifications and a little updating (some of his projections
are already obsolete), the office would be just perfect for a *Finnegans
Wake* scholar. As Grabar says himself, "the changes, novelties, and pos-
sibilities introduced into the surroundings of the scholar in the human-
ities by electronic facilities affect much more than one's scholarly out-
put; they end up by shaping one's life, and thus, probably modify the
very nature of one's actual or potential knowledge." And, if the world
can be brought into one's study, so also one's study can be carried with
greater portability than ever to any spot in the world. The scholarly
community of the twenty-first century will have achieved a state of
information mastery unprecedented in the academy.

   In a sense electronic information technology had to happen. It was
devised as a solution to a growing research problem. The steady accu-
mulation of artifact and of recorded knowledge from time immemorial
resulted in a reservoir of information that was nearly impossible to
search exhaustively. Researchers required a more efficient way to find
what they needed, and the wish was father to the deed. The electronic
technology that we have created can separate relevant data from back-
ground noise on almost any subject and locate patterns of useful infor-
mation in the apparent cacophony. As long ago as 1945, in an article in
Atlantic Monthly, Vannevar Bush described his plan for such a device, a
mechanical pre-computer he called a *memex,* which would locate infor-
mation through analogy and association, like the human mind, rather
than by scanning alphabetically. Bush predicted the development of
"essentially poetic machines," as George Landow notes in discussing
him in *Hypertext* (1992), because he assumed "that science and poetry
work in essentially the same way" (18). Which is to say that the brain
makes discoveries and connections in the same sorts of ways, regard-
less of the subject at hand. It should be no more surprising that human
beings can devise technologies that replicate their thought processes on

the grand scale than it is that they can construct skyscrapers or build vehicles that run faster than the fastest animals they know.

Not that any of this will necessarily console the bibliophile. But, just as photography radically altered the way in which artists approached painting and sculpture, so too the advent of electronic information processing has moved us all into a new and highly self-conscious awareness of *technē*, how we do what we do and how that way of doing things shapes thought.

In his 1987 study, *Electric Language: A Philosophical Study of Word Processing*, Michael Heim worried about the implications of the technological shift away from hand labor: "That we are approaching a paperless society and that computers minimize the involvement of the unique movements of the personal hand . . . touch the ontological foundations of our world, the way we turn to apprehend realities" (199). But almost anything in print moves rapidly out of date, and in less than ten years we can note that handwriting is back in vogue electronically, because computers can now read it. The muscles involved in the unique movements of the personal hand in its scribal function will not necessarily atrophy. In *Hyper/Text/Theory* Landow reminds us that we find ourselves using the latest technology almost before we hear about it. "The advent of pen-based computing, which has already appeared in the hands of people who deliver packages, promises to bring the full powers of the reader-author to the miniature portable computer. Although still in its infancy, pen-based computing shows how a supposedly superseded, once-dominant information technology can blend with electronic textuality" (5). Moreover, voice-command–based computing is on the way, indeed is already at work on our telephones. ("If you wish departure and arrival times, please push 2 or say 'two.'") Thought-based computing, in which the machine reads brainwaves on the surface of a finger, has already been developed, as have programs that use biofeedback to tell whether a learner has learned what a machine has taught. The lag time between the perception of a possible technological improvement and its practical accomplishment is steadily decreasing. In a similar manner the continuing development of electronic texts will enable us not so much to supersede our old ways of doing things as to enrich them. Better and more creative ways of handling literary scholarship will inevitably appear, with inevitable consequences affecting the essence of what we teach and write about. As Lanham says, "The definitive and unchangeable text upon which Western humanism has been based since the Renaissance, and the Arnoldian 'masterpiece' theory of culture built upon it, are called into question, put into play" (73). *Play* is perhaps the operative word. New technology often enters the marketplace as games to play.

What will happen to books as we know them and to those of us who have traditionally depended on books? Those who refuse to be reassured seem to fear that twenty-first-century technology will somehow devalorize or even eliminate the book. But the utterly paperless society dreaded by Michael Heim and others will not likely arrive soon, if ever. Rather, as electronic technology gradually manifests its superiority, it will gradually absorb more of the roles traditionally assigned to paper. (It is also worth noting, perhaps, that paper itself is changing: plans for next-generation computer screens call for thin, flat screen-sheets that resemble paper.) In all likelihood ink, paper, and books as we know them will continue to be manufactured alongside their technologically improved imitations, like fountain pens and glass quill pens today, but it seems inevitable that these will be gradually improved and eventually superseded by more advanced technology that can outperform the book. In an article written for the general reader about the Xerox Palo Alto Research Center's (PARC) innovations in the September 1994 issue of *Smithsonian Magazine,* Richard Wolkimer notes that PARC engineers have developed high-resolution screens on which images and print actually appear *sharper* than those printed in ink on paper (88). Electronic technology is simply more versatile than any tool we have had before. In most comparisons with a book it is superior, except in the tactile and olfactory and visual senses—but, then, those of us who still want books to touch and smell and hold will have the books themselves for as long as their material substance survives, and we will no doubt devise print bindery technologies to enable us to replicate at will any desired first edition or produce a new one. And even for those of us who will continue to prefer books in the hand, a chief compensatory advantage of the electronic texts of the not-too-distant future is that electronic text is always available, ready to be pulled from cyberspace on demand, much as turning on a radio now brings that other gift of the Muses known as music. And, as Nicholas Negroponte reminds us in *Being Digital* (1995), "Digital books never go out of print. They are always there" (13).

Art critic Robert Hughes raises another important issue in the ongoing debate about the relative value of old ways versus new ways in the visual arts. In a rousing bah-humbug to technology (*Time*, 22 April 1995) Hughes complains tautologically that virtual reality is not reality, that an electronic reproduction of a painting is no substitute for the real thing. This is hardly news. The photographic reproductions of paintings that we now have are also no substitute for the real thing. Very few of us mistake them for the real thing, yet they come in handy until such time as we can confront the original. Virtual reality would appear preferable by far. Instead of a postcard-sized reproduction in a textbook, imagine an electronic facsimile that replicates the original in three-dimensional verisimilitude, with paint colors precisely calibrated by microchip, with texture and brushstroke made visible—even tactile. Such an easily accessible replica of an original would surely have its uses, especially as a teaching tool to answer questions and to tell us about the painting in great detail. Imagine a technology that can place Duchamp's *Nude Descending a Staircase* in situ at the 1913 New York Armory Show, complete with surrounding paintings and sculpture, so that a browser can pause in front of it or turn around in virtual reality and look at what was across the room. Suppose this replica of the original could be overlaid, at a spoken command, with Duchamp's more familiar revision of the revolutionary canvas. Imagine a constellation of analyses, commentaries, and critiques, accessible instantaneously at the request of any student who wants more than a minimal glance. Imagine a student who wants to revise the painting still further and does so, without losing the capacity to retrieve Duchamp's originals. Imagine the impact of such a preparation on the student's eventual contemplation of "the real thing." It is hardly an eventuality to be scorned.

Although Howard Rheingold is surely correct to note in *The Virtual Community* (1994) that we "owe it to ourselves and future generations to look closely at what the enthusiasts fail to tell us, and to listen attentively to what the skeptics fear" (276), the electronic future looks rather more encouraging than daunting. For one thing, the vocabulary of the "tekkies" is reassuringly familiar and even playful. The Adam in the electronic Eden who named the *mouse* and the *window,* created *software* from a rib taken from the side of *hardware,* and originated the concept of *user friendliness* is obviously possessed of a sensibility attuned to values that humanists hold dear. Far from facilitating the robotlike uniformity feared by the creators of dystopian literature, the wizards of electronic technology are devising tools for an unprecedented expansion of human creativity. *Anyone* who can acquire the technology—and it will soon be as near as the telephone and television—will have the tools to study and learn and create with unprecedented convenience and at unprecedented levels of sophistication. The implications for teaching and for scholarship are as limitless as imagination. Electronic scholarship will fashion a whole new academic environment. The image of scholarship as lonely drudgery in a tiny space is about to be radically revised. Landow puts it succinctly in *The Digital Word:*

> Before networked computing, scholarly communication relied chiefly upon moving physical marks on a surface from one place to another with whatever cost in time that movement required. Networked electronic communication so drastically reduces the time scale of moving textual information that it produces new forms of textuality. Just as transforming print text to electronic coding radically changed the temporal scale involved in manipulating texts, so too it has changed the temporal scale of communication. Networked electronic communication has both dramatically speeded up scholarly communication and created new forms of it. (350)

A growing body of literature nevertheless attests to the discomfort many people feel with the prospect of change. In a chapter entitled "Elegies for the Book" Lanham discusses six books that consider the problem. They make a good beginning bibliography for anyone interested in pursuing the matter. He takes issue with the late O. B. Hardison's *Disappearing through the Skylight* (1989), Alvin Kernan's *The Death of Literature* (1990) and, in a note, Neil Postman's *Technopoly: The Surrender of Culture to Technology* (1992) and Theodore Roszak's *The Cult of Information: The Folklore of Computers and the True Art of Thinking* (1986). He sympathizes with some of Gregory Ulmer's principles in *Teletheory: Grammatology in the Age of Video* (1989) and with Myron Tuman's fears in *Word Perfect: Literacy in the Computer Age* (1992). He acquiesces in the positive outlook expressed in George P. Landow's *Hypertext: The Convergence of Contemporary Critical Theory and Technology* (1992), Landow and Paul Delany's *Hypermedia and Literary Studies* (1991), and Jay David Bolter's *Writing Space: The Computer, Hypertext, and the History of Writing* (1991).

To Lanham's list of worthwhile readings we may add Walter J. Ong's classic *Orality and Literacy: The Technologizing of the Word* (1982),

Myron Tuman's edition of essays *Literacy Online* (1992), and David R. Olson's *The World on Paper: The Conceptual and Cognitive Implications of Writing and Reading* (1994). In *The World on Paper* Olson worries that the declining influence of books will have an impact on cognitive skills that we cannot yet foresee. The recognition that the mind behind the writing and the mind of the reader have different perspectives on the world—that my view is not the only view—may well be dependent upon reading: "Coordinating them is what initiates the internal mental dialogue which both Plato and Hobbes took to be thinking" (256). That this is a process different from the hunting and gathering of facts, which are the skills privileged by electronic gadgetry, causes him to wonder what alterations in our speech modeling and thought processing may be in store. He is, however, aware that literal thought "is not restricted to the medium of writing even if writing and reading were critical in their evolution" (281). But Olson's notion that we may dissolve the self that depends on reading is hardly self-evident. It ignores the success of preliterate people in antiquity and illiterate people in contemporary society in developing viable senses of self.

Sven Birkerts's *The Gutenberg Elegies: The Fate of Reading in an Electronic Age* (1994) is a recent addition to the debate. Birkerts works his way from an initial grief over the loss of the familiar to a grudging acceptance of the forever altered terrain:

> It was hard, I confess, to square my experience with the hype surrounding hypertext and multimedia. Extremists—I meet more and more of them—argue that the printed page has been but a temporary habitation for the word. The book, they say, is no longer the axis of our intellectual culture. There is a kind of aggressiveness in their proselytizing. The stationary arrangement of language on a page is outmoded. . . . Indeed, the revolution is taking place even as I type with the antediluvian typewriter onto the superseded sheet of paper. I am proof of the fact that many of us are still habit-bound, unable to grasp the scope of the transformation that is underway all around us. But rest assured, we will adjust to these changes, as we do to all others, by increments; we will continue to do so until everything about the way we do business is different. . . . [T]hose of us who . . . are still embedded in the ancient and formerly stable reader-writer relationship, will have to make our difficult peace. (152)

If it is not exactly the ringing affirmation that Tennyson mustered at the end of a similar journey toward acceptance in *In Memoriam* (a work that Victorian scholars are now encoding in hypertext), it nonetheless epitomizes the near trauma of many readers, looking over the edge of the new century and reeling at the shock of what largely resembles an abyss, wondering if they will have enough energy to make it to the other side.

Although there is still nothing new under the sun, Birkerts's description in *The Gutenberg Elegies* is typical of the unease occasioned by the rapidity of the change to the "new" *technē*:

> Over the past few decades, in the blink of the eye of history, our culture has begun to go through what promises to be a total metamorphosis. The influx of electronic communications and information processing technologies, abetted by the steady improvement of the microprocessor, has rapidly brought on a condition of critical mass. Suddenly it feels like everything is poised for change: the slower world that many of us grew up with dwindles in the rearview mirror. The stable hierarchies of the printed page—one of the defining norms of that world—are being superseded by the rush of impulses through freshly minted circuits. The displacement of the screen is not yet total . . . but the large-scale tendency in that direction has to be obvious to anyone who looks. (3)

This enunciation of *fin de (vingtième) siècle* anxiety should ring with some familiarity in the ears of modernist scholars. It incorporates observations that could be applied retrospectively to modernism itself. The tone of his opening statement, which is amplified in the ensuing argument of his book, has striking affinities with the sense of disbelief and unease with which the work of the moderns was met *au debut*. We remember, however, that what seemed so strange at the start of the century has come to be taken for granted, so that Ibsen's *A Doll's House* or Stravinsky's *Rite of Spring* or Duchamp's *Nude Descending a Staircase* no longer generates outrage among an increasingly sophisticated populace, long inured to the shock of dissonance.

Modernists can take heart. We have made this leap before. Inured as we are to uncertainty, relativity, randomness—not to mention the relentless newness of proliferating critical theories—we can be said to be well prepared for future shock. Modernism itself breaks so creatively away from the tradition, refashioning the form and substance of whatever it encounters, that its radical vitality has primed us for a future similarly characterized by changes in the very ground of our understanding and in the cognitive tools that we employ. Long before Landow pointed out the resemblances between contemporary critical theory and hypertext, Walter Ong had showed us in *Orality and Literacy* (1982) that the oral culture that gave us the *Iliad* and the *Odyssey* operated very well indeed without the artificial linearity that print culture derived from the written word. If we are headed for a "new" oral culture, one that processes its information by visual image and by analogy, rather than by the cumbersome multiple codings and decodings that print requires of our mental energy, then we might do well to remember that it is not really a new culture at all but, rather, a return to the familiar. Homer understood hypertextual linkages. Linked *lexia*s are crucial to the structure of the *Iliad* and the *Odyssey*.

Everything old is new again. More to the point, as the motto of the Palo Alto Research Center has it, "The easiest way to predict the future is to invent it," and modernism may be said to have predicted this future we face by inventing it. The advances offered by electronic technology owe a debt to modernism. In fact, the high modernists and their heirs in the literary, visual, and musical arts produced a set of metaphors that not only parallel the scientific insights of the twentieth century but created the mind-set that gave rise to them. The verbal and dissonant structures that they employed, and the blessed rage for order that drove them to create, prefigure the ramifying networks and binary universes of our present mode of information processing, sometimes selecting with uncanny perspicacity metaphors that map deep organic or atomic structure. By making structures—*poiēsis*—they affirmed that a kind of order still existed, even if that order now had to be understood as unconventionally unstable. By using mythic patterns to create a force field, within which bits of information arranged themselves like so many iron filings around a magnet, as Joyce did in *Ulysses*, they enacted rituals of meaning for a world struggling with the fear of entropy.

If a dozen years after Yeats used ladders in the penultimate poem of his career, James Watson and Francis Crick discovered a double helix where all the ladders start, did something of Yeats's imagery feed their imagination, just as Kekulé's earlier discovery of the structure of benzene was facilitated by a dream of six monkeys joined head to tail? Or what are we to make of the fact that one way of stating Heisenberg's uncertainty principle is to quote the last line of Yeats's "Among School Children": "How can we know the dancer from the dance?" What these examples of analogous formulations in Yeats's poetry and in science suggest is that the arbitrary boundaries between different fields of human learning are rather more illusory than we sometimes believe. Both scientific models and the linguistic structures made by poets derive ultimately from the same matrix, the human brain, and they take shape in a culture of ideas that only *seem* to be "in the air," as they were in Renaissance Florence, say, or in the nineteenth-century Vienna that gave us Freud and Jung and Wittgenstein. As cognitive science investigates the mechanisms of creativity—and the importance of that field is growing—modernist scholars can expect greater attention to their writers, musicians, and artists, because the twentieth century can boast some of the greatest exemplars of cross-disciplinary creativity. William Carlos Williams's medical practice and Wallace Stevens's insurance career—and their mutual interest in art and music—are of obvious relevance, as are Ezra Pound's omnivorous cultural range and Joyce's linguistic virtuosity. To the extent that art incarnates intellectual structures or replicates them, the work of modern artists in the twentieth century can be seen as mapping the terrain for the scientists who read and followed them, and we will see more interdisciplinary appreciation for their work, together with a range of studies that attempt to bring the two cultures closer together.

Modernism's appreciation of dissonance, its privileging of the individual act of apprehension, and its detestation of rigidity and conformity seem, in retrospect, to have apprehended an underlying principle of human behavior that predicted the collapse of empires throughout the century and the failure of rigid political systems at midcentury and after. Modernism asserts the value of difference and variety against the homogenizing conformity of industrial mechanization. And, though at first glance modernist writers may seem to be reeling in a world in which the center cannot hold, they did, in fact, continue to affirm the possibility of a center, or multiple centers, by the very act of making art. The order they half-created and half-perceived has come to be seen by scientists, historians, economists, and others well outside the normal bounds of humanistic studies, as the order manifested by nonlinear dynamic systems, in the subject area studied in chaos theory. Real-world conditions, chaoticians note, are not really random. Rather, they mask a deeper kind of orderly complexity at the heart of dynamic systems. Computer-generated images, or graphs, of large-scale phenomena have revealed a visually staggering array of irregular but nonetheless orderly patterns at the heart of everything in nature, from cloud formation to heart fibrillation. And, more revealing still, the patterns from one academic discipline (say, heat diffusion in metals) match the patterns in completely different academic disciplines (say, the behavior of stock market derivatives). From this perspective the word *chaos* resumes its ancient meaning. For the Greeks it meant the substance that was the ground of physical reality, the primal material from which order arises. Chaos, then, is *apparently* random but not really so. Scientists did not see this before, because until the advent of computers they simply lacked the tools for large-scale observation over time and space. Computers make visible to all of us the deep order that modernist writers and artists detected in what seemed to be disintegrating and disordered. But the intuition of such a complex reality was available in modernist metaphors.

The earliest literary enunciation of the principle of chaos theory that I have found—though Gerard Manley Hopkins's instress of inscape prefigures it—is in Virginia Woolf's *To the Lighthouse* in 1927: "In the midst of chaos there was shape; this eternal passing and flowing (she looked at the clouds going and the leaves shaking) was struck into stability" (161). The modernists were drawing the pictures for this radically revised idea of chaos fifty years before the computers showed us fractals, and it was precisely cloud formations and wind-blown leaves and dripping water, phenomena that never reach a steady state, that gave them the idea of a science of real-world conditions, to supplement the science of perfect abstraction. Early modernist writers and artists understood what their intellectual peers in the scientific disciplines were slower to grasp, that the old linear forms of thought were oversimplifications that did not adequately model reality. A new paradigm was needed, and they laid the imaginative groundwork for it. Their work showed the world as dynamic, unstable, changeable, shifting, but not beyond cognition. As artists who had not been overexposed to the scientific focus on predictability and uniformity of result, they could see what most scientists overlooked—namely, as physicist James Yorke put it: "The first message is that there is disorder. Physicists and mathematicians want to discover regularities. People say, what use is disorder. But people have to know about disorder if they are going to deal with it"

(Gleick 68). Modernist writers, artists, and musicians not only understood disorder; they could also detect and demonstrate dynamic patterns within it, and their art showed twentieth-century science a new way of seeing complexity. There might be, for example, thirteen ways of looking at a blackbird. A man-made cylindrical object placed on a hill in Tennessee might induce the appearance of regularity in an apparently random real-world setting.

Poetry is particularly germane to this discussion. Though Wallace Stevens and T. S. Eliot and W. B. Yeats did not exactly foresee a technology that operated by way of nonlinear networks, their poetry modeled the science and technology to come by imaging such things. A poem— or any other work of art—is an encoding of human experience, a kind of microchip, from which others can learn. Poetry itself is a kind of networking. It is grounded in the act of connecting bits of information that might otherwise appear unrelated, whether concepts in metaphors or sounds in rhyme. It is the mental mechanism by which we apprehend anything new, comparison and contrast with what we already know. If we seem to be in midflight through a quantum jump in human information processing, it is worth noting that the work produced by Yeats, Joyce, Pound, Eliot, Woolf, and other major figures of high modernism prefigured it both structurally and thematically, preparing the way for the change.

Not by accident, James Gleick's *Chaos: Making a New Science* is peppered with quotations from poets, including Wallace Stevens's affirmation of himself as a connoisseur of chaos and Conrad Aiken's remarkably on-target observation that "chaos draws all forces inward / To shape a single leaf" (213). The literary applications of chaos theory have been admirably presented in two books by N. Katherine Hayles, *Chaos Bound: Orderly Disorder in Contemporary Literature and Science* (1990) and her collection of essays by various scholars on the same theme, *Chaos and Order: Complex Dynamics in Literature and Science* (1991).

Further, it has become abundantly clear that the next century will privilege those with adaptability and imagination over those whose education trained them for a specific task. The liberal arts in general are now widely praised as a wise choice for a college major, and not just by humanists. Thomas Kuhn, the physicist–turned–historian of science who gave us the concept of paradigm shifts in *The Structure of Scientific Revolutions* (1962), emphasizes the importance of imaginative flexibility, the ability to conceptualize scientific phenomena from within the traditional mind-set but also from utterly different points of view. On another level it is clear that the dynamics of literary systems and literary creativity have cognate models in the sciences, and these are likely to be examined extensively. One recent study even explores persuasively the connection between the modernist dissociation of sensibility and schizophrenia. In *Madness and Modernism: Insanity in the Light of Modern Art, Literature, and Thought* (1993) psychologist Louis A. Sass notes the uncanny similarities between the words of famous writers and the descriptions of dissociative states of mind experienced by people with cognitive dysfunction, wondering "whether there might be something more than mere elective affinities" between the classical definitions of *dementia praecox* and the modern sensibility (357). Literature scholars can expect an opening up not only of the canon but of the criticism as well.

On a more immediately practical level, modernist scholars should not fail to notice that Nicholas Negroponte's observation that digital books never go out of print generates the happy corollary that those books that have actually fallen out of print can be restored cheaply and with unprecedented ease. Quite apart from the accessibility of texts in libraries that are electronically accessible on one's personal computer, there will be ample opportunity for making available out-of-print texts of all modernist authors for classroom assignment and personal scholarly research. Clusters of commentaries and handbooks can be added at will. The utility of such a capacity for the expansion of information is obvious.

As George Bornstein and the contributors to his valuable volume *Representing Modernist Texts* would agree, one primary benefit to accrue from the enhanced capacity of digital machines will be the improved editions they will make possible. The need for reliable texts will not be lost on anyone who has tried to teach from a flawed one, such as the standard anthology (since corrected) that rendered the line from Wallace Stevens's "Sunday Morning" as "*clam* darkens over water lights" instead of "*calm* darkens over water lights." And at a deeper level there are modernist writers whose work will be more precisely rendered by hypertextual editions than was previously possible in printed texts. Yeats learned the limitations of print technique firsthand—earning some of his bread as a notoriously inaccurate hand copyist for others in the British Museum. Given his lifelong tendency to revise his work repeatedly, it is not surprising that, in his frustration with the arbitrary fixity that typesetting imposed upon him, he produced a poetry whose instability strained at the limitations of print and anticipated the technology we are now devising, a technology better suited to Yeats's work than anything he encountered in his own lifetime. As Bornstein has noted in *Palimpsest,* the question "What is the text of a poem by Yeats?" is best answered electronically (167).

Good editions of major and minor works are badly needed, and increasing numbers of them will come from modernist editors. Electronic technology will make it possible for us to restore the modernist canon to an accessibility equal to its first appearance. We will simply pull copies of the original editions from the ether, as we have need of them, and edit them as required. That should greatly enrich our capacity to present, analyze, and evaluate the whole range of modernist achievement, and it will seem a cornucopia indeed to those of us who have struggled with the steadily decreasing availability in print of major and minor modernist authors.

The expertise that we have spent so long perfecting will not go to waste, as modernist scholars should be much in demand as editors of hypertextual editions of our writers. The preparation of multimedia texts calls for teamwork among many experts in manuscripts, scholarship, background and contemporary history, art, music, publishing and other related aspects of the modernist experience. Hypertext editions, incomparably rich research resources, will offer university or independent students a graduate-level saturation in a work of art. The student is free to skim the surface or ask for different levels of depth of preparation. Instead of the intrusiveness of footnotes, which inevitably distract a reader from the meaning of sentences by suggesting that more is to be had and maybe not to be missed, hypertextual links can be invisible. The reader stops at will, interrogates the page, and is offered a range of options for further pursuit of an idea, deeper into the sources or background, or perhaps to parallel concepts in parallel writers or disciplines. The electronic text can be suitably embellished and customized by each potential user. Notes can be added; other research tools can be accessed and excerpted. The result is a personal copy of a text that can have almost infinitely large electronic margins filled with journal notes and data banks and cross-references.

Although much of what we do as modernist scholars will proceed unchanged, then, much will be altered by access to electronic tools that will quicken, intensify, and expand our ability to handle ideas. One will not have to be a modernist, nor indeed particularly a professor of English, to experience the ways in which revolutionary technological breakthroughs will transform research and teaching.

Publication will change. To the established mechanisms and venues we already have, we are adding instantaneous publication in cyberspace. The questions raised by that possibility were debated for nine months on the Internet beginning in June 1994 and will be issued in edited book format as *Scholarly Journals at the Crossroads: A Subversive Proposal for Electronic Publishing* by the Association of Research Libraries. For a while, at least, traditional journal articles and electronic publication will coexist, while universities find ways to design reward systems for less conventional forms of publication, but it is certainly likely that in the twenty-first century we will be publishing our scholarly results where they are most easily to be accessed for the greatest good by the greatest number. We will select what to read for ourselves from the background noise of so many bits of information by designing our own "journals" for our highly specialized interests, and we will do this electronically.

Copyright will change. The topic is much too complicated to be handled here, but it takes only a few minutes' contemplation to see that an electronic medium that dispenses information without regard to international boundaries, allowing each person to assemble a personal collection of data from many sources and to alter them at will, is hardly a world in which the customary fixities and legalities of copyright law will suffice. Downloading the wisdom of the ages onto one's personal computer will create problems for copyright lawyers that boggle the mind. We are a long way from the decision of the early Irish king Diarmuid that the manuscript owner is entitled to the scribe's copy, on the principle that the copy is the offspring of the original: "To every book its copy, to every cow its calf." The parentage of an electronic copy of a given work will no longer be so easily ascertained. The copy is no longer scribal or even printed text but, rather, light on a screen. One doesn't own it so much as borrow it from the air, like a radio or television broadcast. What will happen to bookstores and university presses and publishing houses in the aftermath of such publication is not yet clear, but it will obviously impact modernist scholarship.

Technē. The digital revolution in which we find ourselves need not be imagined as destroying our familiar world. Perhaps the reality will be rather more like the situation that novelist Flann O'Brien describes in *The Third Policeman,* in which he considers, tongue in cheek, the possibility of molecular transfer between bicycles and the people who ride them. By constantly cycling on the bumpy roads of Ireland, he says, people might gradually and imperceptibly exchange molecules with their machines, so that the bicycles become partly human and the humans become part bicycle. That whimsical notion seems uncannily descriptive of the current state of affairs between humans and their computers: as our computers acquire "artificial" intelligence, we become more computerized. O'Brien's humorous and benevolent view of a molecular rapprochement with our inventions reminds us that the possibilities for our kind in the twenty-first century are limited only by our inventiveness. It is also a refreshingly hopeful sight to see that inventiveness addressed not to massive destruction but to the betterment of humankind.

Ten years after the Manhattan Project unleashed atomic technology into our world, the Bavarian Academy of Fine Arts sponsored a series of lectures on "The Arts in the Technological Age." The speaker for 18 November in the main auditorium of the Technische Hochschule in Munich was the philosopher Martin Heidegger. His subject, "The Question Concerning Technology," gave him the opportunity to demonstrate that technology and art are not at war but, rather, inherently interrelated and complementary forms of knowing. Like Plato, he reminds us that knowledge is expression, emerging out of the self. "Technology is," he says, "no mere means. Technology is a way of revealing" (12). In that "way of revealing" it functions just like art. Although we may have forgotten it for a few centuries or so, we have known far longer that technology and art are one and the same, and we have stored that bit of information etymologically in the words *technology* and *technique:*

> *Technikon* means that which belongs to *technē* [which is] the name not only for the activities and skills of the craftsman, but also for the arts of the mind and the fine arts. *Technē* belongs to bringing-forth, to *poiēsis*; it is something poietic. . . . From earliest times until Plato the word *technē* is linked with the word *epistēmē*. Both words are names for knowing in the widest sense. They mean to be entirely at home in something, to understand and be expert in it. . . . Technology comes to presence . . . where *alētheia*, truth, happens. (12–13)

With electronic technology at our fingertips, modernist scholars have new ways to bring *alētheia* into the light and to preserve, extend, and deepen what we know. Truth to tell, the future of modernism is literally in our hands.

WORKS CITED

Birkerts, Sven. *The Gutenberg Elegies: The Fate of Reading in an Electronic Age.* Boston and London: Faber and Faber, 1994.

Bolter, Jay David. *Writing Space: The Computer, Hypertext, and the History of Writing.* Hillsdale, N.J.: Lawrence Erlbaum, 1991.

Bornstein, George, ed. *Representing Modernist Texts: Editing as Interpretation.* Ann Arbor: U of Michigan P, 1991.

Bornstein, George, and Ralph G. Williams, eds. *Palimpsest: Editorial Theory in the Humanities.* Ann Arbor: U of Michigan P, 1993.

Delany, Paul, and George P. Landow, eds. *Hypermedia and Literary Studies.* Cambridge and London: MIT Press, 1991.

Gleick, James. *Chaos: Making a New Science.* New York and London: Viking Penguin, 1987.

Grabar, Oleg. "The Intellectual Implications of Electronic Information." Paper presented at a conference on Technology, Scholarship and the Humanities: The Implications of Electronic Information, at the Arnold and Mabel Beckman Center of the National Academies of Sciences and Engineering, Irvine, California, 30 September–2 October 1992. Text available from CNI/documents/teach.schol.human/papers/Grabar.txt

Hardison, O. B. *Disappearing through the Skylight: Culture and Technology in the Twentieth Century.* New York: Penguin, 1989.

Hayles, N. Katherine, ed. *Chaos and Order: Complex Dynamics in Literature and Science.* Chicago: U of Chicago P, 1991.

———. *Chaos Bound: Orderly Disorder in Contemporary Literature and Science.* Ithaca and London: Cornell UP, 1990.

Healy, Jane. *Endangered Minds: Why Our Children Don't Think.* New York: Simon and Schuster, 1990.

Heidegger, Martin. *The Question Concerning Technology and Other Essays.* Trans. William Lovitt. New York: Harper and Row, 1977.

Heim, Michael. *Electric Language: A Philosophical Study of Word Processing.* New Haven and London: Yale UP, 1987.

Hughes, Robert. "Take this revolution . . ." *Time.* Special issue: "Welcome to Cyberspace" (Spring 1995): 76–77.

Kernan, Alvin. *The Death of Literature.* New Haven: Yale UP, 1990.

Landow, George P. *Hypertext: The Convergence of Contemporary Critical Theory and Technology.* Baltimore and London: Johns Hopkins UP, 1992.

———, ed. *Hyper/Text/Theory.* Baltimore and London: Johns Hopkins UP, 1994.

Landow, George P., and Paul Delany, eds. *The Digital Word: Text-Based Computing in the Humanities.* Cambridge and London: MIT, 1993.

Lanham, Richard A. *The Electronic Word: Democracy, Technology and the Arts.* Chicago and London: U of Chicago P, 1993.

Negroponte, Nicholas. *Being Digital.* New York: Knopf, 1995.

O'Brien, Flann [Brian O'Nolan]. *The Third Policeman.* London: MacGibbon and Kee, 1967.

Olson, David R. *The World on Paper: The Conceptual and Cognitive Implications of Writing and Reading.* Cambridge and New York: Cambridge UP, 1994.

Ong, Walter J. *Orality and Literacy: The Technologizing of the Word.* London and New York : Methuen, 1982.

Postman, Neil. *Technopoly: The Surrender of Culture to Technology.* New York: Knopf, 1992.

Rheingold, Howard. *The Virtual Community: Homesteading on the Electronic Frontier.* Reading, Mass.: Addison-Wesley, 1993.

Roszak, Theodore. *The Cult of Information: The Folklore of Computers and the True Art of Thinking* New York: Pantheon, 1986.

Sass, Louis A. *Madness and Modernism: Insanity in the Light of Modern Art, Literature, and Thought.* Cambridge and London: Harvard UP, 1992.

Tuman, Myron C. *Word Perfect: Literacy in the Computer Age.* London: Falmer, 1992.

———, ed. *Literacy Online: The Promise (and Peril) of Reading and Writing with Computers.* Pittsburgh and London: U of Pittsburgh P, 1995.

Ulmer, Gregory. *Teletheory: Grammatology in the Age of Video.* New York and London: Routledge, 1989.

Wolkimer, Richard. "We're Going to Have Computers Coming Out of the Woodwork." *Smithsonian* (September 1994): 82–93.

Woolf, Virginia. *To the Lighthouse.* San Diego and New York: Harcourt Brace Jovanovich, 1927.

Contributors

George Bornstein (University of Michigan) is the author of several books on modernist poetry, including *Yeats and Shelley* and, most recently, *Poetic Remaking: The Art of Browning, Yeats, and Pound.* He has edited *W. B. Yeats: The Early Poetry* (two vols.), Yeats's *Letters to the New Island* (with Hugh Witemeyer), and several collections of essays, including *Representing Modernist Texts: Editing as Interpretation* and *Palimpsest: Editorial Theory in the Humanities.*

Ronald Bush (Oxford University) is the author of *The Genesis of Ezra Pound's Cantos* and *T. S. Eliot: A Study in Character and Style.* He is also the editor of *T. S. Eliot: The Modernist in History* and (with Elazar Barkan) *Prehistories of the Future: The Primitivist Project and the Culture of Modernism.*

Mary FitzGerald (University of New Orleans) has edited Yeats's *The Words Upon the Windowpane* and *Selected Plays of Lady Gregory.* She has coedited *Some Unpublished Letters from A. E. to James Stephens* with Richard J. Finneran and has published articles on Yeats, Lady Gregory, Sean O'Casey, and modern Irish poetry. Currently, she is editing *The Irish Dramatic Movement* by Yeats as well as works by Lady Gregory.

Michael Groden (University of Western Ontario) is the author of *"Ulysses" in Progress,* general editor of *The James Joyce Archive* (63 vols.), and compiler of *James Joyce's Manuscripts: An Index.* He has also published articles on Joyce, textual criticism and theory, and theories of fiction. Most recently, he has edited (with Martin Kreiswirth) the *Johns Hopkins Guide to Literary Theory and Criticism.*

Holly Laird (University of Tulsa) is the author of *Self and Sequence: The Poetry of D. H. Lawrence* and the editor of *Tulsa Studies in Women's Literature.* Her published work and teaching are engaged with Victorian, modernist, and postmodern writing and with feminist theory. She is currently at work on a feminist study of literary collaborations.

James Longenbach (University of Rochester) is the author of several books about modern poetry: *Wallace Stevens: The Plain Sense of Things, Stone Cottage: Pound, Yeats, and Modernism,* and *Modernist Poetics of History.* His forthcoming books include *Modern Poetry after Modernism* and *Threshold,* a volume of poems.

Christopher MacGowan (College of William and Mary) is the author of *William Carlos Williams's Early Poetry: The Visual Arts Background.* He is the editor of *The Collected Poems of William Carlos Williams, Volume I* (with A. Walton Litz), *The Collected Poems of William Carlos Williams, Volume II,* and *Paterson.*

Vicki Mahaffey (University of Pennsylvania) is the author of *Reauthorizing Joyce* as well as numerous articles on Joyce, Woolf, and modernism. Her most recent book, *States of Desire: Wilde, Yeats, Joyce and the Irish Experiment,* is forthcoming.

Jeffrey M. Perl (University of Texas at Dallas) is the author of *Skepticism and Modern Enmity: Before and After Eliot* and *The Tradition of Return: The Implicit History of Modern Literature.* He is founder and editor of the journal *Common Knowledge.* His forthcoming books are *A Preface to "Theory"* and *Two Windows on Saint-Denis.*

Sanford Schwartz (Pennsylvania State University) is the author of *The Matrix of Modernism: Pound, Eliot, and Twentieth-Century Thought.* He has published essays on nineteenth- and twentieth-century literature, criticism, and intellectual history and is currently working on a book on the relations between art and politics in the decade after World War II.

Robert Spoo (University of Tulsa) is editor-in-chief of the *James Joyce Quarterly* and author of *James Joyce and the Language of History: Dedalus's Nightmare.* He has edited H.D.'s *Asphodel* and her *Kora and Ka,* and has coedited volumes of Ezra Pound's letters, including the forthcoming *Ezra and Dorthy Pound: Letters in Captivity, 1945–1946.* His current research is on modernism and the law of intellectual property.

Hugh Witemeyer (University of New Mexico) is the author of *The Poetry of Ezra Pound: Forms and Renewal, 1908–1920* and *George Eliot and the Visual Arts.* He is the editor of *William Carlos Williams and James Laughlin: Selected Letters,* of W. B. Yeats's *Letters to the New Island* (with George Bornstein), of *Ezra Pound and Senator Bronson Cutting: A Political Correspondence, 1930–1935* (with E. P. Walkiewicz), and of *Pound/Williams: Selected Letters of Ezra Pound and William Carlos Williams.*

Index